Under New Management

UNDER NEW MANAGEMENT

*Universities, Administrative Labor,
and the Professional Turn*

RANDY MARTIN

TEMPLE UNIVERSITY PRESS
PHILADELPHIA

TEMPLE UNIVERSITY PRESS
Philadelphia, Pennsylvania 19122
www.temple.edu/tempress

Copyright © 2011 by Temple University
Published 2011

Library of Congress Cataloging-in-Publication Data

Martin, Randy, 1957– author.
    Under new management : universities, administrative labor, and the professional turn /
Randy Martin.
        p. cm
    Includes bibliographical references and index.
    ISBN 978-1-4399-0695-8 (cloth : alk. paper) —
    ISBN 978-1-4399-0697-2 (e-book)
    1. Universities and colleges—United States—Faculty.   2. Universities and
colleges—United States—Administration.   3. College personnel management—United
States.   I. Title.
    LB2331.72.M36 2011
    378.1'2—dc22

                                                                        2010046506

♾ The paper used in this publication meets the requirements of the American National
Standard for Information Sciences—Permanence of Paper for Printed Library Materials,
ANSI Z39.48-1992

Printed in the United States of America

2 4 6 8 9 7 5 3 1

For colleagues everywhere

Contents

Preface

For all its promise as the noble leveler, higher education today is part of the great divide in the United States. At once an engine of opportunity and disequilibrium, it is at odds with itself. For faculty, perhaps no gulf is greater than that between itself and what is frequently referred to in an ominous tone as "the administration." In the iconic picture of the professoriate is portrayed the paragon of inner-directed existence, a life of the mind answerable only to its own calling, governed by its own rules, and subject to its own review—in effect, autonomous. And yet much faculty work jostles with that image. Professionals in higher education as elsewhere have been swept up in the wave of management that has made itself at home in the workplace as well as in every other place. Indeed, from work to leisure, policy to poverty, child rearing to anger, there seems scarcely an aspect of human existence that is not in need of management. The sense that someone is always looking over your shoulder, measuring your every move for best effect, and inviting you to judge yourself and others by common standards of worth has for many been largely internalized.

Since the sixties, the tremendous expansion of access to higher education has swelled the ranks of professionals. Yet rather than fulfilling the promise of becoming the new mandarins whose knowledge reigns, those who pass through college have increasingly found themselves to be subject to new management. This brave regime bears the conviction that every bone and sinew must be engineered to maximize all manner of output; even job satisfaction must be maximized as all effort is enlisted in the process of generalized accountability. The practice of management has been grounded in the application of rationalizing the knowledge required for greater output, which is measured in the aggregate according to the logic of a standardized mass. Now, such administrative effort effects a way of being that is at once intimate and expansive, where getting the feeling just right results in wholesale transformation, and tightly targeted initiatives or small movements in ranking are leveraged to dramatic claims of victory or defeat.

A reasonable enough impulse in the face of this onslaught is to take flight from the managerial imperative—assuming, of course, there is somewhere else to go or that you cannot or will not take the insipid desire to discipline with you. Another—doubtless more queasy—response is to look inside this calculus and see how it might be figured otherwise. If management is indeed so profoundly formative of education and higher learning is tooled by and toward it, the denizens of academe—students, faculty, administration alike—may do well to consider where else it may lead and what else we might aspire to than obeisance to scarcity-inducing norms of accountability and excellence. If management teaches us to run things, where do we want to go and how should we organize ourselves to get there?

Far from acceding to the mantra "If you cannot beat them, join them," this book examines what else might be done with the surfeit of mutual management in our midst. It seeks to understand what is happening within higher education in order to recognize and value the alternatives that lie already to hand. Rather than seeing administrative work as something to be bemoaned, refused, resisted, or avoided, this is an exploration of what else might be wrought from the generalized condition of management than the dulling drain of overwork. There is, no doubt, a dollop of hubris in this internal or immanent approach to revaluing and redirecting extant capacities for managing the institutional surround. The will to manage otherwise springs from my own experience of more than a dozen years of various administrative charges—to say nothing of the years before I joined the bureaucratic ranks yet subject to the managerial imperative. As a college student, I had been deeply instructed by various kinds of political engagement, including being in a collective that ran a radical bookstore at the University of California, San Diego, where I started my undergraduate studies as a premed student; my tenant organizing in Berkeley, where I transferred to study sociology; and my participation in various campus protests. When I graduated in 1979, I went to work in a paint factory. In 1980, as a teaching assistant at the University of Wisconsin, Madison, I went on strike with the graduate student union, subsequently lost my funding, and finally left Madison for New York to dance professionally. I had written my master's thesis at Madison on worker resistance in the paint and garment factories where I had worked. Returning to graduate school to get my doctorate in sociology at the City University of New York a year later, I wrote my dissertation on a dance company I had performed with. Starting in 1982, I also worked as an adjunct at Queens College teaching hundred-student sections of introductory sociology for several years, including the year after I got my degree in 1984.

After applying unsuccessfully for scores of positions (and perhaps two hundred over the course of my career), I received my first tenure-track faculty appointment in 1985 at Rhodes College, a Presbyterian liberal arts school in Memphis, Tennessee, where I was the only full-time sociologist in a department with two anthropologists and a part-time sociologist. I left my position there in 1987 to return to New York on a one-year visiting appointment in another similarly small and mixed anthropology-sociology department, at Bard, a liberal arts college upstate, before taking a multiyear contract line to teach a freshmen curriculum and an arts and society program at Purchase College, part of the State University of New York system, outside New York City. I then secured another tenure-track job in 1989, at Pratt Institute, an art school in Brooklyn, where I worked for eleven years (in particular to set in place a new undergraduate program in cultural studies). Ultimately, I wound up as professor and chair of the Social Science and Management Department, which included historians, psychologists, and economists, and spent a few months as interim dean in the School of Liberal Arts. In 2000, I moved across the East River to the Tisch School of the Arts at New York University (NYU) in a newly created position as associate dean of faculty and interdisciplinary programs. After six years (during which time NYU graduate students went on strike and lost recognition of their bargaining unit, adjuncts unionized, and non–tenure track full-time faculty lines increased in number), I left the dean's office to chair the Department of Art and Public Policy, in which I held a faculty appointment and launched a graduate program in arts activism.

This meandering trail into and out of and again into research universities, tenure-track jobs, mixed-discipline and interdisciplinary departments, activism, and administration clearly informs my perspective—namely, a conviction that how and to what end institutions are run matters. Fortunately, this is not a unique or original discovery but one that joins daily routines with a multitude of histories and ambitions for what might be. Also, I have been engaged by the ways in which knowledge and organization flow outside campus commitments, where I have served as chair of the Program Committee and faculty at the Brecht Forum, a movement-based adult independent learning center; as a coeditor of the journals *Socialism and Democracy* and *Social Text* (where I have been on the editorial collective since 1984); as a member of the advisory board for Imagining America: Artists and Scholars in Public Life (a national consortium); and as vice-president and then-president of the U.S.-based Cultural Studies Association (2006–2010). I confess to having caught the administrative bug, and this book perchance is my writing cure. Also, this book continues work I have done over the past decade on the culture and politics of finance (both foreign and domestic) and is an effort to extend that prior analysis to an understanding of what the prevalence of financial rubrics and dispositions has to do with the making and unmaking of social class—specifically, the professional-managerial class, whose fate is so closely tied to that of higher education.

These past thirty years in which I have come of age, academia has witnessed the assertion of a potent managerialism associated with the shift in the proclaimed purpose of higher education from a public to a private good, from an end in itself to a means for professional employment as part of a broader knowledge sector that makes intellectual work a form of property. Students of a widening age span continue to attend college in increasing numbers and come away with credentials of uncertain efficacy—to say nothing of mounting debts. These mutations to higher education have been part of a broader array of changes in which the ascent of finance has been deeply imbricated. It is not simply, as we learned in the recent credit and debt debacle, that banks assumed unsustainable risks and disparate kinds of institutions became entangled in the activities of investment. Government sought to get out of the business of providing security for all and encouraged a form of personal risk management, while bellwethers of a reliably safe future—like home ownership, college savings, defined-benefit pensions—were transformed into the gambits of personal finance.

The spectacular sums traded daily—trillions of dollars in exchanges and over-the-counter transactions between firms—made finance seem ethereal and needless rather than fundamental to the conduct of human affairs. In actuality, these financial operations have made far-flung values commensurable in the global economy as well as in the ordering of our lives, where the connections between us are at once deeper and more volatile, distant and mutually entangled. A company that sells clothing to big box stores in the United States may spread its manufacturing from Vietnam, where fabric is cut, to China, where it is sewn, to Haiti, where buttons are applied. The garment can be produced globally because its cost factors have been fixed through a series of contracts that set currency exchange rates for the projected dates when the work is expected to be completed. These agreements to trade currency at particular prices and moments come to have worth of their own when they can then be bundled together and exchanged as separate commodities meant to smooth out the variation or risk of unexpected (but now actionable) changes in markets. What enabled making a particular commodity now enjoys a second life as a small part of global financial exchange. Hedging against risk becomes a business opportunity for those who traffic in the now-legion investment instruments called derivatives.

The logic of the derivative—a portion or attribute of some underlying value leveraged to make for greater systemic volatility in the name of managing unexpected outcomes—is a potent force not only in finance but also in other kinds of social matters. The rippling effect of small variations in value could be seen in the subprime mortgage business, where default on the riskiest investments caught flame through the rest of the economic realm, but also in the war on terror, where small deployments of force on either side multiplied the dangers for all. Similarly, principles of arbitrage, the exploitations of minor variations in an environment that are leveraged to large effect, could be seen in the emphasis on flexibility, reinvention, and creativity that the new management augurs. An organization's success or failure is tied to a few strategic initiatives, and the leaders or stars can make or break an entire institution's reputation, but openness to an unexpected synergy can yield great advances throughout. In this respect, finance is not simply about the marshaling of capital for others. It operates according to certain social principles—logics of association and partition—that travel in other domains. The seemingly arcane perquisites of finance may prove crucial to understanding the more prosaic and profound interdependence among productive endeavors that share select attributes and circumstances. The process by which social logics of finance come to bear on human affairs is known as financialization. The interdependence among strangers whose efforts are coordinated by operational approaches to working together, who amass great wealth that transcends the needs of any alone, also goes by the name "social class."

Class has been variously conceived of as an individual's location on a graded, hierarchical scale of income, education, and status, or as an aggregated mass sharing a common interest, or as an objective situation mapped onto a stable subject position, and even as a future enlightened reign extrapolated from the deficiencies of the present. Alternatively, treating the social logic evidenced in derivatives permits an understanding of class as a principle of association. The emphasis is on how linkages and interdependencies among separable and distinct attributes of persons and things are achieved amid circulating and indeterminate relations while maintaining locational and other qualitative differences. While derivatives render some aspects of spatially dispersed values commensurate (but not the same), they also orient expected or future events as something to be evaluated and acted upon in the present. This is the temporal dimension of risk management.

For an ensemble of labor that is as internally differentiated as the professional-managerial class, beginning with commonality of circumstance, self-understanding, or opportunity may prove difficult. Most professional occupations, from doctoring to teaching, have experienced a loss of autonomy and rise of accountability protocols without losing their mandates of specialized expertise (as was the claim for otherwise interchangeable factory workers). If industrial capital's concentrating tendencies of the prior two centuries placed the image of a massed proletariat on the historical horizon, the expansive centralization of finance has more dispersive but just as significantly associational effects. Derivatives hint at the ways we can be together, affect one another, but not necessarily be as one—a complex class optic that moves from a concentrated mass to a diffuse yet consequential web of entanglements.

While the recent meltdown of stock and credit markets sheds light on high-end finance professionals' inability to use their sophisticated arsenal of mathematical models to reap profit from market volatility, it had long been noted that four-fifths of the hired stock pickers did worse with their portfolios than the broad market average (i.e., doing nothing at all). Professors in all manner of fields may also be confronting their own versions of this knowledge failure, not in terms of an inability to create new idioms but through a loss of control over what happens, who masters the market, or how knowledge is valued and governed. This disconnect between the expansion of professional fields and a confrontation with the limits of professionals' knowledge to govern their own affairs, a conundrum here referred to as the "professional turn," is especially poignant in financial services but speaks to a larger predicament faced by experts in other fields, professors included. Within higher education, the professional turn has reoriented traditional liberal arts disciplines toward market-derived outcomes, while pressing the ever-expanding professional training to consider what constitutes its distinctive knowledge base.

When applied to politics and daily life, financialization introduces a schism between those who can benefit from assuming risks through effective self-management and those who fail to do so—the populations considered to be at risk. Members of university faculties have themselves experienced a version of this cleavage between the risk-capable and the at-risk: the stars and leadership deemed worthy of additional investment versus the casualized full-time and adjunct faculty members who perform most of the instruction despite administrative indifference toward their fate. Yet these faculties, many graduate students among them, have been quite active in organizing themselves in the face of these circumstances, and for them, professional training comes to include courses in the politics of academic labor. If the university, far from being a remote ivory tower, has been a model of new management's labor policies, it has also been the scene of a vigorous response. It has been the ground not only of myriad activisms and mobilizations but also of organizational initiatives, some reminiscent of earlier industrial formations and others promising something still to come.

The shift from permanence to precarity among the bulk of faculty positions makes vivid how broadly the professions are experiencing change. While the old perquisites of prestige become ever scarcer, new kinds of association are emerging among those growing numbers relegated to mere service positions. The autonomy that new management takes away comes back as a claim on how the institution itself should be run. The pervasive administrative logic becomes part and parcel of academic labor. But rather than creating a unity of experience or outlook, the organizational reach and implications of this managerial work result in myriad combinations and potential directions for what knowledge work is, how it is done, and what it is for. The traditional disciplines, academic titles, and institutional and national educational rankings are still very much with us, even as they have become reordered, lost purchase on once secure realms of privilege, or become decentered from prior claims to authority and influence.

While the U.S.-based research university is still touted for its prominence, its limits to serve as a model for global higher education, as it once so confidently claimed to, are becoming increasingly apparent. Constricted access and affordability have cast a shadow over the meritocratic ethos. Proprietary deliverables jostle with civic engagement in defining purposes. Chronic indebtedness compromises the calculus of value added to lifelong earnings. The powers of credentialing to establish professional security are eroding. Expansive and diverse approaches to critical understanding sit uneasily with homogenizing rubrics that measure what education yields. For all this, higher education in its myriad forms continues to be where divergent conceptions of the future are contested, combined, and played out. In the cauldron of pressure and promise, the expressions of active dissent, intervention, mobilization, initiative—both here and abroad—carry a resonance beyond their immediate extent and duration. In this, the university joins a host of other institutions (whether associated with public functions of government or market-based conceptions of trust, such as financial and multinational corporations) whose light as beacons has dimmed. Whether the institutions themselves are in ruins or their shine has lost its luster, conversations about a range of organizational approaches that are now possible, about how we speak for others, about how specific political initiatives can be made comprehensive have opened anew. The volume and range of critical voices can prove both welcome and disorienting—making it all the more difficult to recognize and value the difference that such efforts may actually be making to present dilemmas and future prospects.

While higher education is often spoken of in terms of crisis, this concept might be better treated as a critical juncture or turning point rather than a terminus. Looking at the current complexity, therefore, becomes the grounds on which to effect the direction of that change, rather than being caught in a moment of despair or a narrative of decline. No claim is being made here to speak for all these various activisms and initiatives, even if their scope and reach gestures toward the contours of a more general response to the issues of knowledge making that entangle the financial crisis and the shifting circumstances of the professional-managerial class. While new management is widespread, the organizational prospects it engenders must be located and specified. This book is an effort to navigate between the dilemmas and prospects presented by these still-emerging circumstances to make room analytically for what still appears to be incommensurable. It surveys the landscape from what has been treated as a privileged perspective to see what else might lie within and without.

Acknowledgments

Much has changed in the thirty-five years since I entered higher education as a bright-eyed premedical student at the University of California, San Diego. Tuition bills were negligible and the horizon for what an education could deliver was broad. Now I find myself teaching at a university with the highest student debt in the nation at a moment when higher education is encountering all manner of stormy weather. This book is one effort to come to terms with these changes without succumbing to nostalgia for what might have been or to cynicism for what lies ahead. As a student of higher education, I have been deeply instructed by the institutions where I have worked, the colleagues I have collaborated with, and the many students who have taught me my craft. Queens College of the City University of New York, where I was first an adjunct; Rhodes College in Memphis, Tennessee, where I first taught full time; Bard College and State University of New York, Purchase, where I taught as a visitor for a year; Pratt Institute, where I worked for eleven years; and New York University, where I have spent the past decade, have all provided valuable lessons—especially the exquisite leadership of Tisch School of the Arts Dean Mary Schmidt Campbell, along with my former decanal colleagues Sheril Antonio, Robert Cameron, Elliot Dee, Louis Scheeder, and Pari Shirazi. My dear interlocutors, Marc Bousquet, Michael E. Brown, Bruce Burgett, Patricia Clough, Jan Cohen-Cruz, Stephen Duncombe, Brent Hayes Edwards, Karen Finley, Darlene Forrest, Charly Greene, Stefano Harney, Pat C. Hoy II, Colleen Lye, Toby Miller, Rene Francisco Poitevin, Andrew Ross, Ella Shohat, and Lisa Siegman, have deepened my understanding of what education is about. Some of the ideas that appear in this book were developed through opportunities provided by treasured editorial colleagues at the Edu-Factory collective and at the journals *Social Text, Workplace,* and *Works and Days*. Ginger Gillespie, who has been my partner as long as I have taught, has, as a family physician, provided a window into another profession straining under the changes to its world. Our children, Oliver and Sophia, show me aspects of learning I could never otherwise have understood. Among these treasures, I have been well schooled. Also, it has been a pleasure to have the chance to work with Micah Kleit and Temple University Press again, an editor and press that know what it means to matter.

1

The Ends of Education

Higher education today seems to reside in the two cities of Dickensian fame. More students, faculty, and campuses. Bountiful endowments. Its own celestial beings. A program for every proclivity. Lifelong learning. An abundance of patents, strategic partnerships, and product lines. Whether these attributes make for the best of times or the worst is the subject of considerable debate. The same might be said for escalating student debt, erosion of tenure, commercialization, heightened accountability, and outcomes assessment. The queasy mix of celebratory expansion and fitful proclamations of crisis that comprises the current range of opinion on the topic speaks above all to the challenges of evaluating the purposes of higher education for self and society. What once appeared to be a secure confluence of interest between individual and social enrichment, private and public good, professional and national allegiance, no longer abides the same measures of certainty. The feeling of lack amid such abundance poses anew the question of what education is for.

The characterization of our world as a knowledge society where self-managed professionals reign would seem to settle the matter once and for all.[1] For professionals, knowledge is both raw material and finished product. Enlightened management is predicated on ceaseless learning. The rise of a professional-managerial stratum to the leadership of society serves to anchor the university at the central nexus of social class, nation, market, and state. And yet for those very reasons, the university stands as a bellwether of societal fissures and points to the discrepancies between what is promised and what is possible, between what counts as accomplishment and what points to failure. Nor does knowledge itself guarantee success, a lesson painfully in evidence when experts responsible for managing a range of disasters from the environmental to the economic report that they could not imagine, let alone model, what actually took place. Paradoxically, the number of people who can claim to be university-trained professionals continues to rise. The university measures its success in terms of this expansion, yet both professionals and universities have lost their commanding purchase on the means and end of knowledge production. The professional turn is at once a sign of growth and evacuation, democratization and selectivity, expansion and disorientation in the conditions and applications of knowledge work. Self-rule yields to the proliferation of managerial protocols. Specialized domains of expertise jostle restlessly with the generalized conditions of information processing and judgment. Hence, the university has become more than a strategic industry that explains and encapsulates American global might—or its diminution and decay. It is also key in rendering an understanding of what our society is and is not.

If the university is to teach these lessons to either its denizens or detractors, a comprehensive approach is required, one that looks at what education is for, at who decides its contents and delivers its forms, and at what is taught and how. Yet any effort at a broad understanding quickly gets ensnared in a kind of double bind. Higher education is at once central to the societal enterprise and undervalued for what it offers. Its traditional value derives from the fact that it is exceptional in its norms of comportment and exemplary in its excellence. Yet it is also increasingly captive to external measures of performance and productivity. Higher education is attacked as an ivory tower, yet these parapets can no longer defend it. Indeed, the production, dissemination, and evaluation of what counts as literacy is not contained by cloistered walls but suggests a vast industrial complex of communications media, technoscience, and knowledge-based service in which the university is but one node among many. As a consequence, the neat divide between what is inside and outside the university, whether it be between policy and pedagogy, market-driven instrumentality and education for itself, or worker and student, cannot any longer be sustained.

WHITHER AUTONOMY?

In 1968, two sociologists looked at the university in the United States and declared an "academic revolution." What Christopher Jencks and David Riesman were referring to was not the social upheaval on campus spearheaded by antiwar activists but a shift in the locus of power and authority from the nineteenth to mid-twentieth century, when trustees and presidents ruled to the advent of a "unified faculty" that had an informal veto. Jencks and Riesman found that "the shape of American higher education is largely a response to the assumptions and demands of the academic professions."[2] At its core, this transformation amounted to what they took to be a managerial revolution whereby the upper administrators represented the interests of the faculty—who control the central identity of the institution as its middle managers. Their research was more than a generalization from their own particular experience at Harvard, where norms of faculty centricity are perhaps strongest. Theirs was a report on a societal project, demonstrating that professional expertise lies at the heart of and drives the mission of an expanding range of specialized institutions. From this perspective, modern societies prove to be something of a sociologist's dream, artfully balancing the ideational content of rule-governedness or rationality with the material form of autonomous institutions. The competence and clarity of professional self-rule eliminates competition and conflict over who is best placed to perform socially necessary tasks to make society run smoothly. The university professoriate can rightfully claim pride of place in this system because its institution not only runs rationally but also is devoted to the pursuit of reason as an end in itself.

Writing a few years later, French sociologist Alain Touraine was impressed by the American academic system's ability to balance a range of otherwise contending forces. He noted that it had "the exceptional capacity to combine excellence and massification by various processes of internal differentiation and hierarchization" and to achieve a "complementarity of personal development and collective solidarity."[3] The idea of a society centered upon professional self-regulation of knowledge production has persisted in the sociological literature since Daniel Bell's 1973 pronouncement of the professional as the protagonist of the postindustrial society. Writing two decades later, Harold Perkin confidently proclaimed, "The modern world is the world of the professional expert. . . . The professionals have created this world with its fantastic range of sophisticated products and services, and their leading lights have received and are receiving high rewards, prestige, status and in some cases permanent wealth for their efforts."[4] Accordingly, this dominance of professional expertise amounts to no less than a third revolution that supersedes the preindustrial rule by landlords and industrial rule by capitalists, and that rests upon the centrality of higher education and the replacement of class structure with meritocratic hierarchy.

Not all who see professionals as the harbinger of a new era are as celebratory of this new state of affairs. For critics like Donald Clark Hodges—building on the work of James Burnham, Milovan Djilas, and Alfred Chandler—professionals have constituted themselves in a republic of expertise that undermines democratic deliberation by excluding from participation those deemed unqualified and exploits, in a manner that capitalists once did, the toiling majority. "In postcapitalist societies, as in capitalist ones, an underlying population provides the wherewithal for the overlying privileged layer. Such is the condition of exploited wage earners—human livestock, albeit lords over other animals they in turn domesticate. They, too, are engaged in a class struggle, but one they periodically lose. Today they are lackeys of the new class of professionals in times of peace, cannon fodder in times of war."[5] Knowledge sorts privilege and demands obeisance to its perquisites.

The professions not only support the new order but also constitute a self-regulating system in their own right, an argument most fully elaborated by Andrew Abbott. Abbott wants to demonstrate the fundamental historical continuity of expert control over knowledge that concentrates power in the hands of a professional elite. The mobility associated with career advancement preserves the security and autonomy of the professions. Social change both creates and destroys conditions for professional work. Concentrated ownership of the means of professional production yields greater dependence on organizations that assume a federated character and that can lobby government to create a legislatively friendly environment. Groups compete over control of knowledge and its application and dispute the jurisdictional boundaries of their work. Those who can define old problems in new ways will prevail. Only experts possess what is juridically recognized as knowledge—others merely possess information—and are in a position, as knowledge shifts, to maintain the upper hand as the threshold of what counts.

Abbott's strong concept of professionalization points toward an evolution of "a particular structural and cultural form of occupational control. . . . Culturally, professions legitimate their control by attaching their expertise to values with general cultural legitimacy; increasingly the values of rationality, efficiency, and science."[6] The spread of knowledge production means that the university can no longer claim to be the exclusive producer of these values. Internally, it becomes more of a holding company for professional schools that are closer to professional associations than to university fidelity, and these credentialing centers become battlegrounds for professional competition. Externally, the erosion of the university's monopoly over knowledge-making fosters an explosion in continuing education rather than a one-time conferral of a credentialing degree.

The claims for professional autonomy often rest upon a presumption that the views experts have of themselves are generally shared. Abbott, for example, asserts, "For whatever reason, public images of professions are fairly stable."[7] As publics and consumers gain more information, their capacity to judge the efficacy of professional expertise expands. The result is a less atomized clientele who can create cartels for services that increase competition among providers who nonetheless are able to maintain control over what is provided. Other defenders of the value of professional autonomy have been less sanguine on this point. One, Elliot Friedson, sees the professional's ability to maintain a logic of occupational control against conflicting demands of institutions and markets coming under increasing assault. Placed in jeopardy "is the independence of professions to choose the direction of development of their knowledge and the uses to which it will be put."[8] Friedson, writing in 2001, more than a decade after Abbott, observes that the common assault on professional elitism weakens its capacity to "fend off the pressures of capital and the state," a circumstance that exacerbates its loss of credibility with the public.[9]

These arguments regarding the persistence and centrality of professional autonomy are in marked contrast to two very different sentiments toward the growth of occupational expertise. One is that professionals constitute a new working class and the other is that they comprise the new mandarins, a professional-managerial class aligned with the highest echelons of societal command. Building on the discussion of the new working class broached by Andre Gorz (1964), Alain Touraine (1971), and Serge Mallet (1975), Charles Derber defines professional proletarianization as a "shift toward dependent, salaried employment, in which the labor of professionals becomes subject to the authority and management of others."[10] Derber is careful not to suggest that this process amounts to a convergence with the historical nineteenth-century working class. Elsewhere he articulates the contrary position that professionals have created a "junior partnership" with employers to enhance key elements of traditional authority in what amounts to a mandarin capitalism, a position that follows the influential formulation made in the seventies by Barbara and John Ehrenreich of a professional-managerial class (PMC) in the service of business.[11]

The Ehrenreichs argued that while the PMC was made up of "mental workers," without control over the means of production, the workers served to reproduce capitalist culture by solving the problems of daily life, be these affective or scientific. While the PMC divided between business and nonprofit services, the generalized anxieties about class reproduction or upward mobility meant that "private life thus becomes too arduous to be lived in private; the inner life of the PMC must be continuously shaped, updated and revised by— of course—ever mounting numbers of experts: experts in childraising, family living, sexual fulfillment, self-realization, etc., etc."[12] Paradoxically, this insecurity was the basis for class expansion and hegemony over the working class through self-legitimation of its own expertise, with a consequent anti–working class radicalism. The Ehrenreichs' analysis points to the emergence of the new right at the end of the seventies. While Derber notes that professionals have the power to "enclose the mind," he also observes that the Reagan revolution was hostile to the new mandarins.[13] No longer disinterested or narrowly self-interested in expert autonomy, the professions have become a field where larger social contests are played out. Ironically, this was the very critique of the university that Jencks and Riesman neglected, one exemplified, in 1966, in the Students for a Democratic Society (SDS) position that higher education is a social factory whose commodities are the masses of the knowledgeable, with the faculty as subsidiary, unproductive salaried workers.[14]

Taking up this trajectory in the early eighties led John Beverly to declare, "The autonomy of the higher education system in the United States (and other advanced capitalist countries) is rapidly collapsing, posing new problems and prospects to students, faculty and other workers engaged in this sphere."[15] When all are expected to be professionals and perform professionally, the result is a loss of exclusivity over claims to expertise that secure a unique sense of place and grounding. The costs of generalizing the professions as models of labor have been duly noted. "The price is a loss of faith, trust and sense of order, an increased perception of risk."[16] Professionalization under these circumstances becomes a portal to increasing managerialism, which effects a collision between expanded demands for judgment (when expertise is everywhere) and frustrated expectations that knowledge should but cannot control one's fate.

If university-generated professional expertise is drifting toward managerialism, what direction is management taking? The "frontiers of management" in the words of Rosabeth Moss Kanter, are under the sway of humanistic ideals and emphasize core values such as "empowerment," which is now "part of the conventional repertoire of enlightened managers."[17] In Kanter's view, corporations are now flatter, focused, speedier, customer service oriented, organized through teams and projects, engaged in cross-functional contact. More, they partner with customers, pursue strategic alliances, and embrace social responsibility. All this leads to the erosion of the distinction between managers and nonmanagers such that reputation serves as a principle career resource. Peter F. Drucker, who until his death in 2005 was considered the dean of modern management, defines this field as the practice of performance-based results, which he sees as encompassing the operations of all organizations, not just business. At its heart, organizational survival depends on comparative advantage in making the knowledge worker productive. "And the ability to attract and hold the best of the knowledge workers is the first and most fundamental precondition."[18] Knowledge workers need to be able to manage themselves. They waste little effort trying to improve areas of low competence. They focus on strengths, types of learning performance, and values that allow them to decide where they are going. With lifelong learning at their cores, organizations can be built on trust and not force. Drucker's vision makes the business organization sound much like the university, with the top manager acting something like a college dean committed to recruitment and retention.

Not all writing on management holds such a sunny view regarding the use of management theory and practice as a platform for professionally based or society-wide pedagogy. Henry Mintzberg, longtime teacher of managers, has written a biting critique of the prevailing training of managers via the standard MBA curriculum. In his words:

The trouble with "management" education is that it is business education, and leaves a distorted impression of management. Management is a practice that has to blend a good deal of craft (experience) with a certain amount of art (insight) and some science (analysis). An education that overemphasizes the science encourages a style of managing I call "calculating" or, if the graduates believe themselves to be artists, as increasing numbers now do, a related style I call "heroic." Enough of them, enough of that. We don't need heroes in positions of influence any more than technocrats. We need balanced, dedicated people who practice a style of management that can be called "engaging." Such people believe that their purpose is to leave behind stronger organizations, not just higher share prices. They do not display hubris in the name of leadership.[19]

The first undergraduate program in business started at the University of Pennsylvania in 1881, to be followed by the inaugural MBA at Harvard in 1908. Despite initial criticism from business for being overly abstract and having high student attrition, in the subsequent two decades, nearly two hundred business schools were established.[20] For Mintzberg, the development of the Graduate School of Industrial Administration at Carnegie Mellon University in Pittsburgh, Pennsylvania, during the fifties marked a renaissance in business education that was grounded in an interdisciplinary integration of psychology, sociology, economics, mathematics, and other humanistic studies. This liberal arts approach to training business leaders was replaced in the seventies with one championed by Harvard's Michael Porter—a technical analytics known as "strategy," based upon the quantifiably measurable unit of a decision. The play of diverse disciplinary strands was undone in favor of a singular method that could not inspire innovation or the work of others. Against this hegemony of the American approach, Mintzberg advocates a more intellectually speculative manager, hastening a "time for the agents of change to change" so as fulfills the manager's purpose, "to enhance the quality of leadership in society."[21] Leadership is itself a marker of excellence that links the aims of business and universities.

Leaving aside for a moment the question of whether the pressures to focus on share prices at the expense of organizational or other kinds of development can be resolved through a shift in educational preparation, Mintzberg has sharpened the quandary posed by the confluence of management and education. The imperative to increase share price or add value is not reserved for those who lead organizations, but it is a feature of the demands placed on all who work in them. The push to add value applies now to managerial work and education alike, seemingly placing the model of professional training at the heart of all manner of learning. The emphasis on measurable outcomes, or accountability, is usefully understood along the lines of professional training. What has been described as the abdication of a higher calling is exchanged for technical training of hired hands, something that has hollowed the mission and rationale of the business school, but stands more broadly as a dilemma of the rush to relevance that has overtaken higher education under the sway of this professional model. Surveying the historical mission drift, Rakesh Khurana finds "that with the abandonment of the professionalization project and the idea that managers—not shareholders, labor, the state, or the market—should exercise ultimate control over the corporation, university business education lost the grand narrative that had sustained it from its beginnings."[22] The subordination of specialized expertise to externally derived norms undoes the larger story of autonomy by which professions generally had legitimated their authority.

Rather than being forced upon professional education, its instrumentalization appears with its own appeals to efficiency and innovation that makes it difficult to provide a critical context or more comprehensive evaluative criteria for the changes afoot. Jeff Schmidt sees professionals as conservative, uncritical, and ideologically obedient in the "attitudes they display at work and *in* their work."[23] This is not simply a matter of pursuing self-interest by holding on to a specialized field of expertise, but rather of how professionals learn to labor. At the heart of this deficit in critical capacity is the educational formation by which they become credentialed based upon their test performance. The licensing exams taken by architects, doctors, lawyers, and the like are the mothers of high-stakes testing. Ironically, the very instrument meant to sequester specialized expertise from lay understanding standardizes and generalizes a regime of knowledge management. The qualifying exam becomes both model and measure of an appropriate disposition, a "qualifying attitude" in an "ideological workforce."[24] Whereas intelligence testing causes disproportionate anxiety in nonconformist students because the test question is a fragment of actual, fully contextualized problems, the technical aspect as a mnemonic trick selects for students with a narrow approach—those who can combine boredom with endurance, and glean a sense of personal accomplishment through completion of the test.

IN CLASS

The fates of higher education and the professional-managerial class are deeply intertwined. Both have experienced secular growth in numbers of participants and social decay in the compact by which knowledge was to be imbued with power. Talk of class carries this problem. It is conventionally described by measures of individual attributes that make it difficult to conceive of what class means as a social phenomenon. But if class is to be spoken of effectively, measures cannot simply be refused with the argument that they render the concept of class incoherent. Rather, the numbers become a feature of understanding how class works, of what the concept can do, and where its limits lie. Taking the measure of social class is therefore a more complex proposition than is typically conceded. Class is a manner of arranging persons according to discrete categories within a stratified or hierarchical social order (while begging the question of why or how such an order is maintained). It is assigned by a range of factors, such as income, educational attainment, and occupational status. So conceived, class is defined as an aggregate of individuals. Class has no internal social logic, dimension of collective action, or historical purpose. When class is defined more ambitiously as a way of understanding how a particular kind of society is achieved, of what divides populations internally, and what renders them mutually interdependent, the term takes on a clearer political resonance as a principle of association from which emanates a larger historical project. While autonomy based upon expertise over a specialized domain of knowledge was the founding condition of the PMC, the emergent terms of interconnectedness need to be identified. The attributes of persons that stand in for class as a social and historical formation must be read not only for their statistical sufficiency but also for the traces they bear to a larger collective project.

The most selective measures of the PMC by income or credential would restrict membership to the upper 15 percent to 20 percent in the distribution of households, or to less than 5 percent of the workforce according to those holding advanced professional degrees and doctorates.[25] When jobs are typed by occupational category, management, professional, and related occupations are by far the largest, at more than 50 million of a workforce that totals 140 million (as compared with 7.5 million for "production occupations").[26] By a still more expansive measure of professional and managerial responsibilities across all occupation categories, these jobs comprised nearly 60 percent of the U.S. workforce in 2006.[27] A hundred years earlier, only a tenth of the workforce was employed in professional and managerial fields, and less than 3 percent had completed college.[28]

The first doctoral degree was awarded in 1861, and little more than 50,000 mostly male students, roughly one person in a thousand, attended college. Of course, since that time, for those who finish high school, higher education has become the norm.[29] In 1960, fewer than half of those who completed high school went on to college, now more than two-thirds continue their educations.[30] By 2009, more than one hundred million of those 18 and older had at least some college experience, with more than eighty million holding some kind of degree.[31] Projections are for continued growth. Between 2006 and 2018, associate's degrees are slated to rise 25 percent, bachelor's degrees are expected to increase by 19 percent, master's by 28 percent, doctorates by 49 percent, and first professional degrees by 24 percent.[32] With growth has come a loss of exclusivity but also a greater internal differentiation of institutions that parallels the growing inequality, especially in the past thirty years, that has accompanied the expansion of the professional-managerial stratum, where, by 2004, the top 1 percent of households had tripled its after-tax income gains when compared to the top fifth of earners taken as a whole.[33]

This proliferation of a professional class without allowing for its social significance was already in evidence in the late seventies when a range of Keynesian welfare projects were running aground. Randall Collins spoke of a "credential society" that was a victim of its own success. While educational attainment appeared to predict status and salary, on closer inspection, education delivered mass literacy but could not account for gains in productivity or economic development, which were tied to skills acquired on the job. For Collins, credentials had more to do with normative control, which linked occupational loyalty to monopoly of opportunity, a closed cycle yielding a sinecure sector that perpetuates its own privilege. Yet, he observed that, since the sixties, the credential system has gone into crisis, as education no longer guarantees selective positions. Its confidence eroded, education becomes "a means to a non-intellectual ends" as the "reasons for going to school are extraneous to whatever goes on in the classroom."[34] Consistent with what seemed the Keynesian dilemma of growth unmoored from human development, Collins decried the overproduction and excess capacity that the paper chase generated, or what he termed "credential inflation."[35] The specter of growth without reference to value, of self-absorbing struggles over formal control, of sinecure without calling would orient professionals toward an assault on their own success.

During the same year as Collins, but in a very different intellectual register, Jean-François Lyotard, in his influential report on the postmodern condition—precisely a consideration of the conditions for the valuation of knowledge—highlights as basic features of the emerging situation the loss of university autonomy and education as an end in itself:

> In any case, even if the performativity principle does not always help pinpoint the policy to follow, its general effect is to subordinate the institutions of higher learning to the existing powers. The moment knowledge ceases to be an end in itself—the realization of the Idea or the emancipation of men—its transmission is no longer the exclusive responsibility of scholars and students. The notion of "university franchise" now belongs to a bygone era. The "autonomy" granted the universities after the crisis of the late 1960s has very little meaning given the fact that practically nowhere do teachers' groups have the power to decide what the budget of their institution will be; all they can do is allocate the funds that are assigned to them, and only then as the last step in the process.[36]

For Lyotard, the commodification of knowledge strips it of its abiding justification as the pursuit of truth and as a unifying idea for humankind.

Truth and idea constitute the general accounts, or meta-narratives, by which science was legitimated as the means and end of societal advancement. Science vies with other specialized ways of knowing, all of which are subject to a general doubt or incredulity toward meta-narratives. Each way of knowing must legitimate itself through its own statements and actions, advance its own ideas, and tell its own stories—what Lyotard refers to as small narratives (*petits récits*). While all manner of professional occupations can blossom under these conditions, the professor whose legitimacy was conferred by the institution is displaced and subsequently becomes "no more competent than memory bank networks in transmitting established knowledge."[37] While professions may advance by managing their own rules for valuing innovation—an operation that takes place within language games—when an innovation threatens to change the rules of the game, it is denied minimal internal consensus. And the consequences of exclusion or rejection can be harsh. Anything that might place the system of self-legitimation in jeopardy is considered "terrorist," defined as "the efficiency gained by eliminating, or threatening to eliminate, a player from the language game one shares with him. He is silent or consents, not because he has been refuted, but because his ability to participate has been threatened. The decision makers' arrogance . . . consists in the exercise of terror."[38]

Contrary to the conventional way of understanding the postmodern as a discrete age or comprising a succession of historical eras (periodization), Lyotard sees the postmodern as an anticipatory, nascent state of the modern, a moment of rupture that breaks the consensus around a particular discourse. "The postmodern would be that which, in the modern, puts forward the unpresentable in presentation itself; that which denies itself the solace of good forms, the consensus of taste which would make it possible to share collectively the nostalgia for the unattainable; that which searches for new presentations, not in order to enjoy them but in order to impart a stronger sense of the unpresentable."[39] By this account, the erosion of autonomy at the hands of informatics, which renders the claims of transcendental truth incredulous, might now describe the fate of the professions themselves. The exclusion without refutation that professional convention had arrogated to itself is now visited from without. Incredulous toward specialized expertise, the *petits récits* would subject the postmodern to its own modern moment.

Jürgen Habermas, with whom Lyotard shared a critical engagement, thought that the postmodern suspicion of truth made the self-proclaimed critical currents of those such as Jacques Derrida and Michel Foucault ultimately neoconservative.[40] What would seem to be more accurate is that the neoconservative impulse was manifest as a rightist assault on cultural and intellectual radicalism, which would become formative of a generalized threat in the war on terror. The idea that special interests and particular identities were undermining the tranquility of college campuses coincided with the decaying power of intellectual capital to defend professional legitimacy. Writing on the status of expertise thirty years after Lyotard, Harry Collins and Robert Evans declared, "In today's world the scales upon which science is weighed sometimes tip to the point where ordinary people are said to have a more profound grasp of technology than do scientists. Our loss of confidence in experts and expertise seems poised to usher in an age of technological populism."[41]

The erosion of professional status, along with the decline of the middle class, is now itself a common narrative. Whereas the professional-managerial class was defined in terms of expert knowledge production, the middle class referenced a forward-moving or upwardly mobile mass measured by a rising consumption index. Given the growth imperative built into both of these formulations, they would each be vulnerable to cyclical downturn in fortunes but also susceptible to a more general mission drift if they failed to deliver the privilege and security they promised. The professional-managerial class was always conceived of as being internally divided and subject to split interests and attention, and the middle class authorized racial, ethnic, and gender partition through the geopolitics of segregated neighborhoods. Both conceptions of class were tied in key ways to ideals of the business cycle, whereby fading fortunes are presumed (with proper faith and patience) to swing upward again. Within the closed world of the cycle, more fundamental shifts are difficult to discern. Indeed, between the forces of risk and self-management that have borne upon class formation, the past thirty years have also witnessed a more general class decomposition. The principle of association known as social class is forged by perpetual processes of making and unmaking. The rise of the PMC is accompanied by an internal cleavage between compromised professionalization and rampant managerialism. The utopian promises of emancipating consumerism are swallowed by unending labors of credit and debt. Middle-class anxieties are multiplied between professional services and the industry in self-help. As Micki McGee has shown, the impulse to do it yourself was explicitly at odds with organized labor as a means to collective betterment, as the DIY movement simultaneously expanded the work of reproduction into the spheres of private lives.[42]

Not only does the home become a workplace—or more specifically for the knowledge economy, a research center—under these circumstances but the haven from anxiety promised by home ownership, so fundamental to the American Dream, loses its capacity to provide security in the same way. The corollary of increased participation by women in the workforce is an intensification of the kinds of labor and management that take place at home. Home ownership enters a speculative gambit whereby presumed increase in value is set to compensate for eroding earnings—at least as long as the real estate boom prevails. The home, no longer a bank vault to deposit security, is prized for its liquidity, its ability to transfer credit or serve as an ATM.[43] The bust, evident in the subprime meltdown of 2007, targets newer buyers, especially in minority communities, and exacerbates the disequality of access to resources like higher education.[44] Large lenders, like Citibank, were quick to pare back loans to students at community colleges and less selective four-year schools, effectively redlining nonelite campuses, increasing the hours those students would need to work and diminishing their chances of completing their studies.[45] When the home becomes a line of credit for medical or educational expenses, it is viewed as a source of revenue, something to be managed, and not a respite from management. This is not to say that the decline in the PMC or the middle class is uniform, indeed the professions have themselves become a field that has differentiated outcomes of winners and losers, a feature that Steven Brint has noted, in which the disproportionate growth of professions promotes a "splintering of the professional stratum along functional, organizational, and market lines."[46]

The formalization of knowledge associated with expertise has replaced the moral grounding in social purpose that provided a distinctive place and voice in the public arena. The consequence has been what Andrew Ross characterized as "no respect" for the distinctive function of intellectuals in postwar U.S. public life, to which their own assertion of position and tendency drove a more interested posture that was treated as confirmation of public suspicion.[47] While anti-intellectualism has long be a reported feature of U.S. culture and a concern for observers of higher education going back to Thorstein Veblen at the beginning of the last century, the current challenge to expertise has as much to do with the access to and proliferation of specialized knowledge as the disdain for it.[48] One recent *New York Times* account offered a poignant reckoning of this public sentiment:

> But in the days when a successful career was built on a number of tacitly recognized pillars—outsize pay, long-term security, impressive schooling and authority over grave matters—doctors and lawyers were perched atop them all. Now, those pillars have started to wobble. . . . The pay is still good (sometimes very good), and the in-laws aren't exactly complaining. Still, something is missing, say many doctors, lawyers and career experts: the old sense of purpose, of respect, of living at the center of American society and embodying its definition of success. In a culture that prizes risk and outsize reward—where professional heroes are college dropouts with billion-dollar Web sites—some doctors and lawyers feel they have slipped a notch in social status. . . . Increasing workloads and paperwork might be tolerable if the old feeling of authority were still the same, doctors said. But patients who once might have revered them for their knowledge and skill often arrive at the office armed with a sense of personal expertise, gleaned from a few hours on www.WebMD.com, doctors said, not to mention a disdain for the medical system in general.[49]

In this account, the professions are being squeezed in two directions. They are losing prestige to business ventures that do not rely on a college credential (the reference here is to Bill Gates, Harvard dropout and Microsoft founder) as well as to their clients' presumption of equivalent expertise. Their credentials no longer provide them refuge from performance demands of a different sort: legitimation is achieved by demonstrating value-added knowledge and affirming what the client has discovered. The cited *Times* excerpt moves seamlessly between the professional's own sense of lost autonomy and prestige, the diminished interest in pursuing professional careers (as measured by declines in the applicant pools to law and medical school), the attitude of incredulity toward professional narratives, and the ascent of monetary gain as such over any use value or practice associated with it. As one observer put it, "The biggest barrier to renewing this professional legitimacy is the schizophrenia with which it is viewed. As professionals, people want autonomy and status but as consumers they expect slavish public servants, available 24/7."[50] What is being described is by no means the end of professional expert knowledge but rather a shift in its units of production and terms of circulation. Certainly, "the critiques of the professions as exclusionary guilds of highly educated and mostly well paid practitioners are nearly as old as the professions themselves."[51] But what is presently on offer is more an engagement with the politics of knowledge as such than a critique of privilege.

As with the computer age whose birth Jean-François Lyotard was observing, the professional loses autonomy but does not go away with respect to the proliferation of professional knowledge. So too the university obtains, even as its conditions are generalized with the exercise and claim to expertise trumping the credentialing function. The new economy start-up carries a greater likelihood of failure than a professional practice or small business venture. The terror of being eliminated remains the abiding unpresentable and unrepresented condition of speculatively based success. The impression of instant success without long professional formation, and of turning expertise into moneymaking, would seem to affirm commerce as a meta-narrative beyond what truth and spirit could have delivered. The moneymaking in question is wealth gleaned not simply from making information productive but from making money speak of productivity—something most closely aligned with the ascent of finance over the past three decades. The emphasis on risk over knowledge and volatility over security suggests ways the present condition of knowledge follows features of a financial logic.

Like informatics, finance escapes from particular banking sites and institutions to become a general aspect of commercial production and transaction. As an economic practice, finance is tightly structured around the application of decision to information. Speculation consists in an assessment as to whether a given price for a tradable commodity is overvalued or undervalued. Pricing is a form of grading, of marking what work is worth. But unlike grading, financial valuation need not await the completion of the assignment, the coming to term or fulfillment of required time to assign credit. This financial logic permits a comprehensive management of risk—of gain or loss that departs from expectation—at the same time that it allows expectations to be fully elastic. Rather than assuming the completion of a production cycle before the value of a good can be realized, the anticipation of sale moves the moment of completion into the present. Risk, like Lyotard's lost means of legitimation, presents the professional uncertainty over the utility of knowledge and fosters a proliferation of hedges against unexpected outcomes. Insurance, auditing, re-credentialing, ongoing assessment, quality control—all of these become the sinecures of professional practice. Within the university, the demand to adjust internal policies so that institutions become more selective and thereby improve their rankings, places education in a perpetual war of position where locational improvement is a self-justifying end. An increase in the applicant pool allows a measurable gain in demand to stand for an advance in the quality of supply. At the same time, it makes each individual campus commensurate with others on a scalable standard along which all will move up or down. Paradoxically, just as the university was being modeled on the professional norms of the business school, the business school was trading its own internally generated norms for the externally derived measures of attainment found in the emphasis on rankings.

In what now looks to be a perilous tautology, the inability of the university to justify itself to all who might pass judgment upon it encouraged the adoption of productivity models by which its output could be translated along the lines of a business. One such measurement protocol for assessing output—benchmarking—has been adopted by universities over the past two decades from companies that developed it to meet lost market share. The rationale provided has been to meet the failure of universities' own ability to communicate the tangible product at their core, the question of what faculty actually do, so as to "measure faculty performance in ways that can be commonly understood and—most important—believed."[52] By transcribing educational aims meant to be realized over a lifetime or across a society into discrete units of output, the technical measures readily become an instance of the problem they sought to cure—a discreditable expertise, a product that could be made more cheaply elsewhere, a core mission indistinguishable from that of other knowledge producers. Yet unlike the business sectors from which it was borrowed, benchmarking with respect to the university comes, paradoxically, when market share increases. Therefore, universities suffer a kind of communication crisis whereby increasing demands to judge the value of education lack the evaluative criteria by which accounts might be settled. Caught in the risky embrace of the increasing necessity for education and the uncertainty of what it is for, confidence, in a measure, is to stand for the outcome of education as such. As one apologia for benchmarking stated: "Declining confidence in the academy, combined with increasing scrutiny of higher education by funding agencies, legislators, and the public has compelled academic leaders to improve the extent to which their colleges and universities are meeting goals."[53] At the same time, this explanation begs the question of why an expanding market would provoke a crisis of value and whether devices like benchmarking responded to decreased public outlays for education or helped to justify them.

This market model of education, regarded not simply as a commodity but as an investment with the purpose of adding value to an individual's lifetime output or earnings capacity, is what University of Chicago economist Gary Becker referred to as "human capital." If the goal of education is to provide a private rather than a public good and skills that can be translated into productivity, then the sources or inputs for that training become interchangeable, and universities are distinguished from other institutions by degree not kind. "A school can be defined as an institution specializing in the production of training, as distinct from a firm that offers training in conjunction with the production of goods. Some schools, like those for barbers, specialize in one skill, while others, like universities, offer a large and diverse set. Schools and firms are often substitute sources of particular skills."[54]

This process by which campuses, professions, and knowledge are stripped of their autonomy correspond to a larger historical process of industrialization. The distinction between economic, cultural, and symbolic capital advanced by Pierre Bourdieu assumed that the acquisition of credentialized knowledge would durably hold its value over time. Yet the link between expertise and governance has suffered as economic capital comes to delimit the ways in which the cultural and symbolic are translated into the world.[55] The loss of autonomy in this larger sense has been described as a process of enclosure where localities lose their ability to organize themselves and become subject to productive logics outside their domain. The enclosure of the small parcels of land held by feudal serfs in common in the seventeenth and eighteenth centuries was consolidated into larger plots for raising sheep that provided for the emergence of the textile industry. Subsequently, the enclosure of cottage-based looms pressed small-scale labor into larger manufacture. The loss of intellectual autonomy through the current enclosures of cognitive capitalism has as its opposite number a knowledge commons—a domain of nonproprietary shared endeavor that at times takes open source software as its guide.[56] Far from a fully absorbable and efficient machinery, the new economy paradigm based upon information technology is as Alan Liu has described it, archaically labor intensive in a manner that yields an "incalculable inefficiency and irrationality" not readily governed within the workplace.[57]

What was present in the earlier story that has dropped out in the more recent one is that enclosure also fosters a socialization of labor, the advent of an organizationally promising industrial proletariat. The dispossession of intellectual autonomy meets a repossession or appropriation of fields and ways of knowing—from the indigenous to the popular to the interdisciplinary. Autonomy is lost and other kinds of debt, claims on what is to be known and how it is to be used, are introduced. The incredulity or doubt toward expertise is one symptom of this refracted interdependence, albeit one that does not necessarily generate results conducive to further expansion. The reflections on the creation of a professional proletariat have tended toward nostalgic narratives of decline and have not picked up this dimension of the earlier tale, despite the evident organizing fronts on college campuses, especially among the newly enclosed part-time faculty and graduate students. To offer a more complete picture, the entire process of industrialization of the knowledge sector and the place of the university within it needs to be considered. The advent of information as finance must be combined with the socialization of professional-managerial labor to glean this more comprehensive understanding of the relations that obtain between academic labor and capital.

THE UNIVERSITY IN THE INDUSTRIAL KNOWLEDGE COMPLEX

By now it should be apparent that the loss of autonomy experienced by the academic professional is of a piece with the larger transformation of knowledge production—both as an increasing segment of measurable economic activity but also as a driver for and navigator of prevalent economic trends. Globally, what are called "market-oriented knowledge intensive services" generated $12 trillion in sales in 2005, of which the United States took in about 40 percent of these revenues (this despite losing world market share of high-tech exports from 20 percent in the early nineties to 12 percent in 2005). More narrowly, U.S. companies got some $33 billion in net revenues from intellectual property.[58] Here too, the situation of the university is itself transformed from being at the center of a whole constellation with claims to monopoly on the legitimation of authorized knowledge (through conferral of credentials) to being one land mass in the larger archipelago. No doubt, total revenues and investment returns for postsecondary institutions are sizable. For 2005, more than a half trillion dollars was generated by all colleges and universities ($392.3 billion for public, 140.9 billion for private, and $15.4 billion for proprietary). Except for the for-profit schools, three-quarters of revenue comes from sources other than tuition and fees, such as government appropriations, grants, and contracts, in addition to investment return, fund-raising, hospitals, and sales of educational services.[59] As a proportion of the U.S. economy, higher education quadrupled between 1929 and 1975, after which it stagnated for fifteen years to resume growth relative to all productive activity. Therefore, current postsecondary expenditures account for nearly 3 percent of the total gross domestic product.[60]

Computer software, genetic engineering, pharmaceuticals, petrochemical patents, financial instruments—these constitute intellectual property (IP) with varied and uneven relation to universities and their claims on credentialing and training, research and development, and marketing and licensing. Far from the image of the lone individual inventor that held sway at the end of the nineteenth century, successful patenting today is highly concentrated institutionally. Approximately three hundred corporate and government organizations from around the world were granted more than one thousand patents between 1969 and 2006. Of these large patent generators, only eight were U.S.-based universities (University of California, Massachusetts Institute of Technology [MIT], California Institute of Technology [Caltech], University of Texas, Stanford University, University of Wisconsin, Johns Hopkins University, and Cornell University). The largest of these patent holders, the entire University of California system, holds a total of 5,636. But even the largest research university system is dwarfed when compared to the biggest corporate holders. IBM and GE top the list, each holding nearly fifty thousand patents. The total number can be misleading as individual companies see their capacities for innovation wax and wane according to trends. For example, in 2006, IBM was granted 3,621 patents and GE only 6. On the other hand, the leading universities have all seen their numbers grow from the late sixties to the present. The University of California went from 24 patents in 1969 to 410 in 2006, while MIT saw growth from 31 to 139 in the same period. Caltech was granted only 1 patent in 1969 and the University of Texas none, but by 2006, they had obtained 115 and 107, respectively.[61]

This growth has had significant impact on research universities, even as universities themselves occupy but a small slice of the total proportion of patents granted. While the number of patents increased sevenfold between the early seventies and nineties, by 2006, universities still received only 5 percent of the total:

> U.S. Patent and Trademark Office (USPTO) data show that patent grants to universities and colleges increased sharply from 1995 to about 2002, when they peaked at just under 3,300 patents per year, and then fell to about 2,700 in 2005. (However, this decline contrasts with recent increases in the related indicators of invention disclosures and patent applications filed by academic institutions. . . .) The top R&D-performing institutions, with 95% of the total, dominate among universities and university systems receiving patent protection. College and university patenting as a percentage of U.S. nongovernmental patents grew in the 1980s and 1990s from less than 2% to just under 5%, and then declined to about 4.2% by 2005.
>
> The previous edition of *Indicators* noted that three biomedically related utility classes dominated university patenting in the 1980s and

1990s. In 2005, these same three classes together accounted for more than one-third of all utility patents awarded to U.S. academic institutions: drug, bio-affecting and body treating compositions (15.4%); chemistry: molecular biology and microbiology (13.8%); and organic compounds (5.6%). Other medical and life sciences–related classes of patents, although smaller than the top three in number of patents awarded, also ranked high on the list of top patent utility classes awarded to universities.[62]

Among universities, distribution of financial rewards remains uneven. Most revenues accrue to relatively few patents, while start-ups, which by 2005 had more than doubled over the previous decade to number roughly 400, do not necessarily produce any revenue for the university. Nonetheless, the gross revenues from patents increased from $130 million in 1991 to $1.75 billion in 2005.[63] Despite uneven and limited revenues, the drive to pursue such opportunities spread among research universities:

> A growing number of academic institutions are receiving patents, with growth being especially pronounced during the 1980s. During the 1970s, the number of institutions receiving at least one patent grew slowly, but during the 1980s, the number more than doubled, from 80 in 1980 to 165 in 1994. This development affected both public and private institutions: The number of public universities and colleges receiving patents rose from 51 to 97; private institutions increased from 29 to 58. Patenting by the research universities grew more rapidly than by other institutions. During the 1980s, just as a growing number of academic institutions were receiving patents, the share of the 100 largest research universities (by volume of total research funds) increased from 75 to about 85 percent (where it has leveled off) of all newly issued academic patents. At the same time, a composition shift took place within the top 100: The share of the largest 20 universities contracted, while institutions that rated below 50 in research volume gained a slowly growing share of these patents.[64]

Patents granted is perhaps the narrowest formal measure of knowledge production, and one that is itself subject to much variation and volatility.[65] The rise and fall of corporations and industries, the shift from public to private sector R&D (the U.S. Navy, the largest government patent holder with 13,955, received 498 patents in 1969 and only 270 in 2006—when it made only one new application),[66] international investments shifts, inflation and recession—all play a role. Indeed, by 1979, the number of patents granted to U.S. corporations had fallen by nearly a fifth, down from what it was in the early sixties (1963: 26,633; 1979: 22,504) while foreign firms had nearly tripled their patents, and by 2006 had nearly broken even (77,373 to 78,925). Whereas the number of patents granted to the government has declined from a high of 2,144 to just 792 today, the percentage of total patents given to individuals has gone down from 22.8 percent to 6.8 percent, as the actual number of patents has remained flat (though significantly more individuals in the United States received patents than those in the rest of the world). Ramping up the race to intellectual property seems to have generated its own forms of scarcity. The model of the enterprise university animated by faculty entrepreneurs, enlists ever greater conscripts while sowing increasing disequalities within the institution. The institution in question is increasingly trading its autonomy and privileged mission to join an industry of which it cannot be the master and to chase the epicenter of knowledge production from the margins.

INTERESTS OF STATE

Even this story of the epic shift in higher education from a craft to an industrial model is complicated by the vast internal differentiation that accompanies these changes. While it is convenient to speak of the university as a project, social complex, or site, the scope of its dispersion raises the question of whether it can still be considered as a singular entity, sector, field, or endeavor. While many elements are held in common, how they combine and where they lead varies widely. Surely students, faculty, staff, and administrators run across all institutions of higher learning as instruction is provided, credit is given, and degrees conferred. Research universities are conventionally taken as the model for the whole sector, and yet only about one in fifty institutions of higher education carries this designation. Whereas research now designates all manner of things, other than teaching, as a revenue stream, the influence of the knowledge-making university model extends beyond its actual numbers. Four year colleges spend between a quarter and a third of their expenses on instruction, a range of cost consistent with the proportion of their revenues accounted for by tuition and fees (for-profits are an exception here, as roughly 90 percent of their revenue comes from tuition).[67] Histories of the formation of American universities describe them as hybrids of German research institutions and British colleges whose primary tension is between faculty and student-centered missions as production and transmission of knowledge pose conflicting values.[68] Far from the view of a pristine ivory tower insulated from forces of state and market, William Clark has situated the emergence of the research university in the late eighteenth century from the "joint bureaucratization and commodification of academic practices."[69] While it has become commonplace to speak of the corporatization of the university, Steve Fuller observes that the use of the term "corporate" to refer to universities predates its application to business firms by at least five centuries and that the university had long arrogated to itself proto-state activities, such as pump priming and provision of welfare at a local level.[70] But if the entanglement in states and markets comes early, the more recent shift has been from training a particular kind of professional-managerial labor to generating a species of knowledge-financial capital. This ascendant capital formation effaces the public-private delineation upon which the relative autonomy and authority that had once policed academic productivity had been based.

The rubric of "academic capitalism" has emerged to capture this transformation and the sense that the institutions involved are not the passive victims of a wave of commercialization from without, but are active agents in the wars of position by which they aim to be beneficiaries in what amounts to a kind of industrial self-fashioning. For its formulators, Larry Leslie, Sheila Slaughter, and Gary Rhoades, "the theory of academic capitalism sees groups of actors—faculty, students, administrators and academic professionals—as using a variety of state resources to create new circuits of knowledge that link higher education institutions to the new economy. These actors also use state resources to enable interstitial organizations to emerge that bring the corporate sector inside the university, to develop new networks that intermediate between private and public sector, and to expand managerial capacity to supervise new flows of external resources, investment in research infrastructure for the new economy, and investment in infrastructure to market institutions, products, and services to students. Expanded managerial capacity is also directed toward restructuring faculty work to lower instructional costs (though not costs generally)."[71] The consequence of this integration of the university into the knowledge economy, information economy, or new economy, as Slaughter and Rhoades observe, is that "autonomy, the preferred but perhaps always fictive position of universities with regard to capital and state, becomes less possible."[72]

Importantly, lost autonomy does not diminish but actually expands the realm of self-fashioning by which universities and their denizens chart their courses in the world, and this capacity for action serves to differentiate both the knowledge sector and society more broadly. The interdependencies between universities and other knowledge producers amplify the contingent aspects of strategic decision, imbuing each planning exercise undertaken by administrators with the sense of high volitional charge, as if the enterprise will succeed only if the perfect course gets charted. The heady mix of a strange new world that the university finds itself in and an imperative to land on the right strategic route—what once seemed separable into a language of inside and outside—lend themselves to ungovernable metaphors. Universities cultivate knowledge in the form of categories of labor, classifications of ideas, and bundles of debt. These are harvested by various industrial combines, as the universities mine their own deposits of academic labor and intellectual capital as veins and streams of revenue.

The agency in question is itself one of managerialism, whereby administrators and those faculty who can, exercise discretion that is unevenly distributed. For other faculty and many students, what is at stake is the corresponding shift in education from a public good to a private one, from an investment in citizenship to a means of adding value. University autonomy, on this model, was articulated after the Second World War by Vannevar Bush, the engineer-inventor who had headed the Office of Scientific Research and Development and whose ideas became the template for academic-industry relations after the war (his student Frederick Terman developed Silicon Valley). While Bush himself embodied the engineer as pragmatic polymath who could "develop and apply devices on a grand scale," the partition between postwar academic and industry relations derived from the stated need to pursue pure, disinterested knowledge through basic research, incubated within the cloistered confines of university laboratories, which was then passed on to federal agencies for development.[73] This principle of production presupposed strong partitions between theory and practice (or application). Public interest enshrined in universal norms of science would be kept safe from the madding crowd of instrumentality and policy demands, at the same time that pure research would be insulated from the short-cycled rhythms of private commercial interests. Of course, in actuality, the invisibility of what happened within universities was also consistent with Cold War secrecy and weapons development, and this logic helped to consolidate intellectual and practical affinities between war and financial machineries.[74] As Christopher Newfield has shown so effectively, the intersection and codependence of universities and business has been foundational for the modern versions of each institution, forging not only mutual interests but also a humanistic vision of the properly schooled corporate subject, which he terms "managerial humanism."[75]

But the conditions for producing autonomy as a concept and condition of universities can be understood as one historically contingent solution to managing the tensions in the relations between university, business, and society. By 1980 (along with many other features of the growth-driven citizen-consumer social compact that goes by various names of Keynesianism, the welfare state, and corporate liberalism), the extant state-society arrangements could not do the heavy lifting needed to forge a laboring population that would be consistent with the emerging emphasis on financial services or a knowledge economy. Finance, as has been argued previously, implied a different kind of flexibility based upon the willingness to embrace risk and treat the volatilities of the world as self-making opportunities. Far from taking a diminished role in the organization of economic affairs, the state was a key purveyor of this financial logic. This is the climate in which the Bayh-Dole Act of 1980 was passed. The legislation, the result of lobbying by university officials, allowed schools to keep and treat revenues from federally funded faculty research as income streams, and to see faculty potential for new knowledge in proprietary, commercial terms that the university could lay claim to. For those faculty who could, their discoveries would receive institutional recognition and pecuniary reward as commodities, not public goods.

While the first incarnation of Bayh-Dole was conceived as support for small businesses, its reauthorization in 1983 extended to large corporations. What was initially meant by university managers to preserve their privileged translation of public monies into private gain wound up being a condition that rendered them more similar than they would have been to corporate R&D entities. They moved off their perch and into the fray of the knowledge economy. Universities also became investors in their faculty research, taking equity positions in small business and playing the role of venture capitalists.[76] A stream of legislation continued along these lines. The Orphan Drug Act (1983) provided tax incentives for corporations that developed drugs for diseases afflicting small populations (under 200,000 individuals); the National Cooperative Research Act (1984) removed trade and monopoly restrictions for university-enterprise collaborations, such as Sematech—paving the way for the research triangle model; and the Drug Export Amendments Act (1986) allowed export of unapproved drugs to foreign countries.

In this and subsequent legislation, universities were treated as part of and became the beneficiaries of an increasingly integrated knowledge sector. The Digital Millennium Copyright Act (1998) protected proprietary digital media, helping make distance-learning ventures profitable. The initial requirements in the act, to tie its protections to conventional nonprofit classrooms, gradually gave way to subsequent revisions that abetted for-profit e-learning ventures that could themselves access federal financial aid. Accepting the provisions of digital copyright also meant that universities would be obliged to police students and faculty should a copyright holder charge infringement. The Technology, Education, and Copyright Harmonization Act (2002) further effaced the legal firewall between educational and entertainment inputs and profit versus nonprofit aims, especially supporting commercial development of educational products. The change in regulatory framework encouraged academics to model their innovations on business and permitted universities to integrate themselves into the widening revenue streams of knowledge industrialization.[77]

Not only does this expansive state activity refigure the basis of government subvention for individuals and institutions; it also opens vast new horizons of opportunity for those who might profit from student indebtedness and faculty research endeavors. Tax-free and deferred savings plans are part of a shift from grants to loans that benefit students in higher socioeconomic strata. "Federal loans subsidized markets in students by providing relatively privileged students the funds to choose high-tuition institutions."[78] We could also say that these students constitute a government beneficiary in the prospect of class formation, an anticipation of the high-debt ways that will mark the professional-managerial masses. Lack of student debt is perhaps the strongest predictor for graduate school attendance, given that nearly three-quarters of those earning doctorates in the United States had no undergraduate debt.[79] By 2008, more than two-thirds of undergraduates carried student loan debt—up from the debt of less than half a decade earlier and at double the average debt load. At nearly 90 percent of the student body, education debt is highest and largest at for-profit institutions (compared with slightly more than 60 percent of students at public schools and nearly three-quarters of students at private schools).[80]

At the same time, these higher debt loads seem to be setting targets for public institutions as they raise tuition to compensate for lost government revenues, even at times when private sources are shutting their doors on student loans. Students are invited to consider themselves as mirror effects of the rankings undertaken by colleges, making self-investments as part of a strategy of positional advantage.[81] High-scoring students can think of themselves not simply as consumers but as willing subjects, able to strengthen their market position through investment in test and college preparation. Colleges, in turn, maintain market position by selectivity or by producing high rates of rejection. Where selectivity also results in high earnings capacities, schools are building portfolios of future donors, making their own financial aid decisions part of a larger investment strategy. Whether through lifetime fund-raising or learning, matriculation becomes the loss leader for an ongoing financial relationship.

EDUCATIONAL FUTURES

For what is termed the knowledge industry, education is central. By 2005, more than six thousand postsecondary institutions enrolled 18 million matriculated students—about 13 million in public institutions, nearly 3.5 million in private nonprofits, and more than 1.3 million in the fast-growing proprietary sector (with the largest number of institutions of the three categories at 2,660). Cut another way, almost 11 million of these students were in four-year undergraduate programs, about 6.5 million attended two-year colleges, and some 2.2 million were graduate students.[82] As with other measures, focusing strictly on those within the conventional parameters of the educational field leads to a significant result. At the same time, looking exclusively at matriculated students misses the way in which education is implicated in the labor force and the economy more broadly. This larger population is typically invisible to those within the university, but it constitutes a significant way in which the professional world affects educational institutions and the way in which education is implicated in knowledge industrialization.

Each year, nearly two-thirds of the workforce—more than 100 million people—participate in some kind of adult education. From the beginning to the end of the nineties, the percentage of adults taking an adult education course jumped from 32 percent to 45 percent, with the largest proportionate increase during the period in work-related courses. Given the restructuring and retooling that issues from a volatile labor market, education becomes a medium of lateral labor mobility, allowing those who have lost jobs to retrain and those who hope to hold on to their jobs to re-credential. The higher the formal educational requirements, the more likely the participation in adult education. For example, 71 percent of those in professional-managerial occupations are enrolled in such courses. Yet postsecondary institutions are not the leading providers of such instruction. They provide but a fifth of these courses, while business and industry offer just less than half (with professional organizations and government agencies contributing 20 percent and 15 percent, respectively).[83] On the other hand, while the majority of work-related courses are offered without charge, three-quarters of all adult education is fee based and a third entails distance-learning systems. Median out-of-pocket expenses are more than $1,000 for those enrolled in part-time college and university programs.[84] So again, while postsecondary institutions may not be at the center of adult education, it is a vital revenue stream for them. Further, behind the expansion of professional continued education is government policy, which requires such re-credentialing for licensure but leaves it to the market to dictate how that requirement is met.[85]

It is now possible to return to the Dicksensian double vision with which this chapter opened yet with a greater appreciation of paradox and promise. Higher education and the professionals who dwell within and issue from its quarters are ever more present in the world. But with this growth has come not the touted consolidation of autonomy, or the privileged knowledge makers scaling society's heights, but a vertiginous interweaving of these people and institutions within a larger field that makes a claim on what was once theirs alone. Rather than insist on a return to this paradise lost (as if a return from mass to elite access to higher education were a desired aim of critique), a fuller reckoning with the consequences of the circulation of knowledge in society may prove the keenest route to enhancing the opportunities for agency and intervention on the part of professional academics and institutions with ever more elastic mission envelopes. The larger space of knowledge production invites a more capacious conception of what leads to higher education as well as where does it lead. The irony of focusing on a knowledge industry and an extensive if decomposing professional stratum is that in neither case do we learn what substance or content is borne by knowledge or professional practice. The university's autonomy was once viewed as what underwrote its critical compact. If disinterest was never really an option, a renewed interest in the critical operations of knowledge without the guarantee of idyllic remove may force a more careful examination of the nature of the webs in which knowledge-making and professional labor are spun. If freedom is not a function of institutional privilege, then the opportunities presented by the array of attachments before us may get us farther along the road of an academic agency we would want to live by and for. This route begins before college, in the mutual formation of professional parents and children, the matter of Chapter 2.

2

Getting There

Time was, higher education could trumpet its own new beginnings and govern its own ends. Learning was rigorous, comprehensive, original, enlightening—but above all, autonomous. Whatever values were attached, college could claim authorship. Now primary and secondary education have become preparatory to an unprecedented degree, not only because increasing numbers of people wind up attending university but because the anticipation of college increasingly structures how the early years of schooling are conducted and made accountable to the student's presumptive future. That future is a moving target. And it is getting closer. As higher education loses its autonomy, is no longer a thing unto itself but itself in the service of a professional calling, how has the precollege experience been transformed? There is a flip side to all of this anticipation. For undergraduates whose whole lives have led to their entering the campus gates—whatever their various competencies and capabilities—they carry a roomful of expectations, anxieties, and ways of being and thinking of themselves as college students. Actual instruction proceeds in the face of what it has been projected over years and years of anticipation. Nor do the students come alone. Years of homework, test preparation, and applications to middle schools and high schools have coalesced entire households around demands for what college can and should be.

For students, and for the institution itself, higher education today does not create its own origins but arrives in the middle of something it did not itself initiate, however much it is complicit or in cahoots with its own prehistory. "College-bound" refers as much to a disciplining of primary grades that binds kids to a future as it does to an outcome for a certain demographic of those who can afford to excel. An appreciation of these early bindings is vital if students are to grasp what college life is made of. If winsome days of youth are sacrificed for a student's own future—if childhood, so recently delivered from the grind of labor, becomes its own deliverable—college stands little chance of being a time and place unto itself. Instead, students will enter university as if they were already leaving it. Perhaps, however, this baleful complaint is itself too facile, as is the wholesale dismissal of students as somehow unavailable to the educational ideals that have been reserved for them. If the aim of a critique of current conditions is to help imagine what else might emerge, managerialism will need to be uncorked before serving and its contradictions allowed to breathe. Complicating how students respond to managerial pressures and dilemmas are the experiences they had long before getting to college. Rather than adopting a simple hubris that students must be untaught what they have learned education to be, faculty might get further by learning how students themselves have navigated the contending demands on their attentions and self-understanding.

Ideas of what K-12 education should be is as contested as childhood itself. For those children now invited to enjoy their childhoods, freeing the early years from the clutches of toil took millennia but was formalized in the universalization of education in the nineteenth century and in the restrictions on child labor in the twentieth.[1] Corporal punishment, vocationalism, and standards-driven curricula jostled uneasily with the various progressivisms, holisms, and child-centered freedoms. But mounting drives for accountability spelled the end of childhood as a protected age of innocence. Admiral Hyman Rickover, inventor of the nuclear submarine, had already sent a salvo over the bow of kids' separate peace when he declared, in 1959, that after Sputnik, poor education posed a threat to national security. And with Admiral Rickover's declaration, the war against children had only just begun.[2] President Ronald Reagan appointed Terrel Bell as secretary of education in 1981 with a mandate to dismantle the department. Bell in turn convinced Reagan to commission a study on excellence in education in preparation for the legislative process. The resulting 1983 report of the U.S. Department of Education's Commission on Excellence in Education, headed by former University of California President David Pierpont Gardner (1983–1992), was entitled *A Nation at Risk* and enshrined "risk" and "accountability" as key terms of domestic policy. Reagan's charge instructed that educational institutions, both public and private, exist to assist families in the education of their children; that excellence demands competition; and that school choice had a moral side which would allow "God back in the classroom."[3] The report, principally authored by Harvard physicist Gerald Holton, also positioned the academic performance of school children as a threat to domestic security. It argued that if an unfriendly nation had tried to impose the standards of mediocrity that prevail in public schools, "we might have viewed it as an act of war."[4] This rhetorical move to cast a domestic population as enemy combatants justified an actual federal intervention into a arena once protected as a local jurisdiction. The war would be joined and waged on the ground through mandated testing to produce accountability—the tactical equivalent of the well-managed body count that had prevailed in the war against Vietnam.

Nearly twenty years later, No Child Left Behind, a national framework for educational accountability signed into law by President George W. Bush on January 8, 2002, would continue the assault on childhood as a playful interlude, a time of innocence that celebrates society's affluence before the onslaught of adulthood and its unceasing labor. The imperative to leave no one behind placed children once again in the midst of a war zone and introduced educational reform behind the screen of another military metaphor of saving the fallen buddy in the field. The law operationalized the regulation of the "at-risk," announced as a threat to national security nearly twenty years before. The term "at-risk" appears thirty-seven times in the enabling legislation and effectively renders a wide range of problems of disparate origins commensurate with one another as equivalent risk factors that would be subject to a standard measure of performance and noncompletion. According to the legislation: "The term 'at risk,' when used with respect to a child, youth, or student, means a school aged individual who is at-risk of academic failure, has a drug or alcohol problem, is pregnant or is a parent, has come into contact with the juvenile justice system in the past, is at least 1 year behind the expected grade level for the age of the individual, has limited English proficiency, is a gang member, has dropped out of school in the past, or has a high absenteeism rate at school."[5] Criminality, learning disorders, parenting, immigration status—forms of conduct and states of being—share a calculus by which failure can be predicted and prevented. The failure of each adds to a loss in American competitiveness, even if the meanings of success remain ill defined. After the Cold War, the deeper meanings of strategic victory proved elusive.

The dilemma posed by victory repositioned the enemy so that a sense of national purpose might be forged from countries outside to populations within. Accordingly, the United States was no longer in a race with alternate social systems but faced a world in competition with itself, fighting over who could best the market. Proxy wars slid into internecine conflicts. Not only was the space of the enemy denied a clear geography, but even what counts as triumph became difficult to discern. While reams of evidence were adduced to assess the situation, the larger sense of purpose proved elusive—the mission difficult to define and therefore impossible to complete. Technical measures readily replaced strategic vision. Battles could be assessed tactically by their immediate performance indicators. In this, foreign and domestic policy share a logic of accountability without a broader view of what they aim to account for. The prairie fire that begins with education spreads to all manner of local sites and subjects. Not only individuals but also schools could fail if they were unable to convert exogenous risk factors into measurable performance gains. The Obama administration's "Race to the Top" pits states against one another to provide funding based on productivity gains as part of the American Recovery and Reinvestment Act of 2009: Saving and Creating Jobs and Reforming Education. Echoing earlier themes of education reform, Obama states, "The countries that out-teach us today will out-compete us tomorrow."[6]

Launched in the eighties, the risk wars anticipated in the Bell Commission document proliferate as a series of domestic wars on drugs, crime, and culture. These were a feature of a broader policy shift away from welfare-state entitlements and toward a cleaving of population between the risk-capable and those delimited as at-risk. Defunding or denying government support for those once caught and contained within a safety net redrew the social compact between state and society. The shift of risk to the populace on the basis of each person's ability to bear it contributed to a generalized sense of lost security, a condition that treats troubled populations as predicates of war.[7] For those who successfully passed the test and ascended to the professional-managerial class, their capacity to effectively negotiate risk, to turn knowledge to unexpected gain, would become the measure of those who got ahead in the world. Hence this cleavage of the population between the at-risk and the risk-capable would become the dynamic nexus of policy and self-worth, rendering people capable and culpable for their own failure and removing the guarantees of security, including that of professionalized knowledge itself.

Behind the imperatives of accountability lay a conception of early education which mirrored that of professional credentialing, where, as suggested in Chapter 1, high-stakes testing is the norm.[8] College prep, readiness for learning as an end in itself, yields to a different future, that of the professional. This shift in aims and methods of education—from the self-sustaining and disinterested pursuit of knowledge to measurably interested outcomes of market placement—aligns with what is referred to in this book as the "professional turn." As college becomes reconfigured for professional advancement and development, preparation for it in the primary and secondary grades adopts the protocols of performance-driven knowledge-based deliverable outcomes. While defunded public education was itself becoming a form of tracking, the testing imperative treated all primary education as a kind of college prep. Enhancing opportunity—delivering valuable education—meant orienting all students toward the end of their mandated education. Living the present in anticipation of this expected future accomplishment—itself measured by the caliber of college entrance—would affect not only the orientation of K-12 schooling but also the formation of college students themselves. Freshmen would walk on campus already fully alive to the burdens of instrumentalization. In no small measure, this would serve to increase the number of students who went to college and to expand the proprietary sector happy to attend to these more focused goals and aspirations. Still, it is vital to set the shifting conditions of higher education in the context of what shaped students along the way. Teaching kids that they are the objects of a contest over accounts means that they will be sorted by their grasp of a calculus of risk and reward that is modeled on professional training.

To understand how these pressures operate up close, I want to focus on an elementary school in New York City that in many ways has a history of resisting these very demands and making a dissident claim to selfhood—the whole child—as an end in itself. The school is very much part of the world in which it is placed as an alternative, and it is increasingly populated by professional families keen on meeting performance demands and expectations. It is also a site that makes vivid some of the key fault lines and consequences of what is now termed educational reform in local and national policy discussions. Founded in 1971 through a community-workshop process that included planners, public officials, consultants, parents, community members, and teachers, the school emerged as a child-centered, nonhierarchical school-community partnership. From the start, it featured open, multigrade classrooms and active parent involvement. The arts were viewed as central to a curricular and humanistic holism that permitted integration of various subjects and an emphasis on development of a personal voice. The school was created when it split from an existing neighborhood school, which was deemed at the time to represent prevailing professional aspirations. It moved to an old school building built in 1905 and adopted an even older designation, P.S. 3, a New York public school dating back to the early nineteenth century. Rather than create separate enrollment zones, or catchments, the two schools continued to share the same geographical boundaries within which they would draw their student bodies. Sharing the same neighborhood and providing a local option to choose from engendered a sense that they represented alternative educational approaches to each other. Architecturally the first elementary school, P.S. 41 is housed in a modern facility, and P.S. 3 is cast as having a funky, retro look that provides a visual marker for its moniker, "the hippie school."[9] Beyond its founding, this oppositional sensibility continued at P.S. 3. Hence, the resistance now tells as much about what is possible in the face of standardizing constraints as it does about the fissures in the mandates for greater emphasis on measurable performance outcomes.

In actuality, students' futures are forged not simply in the logics of testing but in the spaces between what standards call for and what they actually do. For a year as PTA president of my own children's elementary school, I had the opportunity to observe the dynamics inside and outside the classroom at close range—from participating in teaching to addressing dramatic policy shifts. Far from claiming that the school or my experience is typical or representative, it is instructive for what it makes legible, through its own eccentricities, in the normal operations of managerially driven school reform. The shift away from curricular and cultural diversity—implicit in the performance protocols introduced by the test-based mandates of Mayor Michael Bloomberg and New York City school's Chancellor Joel Klein (2002–2010)—can be seen in the rhetoric of empowerment found in the enlightened management literature of the past two decades. While the gains have been contested and the implementation controversial, New York City has subsequently been upheld as a national model for what centralized control, scientific management, and strategic investment in schools can yield.[10] Indeed, the solution for public schools is that they reinvent themselves as lean, networked, empowered sites oriented toward continually adding value in the way that a corporation delivers enhanced market share. Rather than simply increasing the percentage of students who meet standards, each school is to demonstrate yearly improvements in scores for all children. In effect, now all are to be treated as if they were potentially at risk of failing if they cannot orient themselves to continual improvement. The logic of this outlook on education as a value-added deliverable is that it will get children to college and shape what they think higher education (and professional life) is about.

THE STRANGERS

Charly Greene's classroom is a beehive—one that at casual glance looks to be a swarm, a cacophonous buzz, but in random motion. Upon closer inspection, however, it is full of intricate patterns, complex polyrhythms, and sweet productivity. She has dubbed her students "the Strangers," and each night's homework assignment asks them to consider, "Is this your strangest work?" It is a class that mixes second- and third-graders of wide ability, some who have been reading chapter books since kindergarten, others who are just getting there. While the school is located in real estate–rich Greenwich Village, it has up to this point been able to include kids from all over New York City. This means that half are white students and the other half black, Hispanic, and Asian students (citywide, 44 percent of the population, but less than 15 percent of the student body in public schools, is made up of white students).[11] This diversity is even more striking in a school district (District 2) where enrollment is on the rise and 90 percent of the increase is from white and Asian students, and average household income increased over the nineties from $150,767 to $169,533.[12] P.S. 3 (also known as the John Melser Charrette School) takes its name and pedagogy from the Charrette approach, used in architectural training, in which students gather around a particular project and engage in discussion and critique.

The classroom gives a sense of a design studio with various workstations. About a third of the room is an open area with a rug and benches. This little amphitheater, into which some thirty kids crowd, is the commons where students and teachers gather together, listening to stories and presentations. Charly is full of questions. When she reads aloud, she asks students why a protagonist behaves the way she does, how the minor characters fit into the story, what they think is going to happen next. There's also a half-dozen tables with chairs—each with its own basket of supplies—where collaborative projects take place. Open cabinets are chock-full of art supplies. Bookcases line the walls with bins and bins of books. Shelves hold works in progress. A board at the front announces the day's activities. These vary from day to day as special projects come and go, but on a representative day, there's independent work, a morning meeting, discussion of a story, sign-language instruction, math, recess and lunch, group projects, more discussion, dismissal. At times, students may be found outside the classroom in the hallway, reading in small groups or working through a project.

In addition, at least once a day, students go to specialized classes in music, art, computers, games, movement, and clay. They also go on field trips to places such as the transit museum or the museum of design. They explore the ecosystem of the Hudson River (a few blocks away) or map and measure the proportions of buildings around the school. These trips are tied to special curricular projects. The creation of a quiltlike woven tapestry to which each student contributes is made of found objects that they have collected in their travels around the city. A video, filmed and edited by one of the parents, features readings and enactments of stories that the children have written about the most extraordinary things that have happened to them. These range from being cut by glass, to being caught in a tsunami in Sri Lanka, to having an adventure in a volcanic lava tube. A study of maps and urban infrastructure draws from different historical periods, scales, and graphic representations. There's often a student teacher in the room as well as a parent and other volunteer helpers who come on a regular basis to work one on one with students. They help with reading, math, games, or knitting, and they assist with setup and planning.

Of the collaborative ethos in the room, Charly reflects:

> Students assess themselves from what they made. You want them to see themselves in what they made. The reason I have so many things in the room is that the kids get to do and make things. We didn't go out so much because they were so into doing things in class. They were really occupied with what they were doing in class, although they also really miss going out. Luis made a comic book and he became known as a comic book artist. We went to the museum twice so that they could see the difference. That was an assessment. There has to be a combination between doing things as a class and knowing what you can do on your own. I was in a class where I felt so frustrated having to do everything at the same time. When I first came here, there

was a philosophy of each student doing what they choose to do. The reason that choice time is important is that kids use skills like they got from architecture to develop their own specialties. But now I think I can't get away with that degree of choice. The compromise is that I introduce more so that they are brought to things more directly. A real choice time comes out of kids having skills. But you have to build that in. Collaboration is really tough, but you have to teach it. Is this an activity that can best be done in pairs? I ask: Why aren't some groups working? How do you say that it has to work? Like anything in teaching, what you emphasize is what comes out. Even when you try to push collaboration, kids get frustrated because they are trying so hard. Some make major breakthroughs when they have to work with other people. The projects really showed who the kids were.[13]

Guests to the classroom, strangers of a different sort, are also common. For a couple of months, Yves, an architect, comes in once a week. He starts by distributing materials to eight groups of three or four children. Some get sticks, others paper, still others sugar cubes. Each group must create a building using all three materials. Trade is necessary, and the students determine the terms of exchange as they go along. Sugar cubes have immediate appeal and those groups that have them are swiftly subject to the attention of those who do not. Exchange rates vary based on the offer, who's doing the offering, and how much remains in stock. Paper, the easiest to work with, garners the least interest. Some groups get their buildings quickly under way. Others struggle to move beyond incessant and internecine barter. Fissures appear when a friend cuts too good a deal with a buddy from another group. Both for those in the midst of construction and those caught in eddies of speculation, the constant requests for materials prove distracting. Still, the structures rise: windows and rooms, front doors, signs, parking lots, roofs. The adults move from work group to work group, asking questions and providing technical assistance, encouragement, and conflict resolution. Some groups work serenely, others founder for focus, still others erupt in disagreement over how to proceed. The children are constantly negotiating all the differences that emerge. After an hour and a half of snaking around the room helping to glue walls and tape ceilings, Charly has the class break for discussion. Some talk about their structures. Others focus on the modes of exchange. A second-grader observes that sometimes free trade feels like forced trade. This is because they are compelled to barter whether they want to or not, because exchange can undermine their concentration and alter their ideas, and because they lack the means to resist the demands placed upon them for materials. Others chime in saying that the pressure to exchange undercuts the ethos of collaborative production. Group composition continually changes over the course of the year. The students learn to partner with the diversity in the room. A few kids are really challenged to work in groups. They break off on their own but are drawn back later or on the next project. Even this changes. One especially volatile boy couldn't sit still with others at the beginning of the year. By the end, he could start a project with someone else, even if he couldn't finish it. He loved to make board games.

Earlier in the year, the class had embarked on a project of creating its own board games. At first, they discussed which games they liked and why. They talked about family dynamics in the context of games, when competition distracts them from the flow of play, who they could rely on to violate the rules or follow them, and when they had the most fun. They had been playing games with dice and cards every morning to help with their counting skills. Now they could make their own if they could figure out how. After discussing the basic elements of a game and comparing it to a story with a beginning, a middle, and an end, a simple grammar was devised. They needed to create an environment and find three ways to move pieces forward and two ways to move them back. Some landscapes were scattered with battling monsters. Others featured the Escher-like staircases of the hundred-year-old school. Still others were populated with imaginary animals or edible treats. Boards were created along with pieces. A distinction was made between games of skill and games of chance. Students debated the fairness of rules, the need to write them down, and the likelihood of equal chances to win. Rules were described as ways of resolving conflict. Some students felt they had too many rules, while others protested that there were too few.

One third-grader devised an elaborate apparatus for throwing dice, convinced that the fanciful mechanism would affect the outcome. This raised the question of objectivity, of forces beyond one's control, and of probability. Dice were thrown dozens of times. Frequency tables were generated. Normal curves were approximated, first on individual graphs, and then these were tabulated together on the whiteboard. Chance was linked to fate in the stories that they wrote and read. Skills lined up with a character's will or talent. Various students provided examples of each from A Series of Unfortunate Events and Harry Potter. Math and reading were in the service of each other. The children took their board games and taught their friends in classes down the hall. The rules, now written down as an instruction sheet, were assessed for fairness and clarity. Explaining, teaching, sharing were reinstated. The children converted their games to fit the scale of the classroom through a series of physical improvisations. They moved themselves as game pieces on giant chess boards. Using the square tiles on the classroom floor, they counted grids and considered how their moves affected others as the space between them grew more or less dense. The shifting landscapes they created were linked to the changes in their metropolitan environment. Some urban history was offered. How had the city changed, toward what end, and how could they find these traces? The timelines they established were woven back into the personal narratives they created—nonfiction tales that required evidence and memory.

The classroom projects were problem based, comprehensive, interdisciplinary. Basic skills, like counting or reading, were coupled with intricate negotiations, spatial and motor skills, turn taking, conceptualization and contextualization. Homework was oriented toward engaging parents in their child's learning process through games, telling of family stories, and collecting of materials. The projects also demanded independent work from the kids. They had to read and analyze stories, providing reasons for their preferences and interests. They did math worksheets and vocabulary lists. They checked for spelling, capitalization, and grammar. They also prepared for their standardized tests. The content of the tests was not linked to what students learned in the classroom. Reading was based on comprehension, identification, and matching, not on demonstrating any particular knowledge base or subject familiarity.

Readying for the test is understood by students to be a thing unto itself. One boy, filling out a multiplication worksheet, was asked how the math was going. He gave a puzzled look and replied, "This isn't math; it's test prep." Consistent with the student's experience, testing, measurement, and accountability are not tied to the rest of the student's classroom education. Rather, testing exists as its own world—its own force—to which pupils pay tribute. Kids may get nervous or excited; they make look forward to the test (one said he liked them because he got to eat candy in class) or dread it. Or they may range across all these sentiments. But tests exist in this otherwise fully integrated classroom as a kind of internal apartheid reminiscent of the separate biblical offerings to God and to Caesar. Early on, students become aware that the teacher is not the ultimate authority in the classroom, even if she is the one they can most access and respect. Charly considers the ways in which the testing affects her teaching:

> The worst thing about tests is that they are so time consuming. They are badly written. Kids get nervous. They think that all of the year was about tests. Kids will say, "I've done that for the test already; do I really need to do it now?" It used to be that the first three months of the year were for getting to know each other, for socialization. Now the testing starts right away. I have to prepare in the summer. I have to figure out how to get around what the test demands. If you say to a parent that your child has progressed and then the test comes [back with a low score], you can't prove it. You can strike a deal with the devil, know that your own curriculum works, and ignore the test. Some children do well on tests but still need help to understand the basic concepts. I feel really sorry for teachers coming in now because before there was a learning curve for them to figure out what works and what doesn't work. As much as you're trying to ignore the test, it's still woven in. You find yourself even on a field trip to the South Street

Museum talking about simple machines and casually mention[ing] that this may be on the test. Your autonomy as a teacher is affected. The principle is that you have to do less test prep, but it's still affected.

I know that if I worked at private school, this wouldn't come up. I wish I had more time to use what I found on the ECLAS [diagnostic test] to help the kids. I won't say that a kid knows lots of math or that I am a good math teacher but that they prepared well and that I am a good tutor. Pretty much you can get anyone to get a three [out of four—i.e., a high enough score to meet grade level standards]. It's soda, candy, chanting, and test prep. You can have a very bright child who can get a three. [Others] can learn to read a short passage but haven't really learned how to read a book and understand it. Whatever we come up with, it becomes about test prep. The administration here is on your side; the parents are on your side. But there are schools where no one is.[14]

Hence, rather than being a comprehensive measure of student performance, a summary of achievement, or a means to measure local learning against an external standard, the work of testing both establishes an administrative demand as a thing unto itself and imposes limits on what such externally applied tasks can demand of the classroom. Rather than learning to resist testing as a kind of administrative labor per se, the classroom teaches its own division of labor as something that both student and teacher must scale.

WORKING PARENTS

In this classroom and many others at the school, there are a goodly number of parents who, rather than just leave their kids at the door and enter their own work-a-day worlds, are heavily involved in day-to-day instructional activities. A manager for the city's environmental protection agency offers science classes, a university dance teacher helps with choreography, and a filmmaker shoots footage of the music classes, creating a documentary film. At the time of my classroom observations (2006 and 2007), the school stood at a double-crossroads. By the late nineties, many of its founding teachers, who had spent their entire careers at P.S. 3, were retiring. Direct nonparent neighborhood involvement was waning, replaced by a gentrification of the surrounding blocks that increasingly came with kids in tow. The school is crossed by Christopher Street, center of New York's most famous gay neighborhood (the Stonewall Inn, the bar at the epicenter of the 1969 gay rights demonstrations, is but an avenue away). The independence of the school's staff to pursue a separate course of instruction was meeting the latest wave of centralized standards and assessment. And yet there remained considerable parent input and opportunity for taking part. Compared with the city as a whole, there is a relatively robust parent-teacher organization, with committees that oversee a range of areas, from arts and curriculum to buildings, library, and safety. Parents maintain a Web site, produce a newsletter and yearbook, undertake fund-raisers throughout the year, and run an after-school program (that has itself become increasingly professionalized). A political action committee keeps abreast of policy changes in the city and state, is represented at district meetings, and helps mobilize public sentiment around key issues.

While the culture of endless meetings may have abated, the increasingly professional profile of the parents offers the prospect of translating specialized knowledge into primary education. That is not to say that professional knowledge translates equally or easily. Despite assistance with homework, curriculum nights, weekly notes home, and a near-daily presence in the classroom as they drop off and pick up their children, some parents strain to grasp what their children's education actually consists of and what it looks like when their kids are learning appropriately. The look of learning is not easily recognizable. If it is a question of seeing how kids respond to what they are exposed to, this can vary much during the course of a day, week, or year. Deeper connections, dispositions toward learning itself, the sense of what to do with what one knows—these are nuanced indicators, ultimately detectable much farther down the road in what the kids come to do in their lives.

There is nothing novel in the indeterminacy between learning and assessment. Rather, what seems pressing is the insistence that any observable moment could be taken as assessable and that parents would expect schools to deliver on this demand. Clearly, not all parents require such immediate certainty. Some report that their kids seem very happy at school, or that they are amazed by all that happens in the class, or that they're glad their kids do not have to suffer the way that they did. Still, there are plenty of parents seeking more structure, more time for preparation, and clearer identification of standards. Teachers are expected to satisfy these demands for more information even though this can sometimes serve to feed parents' anxieties about what is taking place. Weekly notes home from teachers that report on both curricular design and rationale can provoke confusion, even well into the school year. E-mail intensifies labor outside the classroom and carries the expectation of immediate response and unbounded availability. It can also further intensify teacher's attention to those students already receiving a larger share. Most parents appreciate the limits, whereas a concerned few can absorb disproportionate amounts of time.

One parent insisted on viewing a copy of a schoolwide curriculum so that he could see what standards were being set. His review of the document assuaged many of his concerns, despite its schematic makeup and distance from what transpired in the classroom. Public schools do give tours of their facilities to prospective families. Despite a prohibition on active recruitment, these visits can feel like interviews. Parents, aware of the debates surrounding the different approaches to math instruction, ask which model is used. When told that a variety of approaches are synthesized, the questioner wonders how this is possible without creating confusion. One father of a preschooler inquired as to which colleges elementary school graduates wound up at. He was surprised to find that no such records were kept. At the same time, parents are concerned that the tests and the culture of accountability will destroy what is distinctive about the school and that any accommodations to meet those pressures are best resisted. The tours seem to conform to a kind of sensory Rorschach test. When two visitors compared notes after their walk through the building, one was elated at finding classrooms bathed in light, the other distraught at how dark and dingy those same rooms appeared.

Parents who are professionals in the arts can also bring expectations and aesthetic values that may be unsustainable or inappropriate in a primary school. The parent association has an arts committee that draws exactly these professionals into conversation with one another. The tension between supporting and assessing educational programs can surface in this venue. One artist parent bemoaned the quality of the art he saw children create and dismissed the existence of an authentic arts-based curriculum at the school, despite the many specialized art classes and the extensive use of art in regular classes. A gallery owner insisted that teachers should be working artists and that their professional work needs to be subject to review by experienced appraisers such as herself. A proposed program to help diversify the arts by teaching Spanish through theater was met with skepticism. Parents questioned why such goals might not be better met with other language instruction. Another parent suggested achieving diversity by introducing a classically based great books curriculum. Still other parents suggested that professional artists be brought in to give master classes to the children, at the same time expressing concern for the arts teachers, who might not welcome the inevitable comparison. These parents did not reflect on how professional artistic achievements might be made available to young children in a way that students could incorporate into their own learning. Certainly, much can be said for exposing kids in early grades to complex works of art, but this does not answer the question of how to teach the complexity. These did not turn out to be majority sentiments, but they do point to the challenges in bringing professional knowledge into primary school settings. Ironically, it is the intricacy of the curriculum itself and the approaches that teachers take to assessment and evaluation that can elude those parents most insistent on high standards, a demand present in their own professional practices.

The Department of Education funds provide classroom teachers a range of support services for special learning needs, administrative and building staff, and also the means to hire teaching specialists—which includes a full-time movement teacher, a visual arts teacher, and computers, along with necessary training. The relative affluence of involved parents at this school also means that sufficient funds can be raised to supplement what the city makes available. This allows for an increase in the number and coverage of artistic media in the curriculum so that children in all grades get exposure to a variety of forms. Parent monies pay for music teachers and instruments, ceramics instruction and clay as well as other art supplies, costumes for dance concerts, and a science program. Parent monies have also been used to procure supplemental services, like additional school aides and head lice monitoring. These funds have even gone to building and classroom improvements, like drinking fountains, flat screen monitors, and a dance floor. Each year, upon consultation with various committees and discussions at monthly meetings, a budget is devised and approved, and fund-raising goals are set.

The funds are raised through a series of events that both bring the community together and highlight the very different capacities for participation among parents. Those with the flexibility are able to spend many hours organizing events, while those with stricter schedules cannot. This can create a division between the professional parents, especially those who are self-employed or who have their own businesses, and those traveling from afar or with occupations more strictly subject to the time-discipline of others. This is one point where the voluntarism associated with commitment to community jostles with the conditions of labor that would make such time freely available. Community can seem to have a more general aspect, as an environment of equals where all belong, even as it rests upon a more specialized condition of labor that introduces exclusions over which the community has scant control. The parent organization had itself reflected this partition in its own structure. There had been an executive committee of elected delegates who met regularly and made decisions, and a larger body, called the School Community Council (SCC), which met a few times a year and was open to all. The SCC referenced the idea of the school as a learning community but also harkened back to the days when nonparent participants in the institution were numerous and made an affiliative bond as part of the school's community. While anyone from the SCC could attend the executive sessions, only members of the executive committee could cast votes. The defenders of the dual structure found it promoted responsibility and informed discussion. The detractors found it exclusionary and a damper to participation. The discussion as to whether to maintain or change this dual structure took place over several years, until finally a vote was taken to form a single decision-making body composed of all households.

Despite e-mails, newsletters, and bulletin postings, parents would frequently tell officers and one another that they did not know when meetings were held, how decisions were made, or what was going on in general. Others might report that there was a surfeit of information and that it was impossible to keep up with and assimilate all that was distributed. On either side of this divide was a confidence that systems of communication could be improved to the point where participation would be maximized, conflicts minimized, and consensus achieved. Communication in these instances tended to omit the question of the amount of work involved either in becoming informed or in carrying out particular ideas. Conversations about enhanced participation often revolved around preferred methods of communication (e-mail versus newsletter). These could substitute for considerations of content and beg the question of how much detail the community at large might want to be privy to. The ideals of full inclusion and total participation could trade a generic attachment to democracy for an organizational structure by which tasks get done and decisions are made. Such quandaries produce their own rhetorics of accountability in relation to substantive values that can turn out to be divergent from one another.

At one meeting, a decision to provide funds for a class trip was hotly contested by some who felt that monies raised by all parents were being spent on a particular constituency. Others claimed the bylaws were not properly followed. Parents who requested the funds voiced frustration that budgetary decisions were made the year before and that their success in fund-raising did not result in an ability to access monies raised. Parents who had spent long hours organizing fund-raising events on behalf of the school's arts-based curriculum felt it was inappropriate for the yielded funds to be spent on nonarts activities. General understanding of how the budget process worked became an issue, with confusion over what was in savings and what could be counted as a budgetary surplus. The controversy focused attention on who could claim to speak for the interests of democratic participation, and what methods of governance could assure that a balance among flexibility, consultation, and deliberation was achieved. Some parents had every expectation for greater transparency in decision making even when it was unclear how many parents wanted to be intimately involved in the process. For those who clearly wanted to be involved, it was not certain what responsibility they might want to undertake to assure they mastered the needed information.

The volunteer nature of the organization meant that ideas for reform would not necessarily garner the labor required to implement this reform. Some would identify themselves as "idea people" without sensing a responsibility to carry the ideas through. Others felt estranged from meetings because of past conflagrations. It would have to be said that far more of the parent's actual involvement transpired outside of formal meetings than within them. In the end, the bylaws of the PTA were themselves changed to eliminate the organization's dual structure, to introduce greater flexibility, and to assure a proper vetting process for large expenditures. The monthly meetings rarely had a quorum of the parent population (15 percent of some three hundred households was required). A vote was held in the school lobby as parents came in to drop off their children. Just on the basis of how many parents accompanied their children inside the school, this extended the pool of those included in a vote to more than 50 percent. Department of Education regulations, which govern PTA activities, do not permit voting by e-mail or other forms of proxy. Despite the constraints on communication and participation, the new framework to consolidate the decision-making body and eliminate the separate executive committee passed overwhelmingly by a vote of 118 to 7. Along with this change to the organization's bylaws came procedures for making expenditures outside the annual budget process so as to promote initiatives by those active in the meetings. And procedures were put in place for when a vote of the entire community, as opposed to those at a given meeting, was indicated.

The pressures from inside and outside the school congeal in the principal's office. The range of tasks undertaken is enormous, from conflict resolution between students, to staff development, budget planning, data production, interfacing with district and systemwide bodies, working with contractors and vendors, and meeting with parents. The principal patrols the halls and is present at after-school dismissal. She entreats students not to run (they may skip) or scream as they get to where they need to be going. She visits classes and addresses assemblies. As a consequence, she seems to know all of the kids by name and they her. Her familiarity with parents tends to be more limited, constrained as it is by parents she encounters as volunteers and those whose children have special educational or disciplinary issues. Individual parents may come up with wonderful ideas, like an all-school playwriting festival, but they may not consider how the additional program will find a place in the packed school schedule. Parents may also seek greater control over the sense of security in the school—an end to bullying, more separation from the middle school students who share the building, and gentler disciplinary techniques from the school aides who supervise lunch and recess. Some parents assume they can ask the principal for extra services, be they additional security guards or instructional staff, not thinking how they might use their own organizational channels to help communicate and prioritize what is possible.

Given the history and reputation of the school, one consequence of a learning community is the parents' expectations of greater input regarding decision making. This was in evidence when the principal decided to decouple several of the fourth- and fifth-grade classes in response to constant pressure from the Department of Education to improve test performance. Some parents focused on what they say was an end to the uniqueness of the school's culture and a capitulation to external pressures, while other parents fixated on how they were informed: by letter rather than via a face-to-face meeting. Some remembered that, two years before, the idea was discussed in a meeting of just this sort and that it had ended acrimoniously. The pressure from the Department of Education and the principal's efforts to adapt to this pressure can be met with similar skepticism as part of an intractable bureaucracy that will not give parents their due. There are parents who will say that they run the school or that "parents do 75 percent of the work" in it. The imposition of changes from the Department of Education is experienced by them as a loss of autonomy that resembles the erosion of freedom to professionals more broadly. Parents will remark that they chose this particular school because they expected it to resist external pressures altogether and maintain their discretion over their children's schooling. Unfamiliarity with the volume and consequences of the demands that reforms placed on the school administrators elevated the authority that a principal was seen to have. This version of school choice appeared as an equivalent, if local, investment version of the language of choice also touted in the mayoral school reforms that these same parents so disdained.

The principal's attentions were increasingly occupied by Department of Education mandates for reports and accounting. Consequently, there was less time to involve parents as participants in key decisions. The principal is contractually required to improve scores and therefore to find viable compromises that parents need not factor into their own assessments of what is possible and preferable. While parent associations are voluntary, they can contain a cadre of active parents whose work and knowledge position them within the institutional memory and perspective by which challenges and decision points are navigated. There have been cases where officers, such as treasurer and recording secretary, remain over the course of several years, especially where specialized knowledge is concerned. More typically, the PTA copresidents serve a year term and tend not to put themselves up for reelection after going through a cycle. New presidents can come into office with a self-assigned charge to rectify the inefficiencies and, in effect, reinvent the organizational culture through bold measures or reforms. Such confidence that significant organizational change is possible, if only the problems are accurately diagnosed, can be essential to undertaking a time-consuming voluntary position. Seasoned presidents who have just completed a year's service tend to greet the new ideas with a mixture of welcome relief and bemusement, remembering they had entered office with exactly the same round of pronouncements of old ways to be swept aside. Unlike a staff-run organization where certain literacies can be expected, voluntary associations of professionals can proceed with the aspiration to continually liberate themselves from their own histories. They dash ahead by virtue of visionary leadership, even if the individuals in question lack the formal authority to do much more than propose solicitations for input.

MEASURES TAKEN

The expectation of parent involvement, the autonomy teachers enjoyed to devise unique curricula, the diversity of student demographics were all factors that put this school at odds with the city's own schemata for reform. In a previous policy iteration, when schools showed proficiency in meeting standards, the Department of Education rewarded them with exemption from standard curricula. In New York City, two hundred schools had been awarded this designation, P.S. 3 among them. As the public schools became a centerpiece for the national political aspirations of the mayor, attention was focused on how the municipal administration could take over the schools and produce better results.[15] In 2002, the Bloomberg administration successfully petitioned the state to dissolve the New York City Board of Education and bring it into his office as a separate department. Twice in the course of three years, the administrative structure of the schools was reorganized. The reform, called Children First, was given the following rationale: "Schools Chancellor Joel Klein saw school reform as a two-step process. To create adequate schools, he needed to stabilize and bring coherence to the system. To elevate schools from adequate to outstanding, he needed to take a second step: empowering principals by giving them decision-making power and resources and holding them accountable for results."[16] The first phase entailed creating leadership positions more closely tied to the central school administration. In 2003, Klein replaced the district-based structure with ten regional supervisors, each overseeing a cluster of local school districts (there had been thirty). Since principals were to be the line managers in the new schema, it was important to create a fresh cohort tooled in the workings of the new system. Klein, with help from private donors, developed a leadership academy that trained some two hundred principals between 2002 and 2006. While itself a nonprofit, the academy embodies the conviction that the private sector is the best source of ideas for restructuring public goods such as education. Bloomberg himself, who took the mayoralty directly from his seat as media magnate, was the archetype of this belief in the superiority of business models and the heroism of the business leader, who, with his own fortune secure, can procure the civic interest. "The Academy was modeled after successful private sector initiatives such as General Electric's John F. Welch Leadership Center and the Ameritech Institute. The Academy is actively working on building a team of 1,400 great principals who are true instructional leaders, who can inspire and lead teachers, students and parents in their school community."[17] Fourteen hundred is a reference to the number of schools in the 1.1 million student school system. The academy breaks the presumptive career track from teacher to principal by recruiting nationally and tracking trainees directly into the system. It grants greater autonomy to the managerial skill set imported from team approaches to business. By 2009, the effects of the new training were extensive. Nearly 80 percent of the school principals in the system were not on the job in 2001, and the leaders from the academy had three times the teacher attrition of other principals.[18] As if to drive home this point that management skills are best delivered from without, when Chancellor Klein stepped down in November 2010, Mayor Bloomberg replaced him with Cathleen Black, whom he called a "superstar manager." Black was a publishing executive with no experience as an educator.[19]

In June 2007, the second phase of the reorganization was implemented. The regional structure was dissolved and replaced with four citywide supervisory learning support organizations (LSOs). While district and regional frameworks were organized in the name of geography (even if the jurisdictions had been spread out or gerrymandered), the LSOs were ostensibly thematic. The Community Learning Support Organization lists as core values excellence for every child, the importance of homeschool partnerships, lifelong and communal learning, equity, social justice, and civic responsibility.[20] The integrated curriculum and Instruction Learning Support Organization help "schools develop a 'thinking curriculum' that makes cross-content connections and integrates the arts and technology."[21] The Knowledge Network Learning Support Organization "is a dynamic model for student success which promotes continued academic achievement through the implementation of Core Knowledge, a nationally recognized curriculum with a proven record of effectiveness in science, social studies, visual arts, and music."[22] The Leadership Learning Support Organization will "co-construct with each school a Leadership LSO/ School Work Plan to reflect the overall and specific school priorities, needs, and interests, and facilitate collaboration and learning among schools to share successful practices and insights."[23]

Within a few months of being rolled out, the LSO scheme required school principals to choose from among the four options, even if the dimensions of difference between them were difficult to discern. It was unclear whether the LSO reflected different educational philosophies, disciplinary specialization, educational outcome, or other priority—or whether the variation was according to the leadership styles of the supervisors themselves. The parallel form of choice mimicked the appearance of a market without disclosing much about the nature of the goods. Although the terms were of free-willed selection, principals were compelled to choose. The arbitrary character of the distinctions left the impression that the act of choosing was more salient than the choices themselves. While the supervisors were known to many of the principals in the city, the difference in educational approach behind the four options was far more difficult to discern. The LSOs provided consulting services that were priced at different tiers, and the heads of the organizations—all administrators in the former scheme—were assigned the title of CEO. The idea that one could select one's own supervisor created a circumstance of responsibility without altering the relations of authority. The language spoke to the concept of collaboration with the mandate of immediate results hanging like a dagger.

In the name of streamlining the bureaucratic hierarchy, the networks that supported the schools were sundered so that the principals themselves—also newly anointed as CEOs—could be held to higher standards of accountability. The structures of mentoring and professional development that exist between principal and teacher were replicated within the area superintendency between principals and their supervisory staff. Under the previous system, a deputy superintendent would be assigned to work with a particular principal to develop curricular and other resources. Reorganization would shuffle these relations of trust built over several years (or at least since the prior reorganization of District 2 a decade before under Superintendent Anthony Alvarado). Without mediating relationships at the regional level, principals would be more readily encouraged to adopt the central administration's schemes. Rather than being protected within a recognizable network, schools would be directly exposed to the measurement rubrics that the chancellor handed down.

The consequence was to generate a sense of equity of pressure irrespective of the prior performance of the schools. Now, instead of being rewarded for maintaining excellence (as was the case for the two hundred exempted schools), the new schema expected annual improvement from each student for all schools irrespective of their existing standing. The new schema was portrayed as antielitist and democratic. All would be subject to the same performance demands. A year's worth of improvement would be quantified and used to assess the school's teaching effectiveness. While P.S. 3 could demonstrate 98 percent of its students achieving at or above state standards, only 58 percent of students had made what was considered a year's progress over their previous level of attainment. The persistent testing meant that in practice, diagnosis was transformed from naming a goal to be reached to creating a moving target by which productivity would be continually measured and additional value extracted. Education in this reckoning is knowable at each moment as a kind of just-in-time production of value that need not await its own completion. Assigning a score as a quantifiable increment in output, like setting a price on the market, collapses measure, store, and bearer of value so as to stand for educational substance as such.

To put this advanced metric in place, more competition among schools would be required, with tangible consequences for those who could not make the grade. Schools would be placed into similar cohorts as established by competitive performance factors and would be measured one against the other to see which schools would show improvement. Funding would be allocated on a zero-sum basis. Those schools that posted improvements in their test scores—or value-added outcomes—vis-à-vis others similarly positioned, would receive bonuses. Those that could not would be dunned. Excellence was no longer a state to be rewarded but an ever-shifting horizon—a thin and continually disappearing line—to be wielded for constant improvement. Any student who did not show measurable improvement, no matter his or her ability, could place the school in jeopardy. Whereas previously, "at-risk" had meant that those who could not meet standards required additional support, now the entire student population would be treated as part of a risk calculus, and even the most capable could jeopardize the rest of the community by failing to deliver academically. Resources would be pulled away from students who were on the standards margins and applied toward general test preparation. The distinction between those who were certified as having special educational needs (an Individualized Educational Plan, or IEP, not, in actuality a function of capacity for academic achievement) and those who, with extra help, could avoid failure was given a harder edge.[24] Risk was being shifted from the marginal performer to the entire student population.

The rubric for school-based accountability was given the name "empowerment." At first, this designation was difficult to acquire. Subsequently, it was pressed on schools. School improvement was being treated as a proxy for political success and progress in governance. Especially when crime statistics reached a nadir and were likely to rise, demonstrable evidence that the mayor was doing a good job with the city fell to education policy. The takeover of the New York Public Schools by the Mayor's office was predicated on years of purported failure and mismanagement by the professional bureaucrats who ran the schools. Reform would be delivered by a professional for whom experience lay not in educational leadership but in breaking trusts—that is, former federal attorney Joel Klein. Klein understood that garnering public confidence was key, and for this, a series of public meetings was held. At one that took place in the opulent and newly restored Tweed courthouse (adjacent to the mayor's office), where the department relocated, public input was invited. Soon after the meeting got under way, a public interest group stormed into the room and chanted, "Let the parents be heard." The message was unassailably accurate, in that the chancellor had provided little time or space for meaningful input from parents. Yet when the spokesperson of the group did get the chance to speak, he reiterated the slogan that parents should be heard.

The chancellor could emerge as the voice of reason, calming the crowd and assuring that all would be heard while only his existing scheme was being vetted. The scheme for redistributing resources suggested that monies would be allocated to schools in poorer districts and that teachers would take a market incentive of several thousand dollars to relocate in these schools. A union representative sought to show why the monetary incentives would not work (and had not), and was dismissed. Another questioner wanted to know why the reorganization was necessary if all that was sought was reallocation of some monies for instruction. The chancellor admitted that encouraging schools to accept the "empowerment" status was the underlying reason for the reorganization. When asked how principals would find the time to do the additional data mining that the new schema required, he replied that they would adapt by running their offices more efficiently and that no additional administrative staff would be required to collect, analyze, report, and apply the increasing information demands.

While autonomy in the service of producing better test results was prioritized, the discretion to maintain curricular and cultural diversity was not. In a meeting called at the behest of the School Leadership Team, a

principal's council of parents and staff, with a roomful of district administrators, the efforts to preserve P.S. 3's historic demographic mix was met
with shrugs and bewilderment. We were informed by the Department of
Education staff that federal statutes prohibited recruitment to maintain diversity. The unusual circumstance of sharing a neighborhood catchment zone
with another elementary school had presented the prospect of taking students from out of the area and thereby checking the impact on diversity
of the persistent gentrification of Greenwich Village. Several years into the
school reforms, the percentage of African American and Hispanic students
had declined at the city's elite selective high schools, such as Stuyvesant and
Bronx Science, by nearly one-half.[25]

With a construction boom in luxury housing and rents on the rise, more
children were coming into Manhattan, and in 2005, the median income of
white families with toddlers had skyrocketed to $284,208.[26] The focus on
performance preempted an interest in the maintenance of diversity as a jeopardized urban resource. Further, the admission of students from outside the
local school zone put further pressure on scarce middle school seats. A few
years later, the consequences of the lack of planning could be seen in a financial crisis that drove well-healed families to neighborhood public schools
unable to accommodate them. The Department of Education hoped that
additional seats in citywide gifted and talented programs could accommodate
this increased demand.[27] The local problem of preserving uniqueness in one
school quickly bumped up against the multiple constraints of the system at
large. The focus on testing could take attention off of other kinds of planning issues, such as building new schools. Lost in the boom of construction
and test-scores was the relation between new construction in a city whose
economy is driven by real estate speculation, and a larger civic conversation
about what constitutes urban development. Needless to say, in 2010, when
test-scores were exposed as being inflated and, like real estate prices, dropped
precipitously, no reconsideration of assessment principles was on offer by the
administration.[28]

IT TOOK THE VILLAGE

While New York City is often taken as a model of educational reform, and
P.S. 3 would be seen at the edge of that, the reform visited on both are belated
instances of what educational theorist Michael W. Apple referred to as conservative modernization, the use of accountability schemes to teach God-fearing
market values. While the tone of the Bloomberg-Klein reforms are decidedly
secular, they have proceeded with the kind of evangelical zeal that mobilized
a rightist agenda nearly thirty years ago. Apple situates the refluorescence of
homeschooling (which had reached 1.5 million by 1999) in the context of

the rise of a "managerial state," which traded public benefits for domestic self-management.[29] While homeschooled children remain a small fraction of the school-aged population, they serve as a broader model of conduct and consequence for educational reform. Arguments for homeschooling often begin with a move away from regimentation. But also, proponents view the home as capable of greater productivity—as measured by higher standardized test scores—than the conventional school environment.[30] The learning community, parent coordinator, and homeschool partnerships ask children's guardians to view their parenting from the perspective of such enhancements to productivity. The language of empowerment, autonomy, and self-management goes hand in hand with what Linda McNeill calls the deskilling of teachers, whereby "educational standardization harms teaching and learning and, over the long term, restratifies education by race and class."[31] Testing regimes force teachers to narrow what they take as their own capacities for curricular creativity and regulate the process by which teachers are mentored, from the guildlike exchanges between new and experienced teachers to prepackaged curricular bundles assembled by responsible contractors and brought into the classroom.

And yet these schemata, however cleverly crafted and implemented, are nowhere as complete as they would aspire to be. The grab for the center creates much dynamism at the margins, just as the drive to instrumentalize education imbues students and teachers with a keen appreciation of what gets left out. Resistance does not take the form of eliminating the external incursion of accountability driven assessment—whether at home or in the alternative school. Rather, those subject to reforms must constantly ponder and refer to what the narrow instrumentalities left out and leave behind. This peculiar literacy launches students, from an early age, toward a college experience that will prove familiar both in their preparation and their resistance. The students will come already professionalized as students—knowing, if only intuitively, that what they bear is not autonomy or empowerment, but a capacity to turn the accounts back on themselves. Parents, too, will become groomed in the anxieties of measurable accomplishment and professional projections. They will be caught between carving out a separate space for childhood to blossom and preempting its flower by making it accountable to a future known only as a presently measurable outcome.

Importantly, this squeeze play is but one path to socialization offered to professionally aspiring households. The experiences garnered through negotiating the shoals of demonstrable achievement and suspended disbelief suggest that both students and parents gather political experience in how to insulate themselves from these pressures, how to make salient contributions among them, and how to select for what may be of educational value amid the demands to ignore the present for a promissory future. In this circumstance, professionalization is rather selectively applied, an unaccountable expertise that makes educational value demonstrable but unknowable. Yet a knowledge is sought of just how to stave off this anxiety and put it in its place for the immediate engagement of and full participation in learning. Let us turn to an account of that future present—the college students themselves—and see how these formative antinomies play on the field of higher education, especially as colleges themselves are being invited to incorporate these models of success into their own conceptions of excellence.

3

What Is a Student to Think?

Students seeking a self-made college experience find themselves navigating between implied market coercion—higher ed as obligation—and sustained cultural criticism, which says education is hopelessly compromised, not worth the cost, and a waste of time. Yet beyond the pincer grasp of economic instrumentality and wholesale devaluation, there remain many reasons to go to college and many aspirations to be realized by it. While long touted as an engine of opportunity, higher education is both highly stratified and stratifying. Enrolling older students and those who would not have attended college, propriety schools now enjoy huge growth, as state schools and community colleges had during the sixties boom. Selectivity—the push to reduce the ratio of accepted students to applicants—has launched a national contest by which more students apply for more schools and small movements on the list of rankings are counted as major victories. Almost all high school completers plan on college. More than three-quarters enroll. Still, the median age of college students is on the rise, and, as Chapter 1 indicates, the hundred million students in adult education eclipse by far the roughly eighteen million matriculated students. Given the volatility of careers and employment, university extension and lifelong learning chase the shift from upward to lateral mobility, as even professional workers need to return to the classroom for retooling. For many, the credential of an undergraduate degree loses its longevity.

When higher education was restricted to the elite, the liberal arts promise of education as an end in itself could set the university apart from the world to which its graduates were practically guaranteed entry. An education in the classics could endure an eternity and signal a stature and enduring value that the hurly-burly of the marketplace would find hard pressed to bequeath. In practice, there were many strands of impatience with liberal learning, and business was from the start entangled with the elaboration of the modern university. Yet now, even liberal learning has adopted the professional model, delivering measurable worldliness and agreed-upon content and skills, along with the capacity to intervene. While liberal arts degrees have declined as a proportion of the total and professional degrees have held sway, students have had to think about college as a way of locating themselves in the world. During the four decades following World War II, when colleges and students were more substantially supported by federal and state funding, higher education looked to be a public good along the lines of preparation for healthy citizenship. Most famously, with the GI Bill and subsequently with aid such as Pell Grants (need-based grants for low-income undergraduates), college was linked to national service and civic entitlement as part of the claims to a free society. Even as these programs limited access to education, they could be the objects of correction through subsequent ameliorative legislation, like affirmative action.

The dismantling of the social compact that supported universal access combined constructs of scarcity and fiscal crisis (as in the case of open admissions), with moral imperatives that only markets deliver authentic goods. Defunding was driven by the notion that public monies merit no place where personal preference can reign. When education is recast as a private good, the higher calling of a debt to society drifts toward more prosaic versions of debt. Tax-deferred annuities have replaced grants and entitlements as the preferred mechanisms for public policy to advance college access. Admissions offices can resemble brokerage houses that retail bankers' wares. Admissions offices can also face potential conflicts of interest they never had to navigate before. The precollege experience of managing credit is converted into the blunt instrument of living with debt. As a private good, colleges must look to the quality of the services they provide, whether their facilities are state of the art, or at how effectively their staff engender an appropriate affective bond to the college community. The full-service model of education attaches most strongly to the selective residential college, where the aim is to create brand loyalty that repays over a lifetime. The investment in the student promises long-range return. The transactions for distance learning and other proprietaries exist in the here and now.

It would be tempting to sketch a caricature of the contemporary college student as conservative, narrowly focused, fully instrumentalized, disinterested in the social environs, and disinclined to participate in public affairs. While easy to draw, such cartoons are at odds with broad measures of the student's own self-understanding.[1] Nor can the portraits of solipsism explain the range of activisms, whether they be the David Horowitz–inspired Students for Academic Freedom that monitor professors labeled dangerous, or the No

Sweat or Anti-Coke campaigns that weave together the ethos of campus consumption with international labor conditions. Suffice it to say that the social
world of which the university is unabashedly a part gets figured in through
complex and wide-ranging ways for college students. The question of how
this worldliness becomes part of what students actually study and how they
learn is equally intricate. The well-rounded student who is a good candidate
for admission to a selective institution has a portfolio that includes community service—a term that also negotiates often tense town-gown relations that
service learning would enlist students to ameliorate. But notions of social
responsibility, civic engagement, and ethical sensibility pepper many a college mission statement. Preemptive cynicism will not be useful to divine the
significance for the actual educational experience students seek or are able to
embrace.

In this chapter, I want to again draw upon my own experience, this time
in curricular design. Here, too, the students at the Tisch School of the Arts
(TSOA) where I work are not typical, but the challenges they pose are instructive. One case is a core curriculum for students of the arts that collaborates
with the university's expository writing program to position them as public
intellectuals on behalf of the arts. While core curricula are readily dismissed
as rearguard actions to stanch progressive initiatives, they are also occasions
to frame and interrogate what a critically minded education requires and how
politics addresses these very questions. A second example is a small graduate
program in arts politics that also seeks to provide a space of critical reflection for the professional engagements that students undertake. While highly
specialized and specific, this degree program allows for reflection on the links
between student activism and professional engagement that suggests different routes and bases for drawing the social world into the university. These
are practical responses to what can be understood as the professional turn in
higher education, in which professional fields overtake liberal arts study and
liberal arts comes under new pressure of demonstrable professional outcomes.
This development shifts the social frame of education as an often unspoken
public good to one in which more strategic advocacy is required. Getting to
the stakes of these particular examples will require some contextualizing of
contemporary college students and curricular planning.

PROFESSIONAL TURNS

Considering the situation of students today and all they are caught up in, it
is tempting to cast an eye to the sixties as a point of reference, when students
battled constraints on many fronts. Indeed, one of the legacies of the sixties is
to continue to think in generational terms to explain cultural characteristics
of current cohorts. The idea that students' distinct and relatively homogenous
social position accounted for their radicalism lent explanatory force to the

generational concept. Illustrative of this line of argument, whose pedigree lay in the thought of Herbert Marcuse, Erich Fromm, and Paul Goodman, was a sociological account by Irving Louis Horowitz and William H. Friedland called *The Knowledge Factory: Student Power and Academic Politics in America*.[2] The book made a case for students as a distinct social class. "The most intensive conflict in contemporary industrial societies is not among religions, political parties, workers and management, or even races, but between youth and adults."[3] Accordingly, "students as a group have most of the characteristics of a revolutionary class, the essential difference being the substitution of a generational base for the poverty base."[4] Among the positive attributes, this shared foundation consists of a common occupation, housing, and style, along with a negative identification that includes alienation, lack of property, absence of political legal status, and close and intensive interaction. Horowitz and Friedland saw youth as an emergent sociohistorical stage in the life course, one with "no formal role in the world of work and politics."[5]

And yet when the book was published in 1970, these two features of student autonomy were about to come to an end. The Twenty-Sixth Amendment to the Constitution, which formally enfranchised the bulk of college-age youth, was signed into law on July 1, 1971. State after state followed suit by lowering to eighteen the age of consent, along with the right to vote, and, for men, the military draft. The antiwar movement could take credit for ending the draft in 1973 (with its gendered logic of college exceptionalism), and the ascent of the new right rolled back the drinking age from eighteen to twenty-one with the National Minimum Drinking Age Act of 1984. While extending suffrage eliminated one basis of political disenfranchisement, the sense that students were economic dependents who could be located outside the realm of work would undergo an even more substantial reversal. If in this portrait, the sixties radicalism issued from a critique of the numbing effects of joining the knowledge factory that was sustained by students residing outside of work, the transformation of what they would study and how they could pay for it altered the very way in which students would imagine themselves.

Casting a college degree as yielding twice the annual income as a high school diploma provided good cover for the dismantling of the social compact that had supported tuition subsidies to students and institutions (even as the past decade has seen graduates' wages flatten as debt and tuition costs rise).[6] The arithmetic would mean that for the poorest students, the 25 percent tuition increase over the nineties would effectively double the slice of household income required. College would come to be seen as a necessity, but so too would working one's way through it. For forty years since the sixties, as more of the children of laborers turned to college, more and more of the student body would find itself at work. By 1998, nearly four-fifths of college students were holding down jobs (50 percent were working to pay for school and another 29 percent were going to school to improve their prospects at work).[7] Again, nearly two-thirds of all high school completers go immediately on to college in the fall following graduation. More than one-third of students going to four-year schools also work. Sixty percent of students attending community college and the like have jobs.[8]

While an increasing proportion of high school students now go on to college, greater numbers of delayed, interrupted, or returned students are in attendance as well. Between 1970 and 2005, total enrollment at degree-granting institutions of higher education more than doubled, from eight and one-half million to more than seventeen million students. In 1970, substantially more than half of the student population was younger than twenty-one. By 2005, those twenty-one and younger constituted about 42 percent, with those thirty and older increasing from 15 percent to 25 percent of the student population and a median age closer to twenty-five.[9] Not only had the autonomy from work and political enfranchisement associated with the category of youth eroded but the campus population had also aged.

These statistical profiles can reference broader demographic changes, but they can readily miss the content of the historical shift that has taken place. Education as an end in itself is the clarion call of the liberal arts. The pursuit of knowledge for its own sake must hold some appeal for anyone who takes teaching seriously as both an intrinsic good and as contributing to the sort of well-roundedness said to prepare citizens for democratic participation.[10] Yet what persistently places the in-itself/for-itself injunction at risk is the presence of the commodity labor, either as the goal of education, or as its means. It is worth remembering that the arguments for autonomy that provided the foundational idea of the modern Western university in the nineteenth century, were made against the subordination of learning to labor, either as apprenticeship in a guild, or as an occupational response to a religious calling. Now as the market appears to have stolen education's innocence in the form of the preponderance of professional training, it is tempting to see what might look like a one-hundred-year interregnum of the liberal arts as a golden age of uncompromised pursuit of knowledge, and not as a historical aberration in which higher education demarcated social privilege. Along the way, the liberal ideal was already challenged by the model of the research university, where education was to serve the advancement of knowledge as a kind of global mastery—the multiversity. This model represented a conglomerate of interests whose chief practitioners, after University of California President Clark Kerr, were administrators, in contrast to the corporate university, whose intellectual properties were meant to fetch a good.[11]

When one moves from ideals to demographics (as rehearsed in Chapter 1), it is hard to argue for a return to the glory days of, say, 1869, when, for example, in the United States, 563 institutions graduated fewer than 10,000 baccalaureates at a ratio of nearly 8 privileged (preponderantly white) men to every woman, and where, proportionately, men were more than twice as likely to make it through to a degree (although women have outnumbered men since 1980). By the dawn of the new millennium, a majority of students were women and more than one-third nonwhite or Hispanic. Some 1.6 million bachelor's degrees, more than 625,000 master's degrees, and about 63,000 doctorates were conferred—with women overall receiving the majority of these.[12] As human services came to define the job market, the very character of the degree shifted toward professional education. In 1970, bachelor's degrees in the liberal arts were still approaching half of the total (at 46 percent). Thirty years later, the liberal arts disciplines as a proportion all baccalaureate degrees conferred had fallen to just one-third. Among the professional fields, degrees in business gained the most (114,729–311,574 between 1970 and 2005), and those in education suffered the greatest decline (176,307–105,451). Literature, math, and physical science all graduate fewer than they did thirty years ago (although the social sciences and history, which suffered steep declines in the eighties, are back to where they were in 1970).[13]

Even the categories have changed to reflect the professional orientation under which knowledge cannot exist for itself but must be applied to something serviceable. Life sciences have become biological and biomedical sciences, math is now math and statistics, physical sciences now include science technologies. Within the liberal arts, emergent interdisciplinary domains—such as area, ethnic, cultural, and gender studies—are small but have enjoyed steady growth from 2,500 to 7,500 degrees, and general studies and humanities have also grown from just less than 7,500 to more than 43,000 degrees. The visual and performing arts have also seen a substantial increase, from 30,000 to more than 87,000, now surpassing degrees in engineering. MBAs comprise nearly a quarter of the master's degrees awarded, and more professional degrees (e.g., MDs and JDs) are granted than PhDs. Even the growth in doctorates—which has reached a plateau in the past ten years—reflects the preponderance of degrees in fields with professional applications, such as education, engineering, life sciences, and psychology, which are the fields that have the greatest number of degrees awarded.[14] Whatever the (re)turn to professionalism means in higher education, these few figures indicate that it has all the features of durability.

CORE POLITICS

Putting the demographic and disciplinary shifts together, much of the change reflects who college students have become, but also what has happened to the fields themselves. The basic grammar of higher education was a move from a general experience toward some disciplinary specialization. The former was seen as core, or common, and reflected the collective judgment, or cultural values, of a particular faculty. The difficulty of articulating a core speaks directly to the challenges of delimiting a determinate content in which education is judged on its ability to create professionals. Reflecting on the fate of the core curriculum, Stanley Aronowitz has observed:

> In none of the documents I have seen are the various components of the core and their corollary, the "skills" components, justified on intellectual grounds. Rather, they are presented as self-evident, equivalent elements of a well-rounded curriculum. Nor is the much-invoked criteria "coherence" explained. Needless to say, there is no attempt to justify, whether on the basis of learning theory or of educational philosophy, the choice of domains, except on the criterion of comprehensiveness or breadth. Taken for granted, and left unexamined, is the nineteenth-century German understanding of division of academic labor, in which knowledge is segmented into natural, social, literary, and arts domains and subdivided by convention into disciplines. And the idea that the student is best served by a sampling of the various disciplines, to which a skills menu has been added, is never questioned.[15]

In this regard, the core curriculum could be said to stand for the unassailable declaration that one is an educated person—that this is self-evident and that status, in and of itself, has been achieved. With such status under pressure, the performative force of a core curriculum would yield to the inductive protocols of accountability, an assessment of outcomes that treats a student's standing among the educated as readily falsifiable. Instead of the noble confidence that students have taken a great books course and can declare themselves educated, they are continually called upon to demonstrate not what they know but what their knowledge is for.

Given the difficulty in establishing the content of a national curriculum, elite programs that created a core could allow their institutional prestige to stand for the general value of their particular course design. Far from enshrining received universals, these initiatives bore all the idiosyncracies of the circumstances under which they were implemented. Columbia University, for example, dates its core curriculum to 1919, when it adapted the course on war issues developed for its Student Army Training Corps to what would become Contemporary Civilization, which in then-president Nicholas Murray Butler's words would focus on the "insistent problems of the present."[16] What began as literacy for national service and an interest in postwar reconstruction would only subsequently morph into a universalist competency "with wide-ranging perspectives on significant ideas and achievements."[17] The more pragmatic basis of this common requirement was that small class size was needed to develop potent intellectual relationships with faculty early in a student's college career. The core is framed as a transmission from the great minds of the faculty to the students, even if the faculty or graduate students actually providing instruction are not benighted with such greatness.

Two schools that frequently serve as models for core curricula, Harvard and Chicago, have seen significant changes to their curricular commons and even an erosion in the degree to which they inspire and are emulated.[18] In 2002, former Harvard President Lawrence H. Summers launched a curricular review that aimed to displace the collapsed core curriculum with an emphasis on science and globalization, an unspecified commitment to greatness, and requirements for a formalistic flexibility, breadth, and choice.[19] Harvard's faculty issued a new report on its core curriculum that entailed moving from disciplines to subject areas, such as aesthetic and interpretive understanding, the science of the physical universe, and the United States in the world. The faculty affirmed the familiar aims of a liberal education, which was to be "conducted in a spirit of free inquiry undertaken without concern for topical relevance or vocational utility . . . free from most of the constraints on time and energy that operate in the rest of life."[20] The report called for more electives from departments outside students' concentrations, writing-intensive courses, more interdisciplinary courses that employed novel pedagogical approaches, activity-based learning, and contact with long-term faculty. Above all, Harvard's faculty report promoted liberal learning against the threat of professional education that deliberalizes students and prevents them from critical thinking and action outside the framework of career and profession. General education and core requirements are the public face of this learning capacity insofar as they connect what is learned on campus to the world beyond. From the other direction, activity-based learning refers to extra-curricular engagement that could be integrated in some more formal academic evaluation process.

The University of Chicago made a 40 percent reduction in its core requirements in response to reduced undergraduate demand. While the curricular space of the core has been reduced at Chicago, its educational underpinnings remain, according to the catalog, "roughly the same curriculum that the famous educator Robert Maynard Hutchins implemented at Chicago in the 1930s"[21] Like Harvard, the function of Chicago's core curriculum is to constitute a community within the college that can simulate and impart the thinking skills required of participation in civil society. Close readings of original texts in small seminars are the means to this goal. Like Columbia, Chicago's intimacy rests upon a relatively small number of undergraduates and a large presence of nontenured faculty, preceptors, and graduate assistants. This is not a labor model that many schools are in a position to emulate and such a model might divide large public institutions from the private instances that serve as models. Prominent public institutions like Berkeley, rather than a core curriculum, have only writing and American history as common undergraduate requirements. Michigan focuses on unique learning communities. Virginia has distribution requirements. Pressure on seats at public universities has resulted in community colleges serving to fulfill general requirements of a core curriculum before students transfer to complete specialized studies. For example, like Harvard, Shoreline Community College in Washington State divides its core into "broad knowledge in various areas of human learning" as opposed to disciplines, but it also uses a language of "outcomes" for civic engagement as lifelong learners.[22]

These directions in core curricula suggest a bifurcation of a putative transcendental content that includes the knowledge a cultured person needs to acquire in order to be affirmed as literate or educated and formal requisites that students can perform recognizable skills in analytic thinking, moral reasoning, civic engagement, and recognition of other cultures. The former legitimates education as an authentic representation of culture as a whole—a coherent totality—and the latter invokes a notion of relevance that enables students to integrate specialized professional knowledge with a sense of national belonging. Proponents of great books, canon, and other content-based programs are utterly confident that these curricula deliver depth to young minds. It is believed that the profundity of the texts, the originality of their ideas, and the potency of their presentation place students in the seat of genius from which they may measure and acquire their own. Critical skills, modes of inquiry, area coverage—all are meant to reference breadth, well-roundedness, holism. Hence, the required courses are something of a simulacra of the knowable world, and the student must be stretched to fit into this expanse. As ideologies and points of departure for curricular design, both approaches are not without their appeal. In actuality, the success of a great books curriculum rests as much upon the protocols of reading, interpretation, and writing it engenders as the logic of selection or qualities of the particular texts. Likewise, the question of what course materials, examples, or problematics most effectively move students from the particular to the general lie at the heart of any breadth-driven course. With more critical variants of a core, particular and general would not be taken as a priori values. They would instead pertain to the ways in which students are able to locate themselves in the world and make demands on their world that extend beyond themselves.

Whether through coverage or critical procedures, such programs would seem to lead students and faculty to the heart of the labors of learning, specifically to considerations of how it happens and to what end. As Derek Bok has observed, in his quintessentially reasonable brief on behalf of a continued project for the liberal arts in undergraduate education, that both the criticisms and the defense of higher education suffer a kind of crisis of reference. Regarding the scathing attacks of the eighties that signaled the culture wars, he notes:

> Unfortunately, the widely publicized critiques of the past 20 years are not a particularly helpful guide for deciding what needs to be done. Indeed, there is something very odd about their indictments. If they were anywhere close to correct, prospective students and their families would be up in arms. After all, going to college costs a lot of money,

even in public universities. Those hoping to attend and those who pay the bills presumably expect a first-rate education in return. If college were truly in crisis, burdened by incoherent curricula and uncaring professors, students would hardly be applying in such large and growing numbers. Nor would parents be seeking out well-paid counselors to help with college applications or paying for special tutoring to teach their children how to get higher scores on college entrance exams.

Critics may reply that students are not affirming undergraduate education in its current form but are merely anxious for an impressive credential now that a college degree has become so important to future success. But this response will hardly bear scrutiny. Survey after survey of students and recent graduates shows that they are remarkably pleased with their college years. Americans may dislike their government and distrust most institutions in this society, but 75 percent or more of college alumni report being either satisfied or very satisfied with their undergraduate experience. Just after many of the hostile books appeared, a nationwide poll found that more than 80 percent of undergraduates expressed satisfaction with the teaching at their college. In subsequent surveys, large majorities of students have reported being satisfied or very satisfied with their contacts with professors. Two-thirds would choose the same institution if they had to make the choice again. Among the most selective colleges that are repeatedly singled out by critics for special scorn—the Stanfords, Princetons, Harvards, and Yales—the percentages of contented graduates are even higher, and alumni support their alma maters with exceptional generosity.[23]

These data about satisfaction are for Bok the reservoir of good will upon which the denizens of the university can be encouraged to improve students' reasoning or practical capacities for civic and global engagement. He is convinced that ongoing curricular revision can mediate the rift between faculty's desire to teach what it knows and believes should be known, and student's demands for relevance in the face of job pressures. Bok's willingness to take seriously what goes on inside the university reminds us that the criticisms are less about academic labor and more about the location of higher education in society and the discomfort with its lost privilege and presumed entitlement.[24] Whereas the very particular ideological concerns that a critique of cultural traditions and disciplinary authority indicate a larger civilizational decline, the contrary appraisals point to a crisis not of satisfaction but of autonomy. After all, the debate about cultural traditions, canons, common values, and the like is of a piece with the history of higher education, and the replacement of requirements with choice or vice-versa has long elicited concern that the institution had lost its way.[25] The pursuit of what Bok terms "genuine learning organizations"[26] is hampered by the instrumental pressures that keep students from valuing a more comprehensive holism. This pursuit is also impeded by professors who are inattentive to pedagogy and unable to devise the means for recognizing student learning. Besides selective use of student evaluations in course revision, "professors seldom receive clear evidence of how much students are learning" and "papers and exams are not terribly informative either."[27] The difficulty of quantifying how much students have learned reflects a curious drift toward the kinds of externally driven market standards that Bok has elsewhere voiced grave concerns about.[28]

The slippage from qualities (analytic and civic) to quantities (designated value-added dimensions) perhaps accounts for the administrative crisis in confidence that faculty are able to recognize student learning in the assignments they devise and the work that students produce. With the enormous apparatus of assessment research and instruments of measurement that have emerged in response to the crisis of attainment signaled in the 1983 report *A Nation At Risk*, the aim is to render assessment an integral and ongoing feature of teaching itself. Looking at the state of standardized testing in a national context since the Reagan-era report sounded its alarm of an achievement gap, Donald M. Stewart concluded that "much of the current research on testing technology is focused on just this issue: how tests can be 'seamlessly' interwoven with instruction so that the learner is not even aware of when instruction ends and assessment begins."[29] Assessment would thus precede course completion or credit conferral, placing the students' judgment of what they are learning in anticipation of their actual attainment of educational competency. Students would be poised to judge their experience in prospect, not retrospect. The ensuing confusion is likely to result in an unhappiness with the assessment instrument that sees the teaching as deficient.

Conversely, it would seem that student work, rather than the measure of student attitudes toward the work they have undertaken, is the best means available to faculty of recognizing what students have learned. Especially when that work provides evidence and expression of contextualization of course material and articulation of student self-understanding, faculty can reflect on student ability before and after a course. Courses that challenge not simply students' world views but their approaches to their own ways of understanding and expression can be particularly unsettling. Students may not themselves notice what impact the course has had until it becomes integrated and incorporated into other abilities, which they will develop over time. A denial by the student at the close of a semester that the course was effective is not necessarily surprising or a measure of that curriculum's coherence or effectiveness. Rather, this circumstance of student anxiety is an occasion for faculty to convene and engage in the task of teaching evaluation based on the relation between what students can do and what they are able to recognize at a particular moment. This will not be the case where "papers and exams" are merely mimetic moments—and pale reflections at that—of the professor's own disciplinary mastery. Such might be a limitation of the liberal arts model that treats undergraduates as specialists in embryo, rather than helping these students develop modes of work that allow their competencies to emerge. This more worldly conception of work is closer to what the professional turn suggests, whether it be through the capacity to textualize the social world through engaged readings or through the materialization of cultural forms in the kinds of inscription, process, and project that students are asked to undertake.

When Harvard President Charles Eliot gave his 1869 address defending a laissez-faire approach to course offerings and selection that would enshrine an entrepreneurial spirit, the core function was performed by demographic exclusivity. With few of the nation's elite in college, its imprimatur demarcating the educated person might be treated as a simple tautology. The publishing of Harvard's Red Book nearly a century later bespoke an anxiety, as access to education was undergoing marked expansion. The prescriptions were largely for high school and never adopted for Harvard itself. The core, in this instance, was meant to govern what might be contained within the masses as a commonality, while the elite would remain free and self-professedly educated. When, in 1978, Harvard sought to resurrect its core curriculum in an effort to inter the critical spirits unleashed by the sixties, it invoked this authority of disinterestedness on behalf of a kind of transcendental arrogation of power—a philosophical logic meticulously examined by William V. Spanos.[30]

Yet by the 1980s, the demographic expansion and economic implosion in higher education meant that a core could not adjudicate what was taken as a shared consensual domain of knowledge and culture either inside or outside the institution. Enormous pressure was placed on the notion that a core could serve as a point of reference that, by settling epistemological accounts, could resolve social conflicts. The core was taken to be a rearguard action, compensating for the narrow mercantile pursuits of students. It represented the martial imperative to hold out against non-Western values by teaching them selectively—a therapeutic foil to youthful anomie and an evangelical advertisement of traditional disciplinary knowledge. One critique, gathering a range of voices in opposition, stated that the "knowledge imparted by a core curriculum is far too unimaginative and inflexible a standard" for a diverse population that was seeing more adult learners in higher education.[31] The older students were too sophisticated for such curricular prescriptions, and younger students needed the experience of choice for the benefit of their own maturity. Reformers devised a range of alternative approaches, including clustered themes to convey a sense of common fate, skills-based common tools that emphasized general as opposed to liberal learning, a common ground approach based upon shared assumptions, and a decentered, extra-institutional model oriented toward the uncommon individual.

While the alternatives to core curricula ask that we not take for granted what should be common in education, or that we replace commonality with choice, they can still beg the question of how curricula get devised, taught, and engaged in by students. Replacing lists of exalted readings or torpid introductory texts with themes does not account for how the themes get generated. Nor does a generic assortment of skills address what it means to be skillful under present circumstances. An inquiry into shared assumptions does not necessarily account for where the question comes up, and an education based on individual choice can misunderstand course selection for something like free-willed self-formation. If the core names a problem of reference, it cannot be resolved simply by noting the absence of a taken-for-granted orientation. The problem of how students can learn to orient themselves in the world remains, if this takes place not apart from their professional engagement but through it. Hence, rather than setting themselves in opposition to professional studies, the liberal arts briefs for core curricula and general education may get further in establishing what education does and what it is for by incorporating certain features of the productionist approach assumed in the professional model. This would entail a shift from an unremarked liberal or general education to one that asked how students generalize themselves—how they locate and project themselves in the world. In this respect, the positions in the canon discussion that accuse challengers of politicizing curriculum planning avoid not only their own politics but also the politics of mobilizing faculty and students through the conception and implementation of a curriculum.

The core, therefore, is not simply a conversation about what should be common or required. Rather, the force of requirement carries with it the occasion to ask how learning links with its social world. The core, in this regard, is the vehicle for sustaining the politics of the curriculum, not the consensus through which differences are resolved. Surely, students and faculty will be unhappy if they are being asked to shield their differences in the name of agreement, but the unhappiness that accompanies a requirement is also what maintains the obligation to engage, revise, and articulate the means and end of education. It may prove useful to distinguish between core curricula that seek to discern what is common to a culture and should be transmitted to students, from those that pursue the question of what is public in the operation of their educational experience. Whereas the search for commonality might yield a course that is deliverable conceptually, the underlying premise that commonality produces appropriately ordered minds and conduct is a more dubious proposition. If preparation for citizenship entails learning the nation's compact so as to obey it, it is not clear what kind of prescription makes this possible. Lesson plans that convey their disinterest in students to students tend to result in opposition to schooling, not the disciplined minds of a compliant citizenship, as Paul Willis observed for British working-class education.[32]

All this suggests that if an organizing rubric of what constitutes "public" is to operate differently, it is as a project that takes stock of how students are positioned socially, of how they might be oriented to their worlds, and of how courses enact effective placement of students both civically and politically. Less helpful is a notion that treats public as an already existing social good bequeathed by a democracy or as a civic ideal realized by informed practice. As a means to diagnose how students constitute and make demands on a public realm beyond their disciplinary expertise, the core cannot stand as a center awaiting discovery in some giant orb called culture. The public that students encounter is not some idealized space of civic virtue but a realm of formulation and decision that is frequently hostile to them as students, youth, workers, and citizens. Bipartisan administrations have been key purveyors of the idea that the "private" is the source of solutions to what ails society and have cut resources to higher education accordingly. These dangers and hostilities, the forces of normalization and of punishment or banishment, and the questions of professional opportunity and agency are the issues that the core must weigh with respect to a specific student body.

The commitments to service learning, civic engagement, and worldly experience must still address how participation is made available to students and what they will possess by way of response. For students in professional fields, the tensions between specialized knowledge and worldly reception, which is now manifest in the skepticism toward the particular narratives, will frame how students get positioned publicly and what they will be able to bring to the encounter. This public voice is located between the particular expertise granted by specialization and both the demands for and doubts about what counts as the space for that expertise. In short, a core curriculum needs to speak to the predicament of the professional turn and to make use of the partial citizenship—committed and nonexclusive—that university training in a field can engage and reflect upon. The core enacts a kind of worldly intervention where the world may be un-welcoming, and the ground for specialized or disciplined knowledge needs to be part of what an educated person can articulate.

The core attends to the question, what is this education for? The presumption is that the content and condition need to be demonstrated and not simply assumed by institutional access, disciplinary convention, or credentialing. The question of worldliness, therefore, is not simply one of how a market demand gets met (how a job is obtained) but of how a delimited knowledge domain makes a place for itself in the world. Public becomes the realm opened by a kind of knowledge, and the occasion to combine, create, or join is accomplished through the ability to practice something based upon that knowledge. The public is not a passive space that welcomes and waits for utterances to fill it. The very public controversies surrounding education itself suggest that the domain of civic discourse can actually be hostile to various kinds of critical knowledge. Unlike a job that can be given or taken by somebody else, the public must be made and, in so doing, is self-making. As easy as it would be to abandon the question of the core as reactionary, impractical, or incoherent, the challenge of realizing its potential can prove still more fruitful.

LOCATED GENERALIZING

The very idea of a core is enough to agitate allergies from any number of quarters. The hubris involved in what is asserted to lie at the center of an educational mission, and the accompanying conviction that faculty and students will be left in a position to do their most effective teaching and learning, has crashed many interdisciplinary vessels. The core is perhaps at its most brittle when left as a general idea. Tisch School of the Arts' core, and its curricular location, tempts these fates of convention and reaction but hopefully points students in a different direction. It partners the art school faculty and graduate students with the university's program in expository writing. Plenary lectures taught by senior faculty are paired with small writing sections staffed by nonpermanent full-time, but ongoing, faculty appointments. But some aspects of the curricular design countervail convention. The large lecture functions more as a recitation section in the strong sense of the term—here ideas are rehearsed and students must figure out how to attend to the work of composition. The lectures use a range of art examples to model analytic approaches to interpretation, analysis, and composition. The evaluated writing is done in the smaller sections and students apply the ways of understanding developed in the lecture to artistic works of their own choosing. The large lecture is not a center but is presented as an instance of a public sphere, where the students are invited to consider themselves public intellectuals on behalf of the arts. The essay work engenders the kind of voice required to represent and open a space for the arts in a world often hostile to it. The importance of finding one's voice is part of the art school's own narrative, and the challenge is to complicate the freshmen's sense of self so as to open them to the voices of others. These strategies, worked out in the university setting for thinking about the encumbrances of professional communities for civic action and engagement, are termed artistic citizenship.

Unlike its national cognate, artistic citizenship is partial in the double sense of committed and nonexhaustive. Instead of beginning with the stable mimesis of whole person and universal interest in the world, students are asked to reflect on how they generalize themselves from their given productive and contingent positions as artists and professionals. Some faculty wrote essays that were collected into a volume that accompanies the course—as well as a specially prepared reader. The brief for artistic citizenship is described as follows:

Artistic citizenship is a paradox. One that artists may be well served to embrace. The divide between the private world of esthetic creativity and the public realm of exhibit has been unkind to many artists. Under such circumstances artists are left free—or alone to make their work—but stripped of their concern to make room for it in the world.

Understandably, artists could be burned by the public—unless they develop the means to shuttle between worlds, to create room for their art, to affirm by acts of speech the work that images should be left to do. Public art would become that aspect of the artist's work that concerns how the world is made as art makes its way into the world—how spaces of attention, hope, interest, affiliation, entanglement, commitment, passion, empathy, possibility, imagination are crafted when people pause to reflect on what it means to be together. This is art's public project, one that can embrace all manner of spaces and interest, all the more so if the public is to be an achievement and not a passive environment that artists and audiences take up. This public project for art rests upon a partial citizenship—both grounded in a particular experience and committed to a specific means of civic participation.

Art schools have become the commons for artists, the place where their responsibilities to one another are posed, where rights of practice are exercised, where ambitions for the world are honed. The university is no refuge from the professional world. Rather, the professional school invites the student to take up the development of their own competencies as a means to operate in the world. Poised between affinities, to cultural communities, to professional and esthetic attentions, to civic engagements, the art school's curriculum should incorporate the commons within it that it would wish upon its graduates. The larger trends toward credentialing and professionalization that have brought artists into higher education present an opportunity and a challenge for art schools. They can be precisely the arena where ethical responsibility and artistic excellence intersect, where a commitment to an artistic community is harmonized with civic interests, where art earns its freedom to practice by being worthy of worldly attention. In this the art school might aspire to confer on its graduates nothing less than artistic citizenship itself.[33]

The essay writing is positioned for this public voice, one that is distinguished from the student's own artistic professional training as well as from the disciplinary writing that attaches to their liberal arts requirements. The essays ask students to position themselves in a broader field called art, one that moves beyond their own professionalization, that appears as a public persona of a cultural conception of the artist, that moves across valences of high and low, critical and commercial, local and global, community-based and conceptual, and so forth. The art that serves as a prompt for each of the essays is to be found in the city beyond the university's walls, hence an enactment of a move into the world where the physical and geographic are stitched into a conception of the social. Art is also employed as a kind of conceptual lens in which to grasp something of worldly dynamics.

Over the year, students write five essays. The first takes a work of art that they can access directly in New York City and asks them to use the piece to inspire a critical idea. The second focuses on the critical reception of an artwork and asks students to negotiate among a series of reviews. The third establishes a series of contexts for the work that the student must navigate. The fourth focuses on the idea of the public as evidenced by public art, and the last explores the question of creativity, now as a feature of broader cultural processes and not simply the individual experience of the artist. In short, the essays move the student progressively into a more complex, ambitious, and extensively arrayed sense of the public realm. The framework for the essays has been devised by Pat C. Hoy II, director of the university's expository writing program who also serves as one of the plenary lecturers. Hoy's pedagogical interest is in getting students to attend to the generative space between what is said and what is unsaid, in what can be done with words and is inferred from an encounter with them. His own lectures are careful enactments of essay composition. He assembles art works from a range of media, at times with very little said or a simple question asked, where students come to realize that he is displaying the principles of essaying before them, and they are impelled to translate this technique to their own work.

The essays are crafted through a series of etudes in reading and writing, collecting, revising, and reflecting that are coupled with an intensive pedagogical process that the faculty undergoes. Certainly, some students write expressly of their experience in the lecture, as for example in the opening to this essay by Shannon McKenna: "The lecture tonight is on taboos. The lecturer, Larry Maslon, invites us to shout out the different taboos in American society. Without missing a beat, a comedian on the left side of the room yells, 'Cannibalism!' Genius. Pure genius. Acknowledging laughter confirms it. However, the room is quickly brought to order, and the 'right' answers are written up on the board. Race, religion, sex, and politics shove cannibalism out of the conversation. If eating human flesh is excluded from a talk on things you're not supposed to talk about, it must really be taboo."[34] The student's provocation leads to a reflection on the difficulties of talking about death and about how the effacement of this difficulty in memory and time passages is displayed in a public sculpture, *Metronome*, across from New York's Union Square. Connecting this artwork to other essays she reads that show how the annihilation of time reduces what can be made of life, McKenna concludes that they "are unchained cannibals, eating away at life, and at the same time giving me the space to become something savory."[35]

Many of the essays recount students' travels in the city, in search of their own location by a tour of its art. Another essay recounts a student's visit to the Bethesda Terrace and Fountain in Central Park. The spot became iconic in Tony Kushner's play *Angels in America* and its familiarity adds to its lure as a tourist destination. The student, Ryan Chassee, first saw the fountain when, home for a visit in Louisiana, he viewed the film adaptation of the play with his family. "For me, a gay man now living in New York, the film, and, in turn, the space took on a personal significance. When I returned to school and arrived at the top of the terrace for the first time to take in the view, the feeling that I was connected to the space, that it held an important place in my memory, even though I had never actually set foot there, surprised me."[36] His surprise leads him to explore the fountain's history, designed by lesbian sculptor Emma Stebbins to commemorate the opening of the Croton Aqueduct in 1842 and subsequently rededicated as a memorial to the naval dead during the world wars. The recast notoriety of the fountain offered by the broadcast of *Angels*, strikes Chassee as an ironic effacement of these various histories. "What makes Bethesda Terrace *the* Bethesda Terrace is the clashing of various peoples, histories, and cultures. Different groups will therefore struggle to identify with the space on their own terms, to mark it, to claim it. This is the battle for public space that must be fought but never won, for once a victor emerges, the space becomes clouded in a particular consciousness. To remain a truly public space, meaning and understandings must continue to travel and churn, like the threatening weather that passes behind the angel's outstretched wings. As I turn to leave the fountain, a fat raindrop moistens my shirt. The downpour that will wash Bethesda clean has begun."[37] This disjuncture between a mediated public sphere and an encounter with a setting for public art—the surprise that the two do not nestle neatly within one another but jostle for attention—leads the student toward a conception of the public as a kind of renewable resource that sustains contention by both occasioning and unsettling memory. The affirmation of identity that marks the spot contains an unstable historical echo that remains unsettled in the present. The public in this regard becomes a technology for achieving complexity.

Achieving the complexity of the course—both in its design and its application—was also some time in coming. The opening for the venture came in 2000 when the university cut its freshmen composition requirement back from two semesters to one. For several years prior, there had been a supplementary lecture that students could sign up for where several faculty each gave a few lectures on the topics of art and society to around seventy students. The reduction of the university-wide requirement meant that the art school could, in a sense, return the credits to its students as an additional elective or reserve the course space for the core—alternatives wholly consistent with the history of curricular reform. This question was put to the faculty and fell within my own portfolio as the newly appointed associate dean of faculty and interdisciplinary programs. The idea of interdisciplinary programs in this context meant both an opening for faculty members to teach outside of their professional fields in areas that featured the relation of their work to various kinds of civic engagement (documentary, community-based arts, mixed-media, or cross-departmental collaborations), and for a space that would bring together academics and practitioners in the arts.[38]

The school's academic affairs committee, cochaired by a member of the faculty and the associate dean, was the venue where the initial curricular planning took place. A syllabus was devised for the year with the fall focusing on various approaches to the contextualization of art in society and the spring devoted to employing art as an analytic lens by which to gain insight into the social world. The idea of issuing a syllabus and its particular design and contents proved to be highly contentious. The notion that a syllabus could be centrally prescribed raised concerns about academic freedom. The suggested topics and readings were criticized for presenting at once a romantic and essentialized view of artistic selfhood and for eviscerating the creative process borne by the artist. The mutual suspicions represented as basic to the divide between artistic and academic faculty within the art school looked like they might overtake the discussions. But this was not the only partnership that had to be sustained. The syllabus was focused on the school faculty but did not incorporate the pedagogy used by the expository writing program, which provided the basis for the students' evaluated work. The planning sessions with the directors of that program begin with this omission.

While faculty within Tisch did feel that more writing was important for the students, there was not consensus regarding the form and aim of this writing. Some wanted preparation for further academic work. Others sought good writing as it would translate into their own classes. Still others wanted a foundational course in art history or cultural literacy. In short, the syllabus revealed extant differences among faculty while uniting them in opposition to a syllabus. Further, it permitted agreement around a framework of instruction and a commitment to ongoing reflection with each undergraduate department about what such a curriculum should consist of. Faculty members were surveyed as to what they saw as exemplary writing. They were asked about the works of art that spoke to their own aesthetics. They were posed questions about content, format, and method—even about what plenaries themselves might hope to accomplish (given their own and their students' suspicions of large-format lectures). This generated a series of framing questions, including the relation between cultural and aesthetic diversity, differentiation of conception, creation and dissemination, and the political legibility of art, as well as a reading list. The fact that the university requirements would be changed within a year created a tight timeline and sense of "use it or lose it." The support of the dean, meetings with individual departments, creation of incentives for participation (in the form of additional research funds and compensation to departments for borrowed faculty, and support for graduate students who would teach the writing sections), as well as a release from any fixed structure for plenary lecturers ultimately coalesced to allow the course to be approved on a one-year pilot basis, with the faculty to evaluate efficacy one year on. The pilot was itself underwritten by a university curriculum grant. It was, in other words, possible to garner sufficient resources to attend materially to concerns raised and to provide faculty with a way out if the project proved ineffective.

As it turned out, such a measure was elusive, especially at first, when so much remained to be disclosed about what was being undertaken. Faculty from virtually every department in the school did participate in the course. This included filmmakers, choreographers, playwrights, directors, performance artists, photographers, and scholars of screen, stage, and recorded music, in addition to several deans. Yet while faculty participated generously, the fact of this interdisciplinary mix did not by itself answer the question of what work the lectures were actually able to introduce for the students. The lecturers could speak of many things, but often students were confused as to how to incorporate what these learned bodies shared into their own corpus of essay writing. Their relation to the material was not mimetic in the superficial sense of copying back what they were told, or taking the lecturers' art examples as their own. Students were being asked to abstract the lecturer's analytic method from the examples and topics, to see past the what to the how of the presentation. Recognizing how a lecture was assembled—what principles of composition it displayed—suggested a more strictly Aristotelian mimetic faculty, a divination of the form immanent to a given expression, and a correction or revaluation of that form in the materials that the students were working with in their own writing.

The lecture needed to have legibility as a text for interpretation rather than serve as a vessel for information that students would assimilate. Such formalism was not for everyone, even when it was framed not as a purity of what lay within the text but more as a kind of cultural materialism—a weave of what students could apprehend in the intersecting publics of the large lecture, the city, and the pressing social world. For many students, the first aperture was identity—did they like the work that was being shown to them? An untoward aesthetic, an avant-garde of another era, or a raced queerdom seemed to invite endorsement (or more commonly, its opposite), rather than a critical appraisal of its conditions of possibility. The lectures move from definitions to fields of operations, from what to how, from precoded judgment to a willingness to be both drawn in and overwhelmed. Why does this piece work this way? What is it asking of you?

Faculty not teaching in the program had to field anxious complaints from students accustomed to excelling at what they did. The students were working so hard, yet they were still uncertain about the outcome. Triage was ever tempting. Denied the certainty of a five-paragraph essay, of a form to fit an inevitably affirmable thesis, students were right to observe that their writing would get worse before it got better. The immediate reaction that the students did not like the core prompted faculty to consider whether likeability should be criteria enough for sustaining the program. The directors of the core from expository writing met with faculty of each department and took the concerns where they could into adjustments in the format and structure. Lecturers and writing faculty convened after each session to rehearse how the lecture could be used in the individual writing classes. The lecture itself was pared back from running the entire year to the spring semester only so that the students could focus on developing their writing before taking on the added complexity of a weekly lecture. This also alleviated the burden of a seamless progression over the year if the content of the fall and spring were not fixed. Instead, during the fall, students would attend four plenary experiences—a performance, a lecture, a film, and a discussion about a museum visit in which their writing teachers would read out their own responses to seeing the assigned exhibit.

Over ten years, with considerable continuity among writing faculty (and even greater consistency among lecturers), the year-end evaluative discussions turned substantially. Initially, the concerns were linked to status considerations, such as who would be responsible for taking attendance in the lecture hall and how to keep senior faculty from referring to writing sections as recitations. After a few years, the conversations shifted to the various interpretive strategies employed by faculty to make sense of the lecture and a general consideration about what students could do at the end of the term that they could not do at the beginning. Some students could clearly articulate these gains in perspective for themselves. Others would insist that they gained nothing from the lectures while still being able to identify questions and issues presented therein that they would continue to think about (not something many students could do when the course was first launched). Lost is some of the initial fluidity of faculty from around the school when dozens tried their hands at teaching the lecture. Yet the continuity among faculty who teach year after year has made for a deeper understanding of what it means to teach without relying on the authority of discipline, grading, or being at the center of the course work.

The hour lecture has to account for itself if it is to be serviceable. It must at once essay its examples of art so that students can read the logic of composition in their principles of presentation. The students must learn to read the lecture itself as a text, to take seriously its formal composition and rhetorical strategies, to treat the art arrayed before them as a lens for observing the social world. It becomes possible to show music videos of Paul Simon's fall 2006 performance of *Graceland* in Zimbabwe (twenty years after the initial recording) and a 2000 remix of "Snap—The Power of Bhangra," and ask, if these stand as definitions of globalization, what is it? Students see the smooth homogeneity of the international rock star's movement across the planet and the pastiche of South Asian and hip-hop soup-to-nuts exoticism of sheer heterogeneity as somehow mirroring one another. They see the unobstructed openness of Frank Lloyd Wright's public and private interiors in the Guggenheim Museum and Fallingwater, Wright's house outside Pittsburgh, Pennsylvania. Students see the fractured surfaces that no longer delineated the depth of interiority in

Frank Gehry's Guggenheim Museum Bilbao, and his Santa Monica residence as depicting different conceptions of space and subjectivity associated with the modern and postmodern. They trace the shared kinesthetic sensibility of decentered movement in examples of capoeira, krumping, and Z-Boys' skateboarding. That is, they practice reading across instances of artistic endeavors that share affinities of form and context, and they apply these approaches to association in the way their essays will be generated. Students read the lecture as a multimedia assemblage that will get translated into writing in their own compositions.

Aside from the work that they generate, students respond variously to their experience of the course. Some are immediately hailed by the course project and participate avidly. Others are disconcerted at the loss of mastery over writing forms presented in high school or doubtful that the effort expended to generate these essays will carry over to other writing. Still others will resist the demands placed on their writing and express a desire to write unfettered by such demands. Toward the latter part of the year, as they gain fluency in the pedagogical process, these concerns abate for many. Years on, they gain appreciation for what they are able to do. As Pat Hoy, who has tracked these students' deferred responses in follow-up interviews and focus groups years later, closely observes, "This is a demanding course. We expect students to complain about it, but it is a known fact that in the end they tell us a very different story from the one they tell one another. The vast majority of them express clear satisfaction with what they have learned about writing essays. They may not like the intellectual suffering, the incessant challenges accompanied by moments of temporary uncertainty and confusion, but they like the results. When they learn to make something new of complex evidence, they cannot help being satisfied. Creativity fosters its own reward."[39]

Where these rewards are manifest, the core will travel with the student in a way called for by the conventional curricular model but unavailable through its design. The problem of how one essays the public domain and composes oneself accordingly is an emergent accomplishment contingent upon the circumstances students encounter. The traditional core imagines that education emanates from its center and is borne by the student through life. This critical variant appears as a kind of found object, unwilling to relinquish the occasion offered by a core to question means and end. It is meant to anticipate the public operations of students and their predicaments, a feature that makes it difficult to judge in the moment, and as such, its value becomes sensible and usable in response to what students find over time.

TURNING POST-PROFESSIONAL

Yet what students find, or make for themselves, may invite them back to the university from a professional world that demands much and leaves much out. The question would be how the university is prepared in curricular terms for this state of return. Graduate work that is professional assumes it comes before the work it names (whether here professional refers to academic labor, as in liberal arts and science, or the credentialed occupations of law, medicine, engineering, education, social work, and the like). Adult learning—continuing education—represents work on its way to more. It is either a maintainer of currency, retooler of occupations, or enhancer of the learning that jobs leave behind. This enormous learning sector is considered post-professional in a rather passive sense of the term—namely, as after-work (in the double sense of when it is done and when it is being sought). In this, continuing education is asked to do little more than be a translation medium (or holding tank) to more professional activity. Alternately, the post-professional could figure what is left out or remaindered in the present. The core curriculum represents a kind of future—an impulse to return. The conditions of reentry require some negotiation with and reflection upon the university. If the contradictions of professional work offer particular kinds of politicization and activation—of knowledge that must be rejustified and relegitimated because it lacks the autonomy to do so on the basis of a credential—then a post-professional education pertains to what professionals need to know once their expertise no longer suffices. As with the core, a diagnosis of what gets in the way of work is required, an account of the obstacles to what professions promised to realize through knowledge but must now be negotiated through a political thicket.

This post-professional sensibility informed the creation of a new graduate program in arts politics. Offered in the same department of art and public policy as the Tisch core curriculum, this program raises interesting questions about present educational circumstances. With a small number of highly specialized students, the program cannot possibly serve as a model to be replicated by others. Rather, its example is of how a given specificity is achieved. The aim of the program is to convene a space for activists where questions surrounding art and politics are kept open. Hence, rather than adjudicating disciplinary boundaries, the arts politics program maintains a kind of agnosticism toward its objects of analysis. Besides this program, there are a whole range of curricular initiatives pertaining to art and politics, and these are marked by a particular institutional location and history. They may be inside an art department and therefore retain a relation to visual art, performance art, new media, music, and so on, or they may highlight a genre of political art, be it conceptual, community based, or interventionist. Given this rich, if limited, field of places to create political art, how might one take account of the field as such? This is not simply a question of constituting a discursive or epistemological domain, which, as Howard Singerman has shown, was crucial to the formation of the master of fine arts degree after World War II (i.e., in a shift from an apprentice and craft-based manual production of art objects to the installation of a conceptual field with a way of knowing and a delimited object domain).[40]

The field in question is one of practical intervention, political projects, and institutions wholly or partially engaged with political art. This mix of the ephemeral (like protests or performance pieces) and the durable (public monuments and institutions) may be mapped cognitively for any given moment, but the political art field also needs to be informed by the imaginary and the invisible, the prospective and the desired. Whether one makes a life of arts activism, such work rarely conforms to something as continuous or progressive as a career. Both activism and political art are liable to be episodic and indeterminate in opportunity and occasion and therefore rely heavily on diagnoses of the moment, valuing what was incomplete or incompletable in a given endeavor without falling prey to a sense of insufficiency or failure. This situation for arts politics suggests an educational brief, for the response of what is to be done is not to simply do more but to evaluate what has happened and what can be done next. This predicament requires a theoretical intervention that permits a valuation of practical engagement from within.

The one-year master's program in arts politics at the Tisch School at New York University (NYU) is thus conceived as a break with the demands of activism that threaten to derail it—namely, the sense that whatever we are doing, it is not enough to transform the world into the one we want to see. The program is a conceptual pause and refresh for activists, a reason to return to the university to enhance the means to recognize and elaborate the significance of the work they are already doing. Arts Politics is post-professional in this specific aspect. As such, it does not assume a single professional location or reduce the professional to the occupational. The idea is to join artists, scholar-critics, and those working in the institutional fields of art (even if these are aspects of the same person) in a conversation with a strategic and planning focus. The conceit of the program is the premise that far from a crisis in art or politics, we face a crisis of critical evaluation that minimizes the way we think about the efficacy of our own contributions, thereby rendering them more difficult to sustain. Students need to come with a project in mind and leave with a plan for intervention that changes its terms and conditions. The idea of keeping the program to a year reflects a sense of what it would mean for activists to have something like a sabbatical inside rather than outside the university. Also, it recognizes the high tuition fees and cost of living associated with a private New York City university education. But many are excluded by the limited financial aid that attends to programs that are not part of a teaching or research operation. The formal entrepreneurialism that makes it possible to argue both an educational need and the existence of a market (a group of students able to attend) also delimits who can move inside the university. Negotiating this structural limit becomes one of the program's educational aims.

The planning process for this program initially drew some skepticism from other schools as to the appropriateness of housing an intellectually based program in an art school. The program was initially designated "cultural politics" in reference to its most proximate epistemic domain. Another concern was that the program adequately distinguish itself from professional programs in fields such as public policy and arts management and administration. The name of the program—arts politics—emerged as a condensation from other terms that had preexisting institutional homes or markers. The politics of naming, framed in terms of a scarcity of identity, became a kind of organizing device to enlist the participation of others. When the program went for interschool academic approval, there was a request to clarify the academic standing of activism—to pinpoint its epistemological status. Unfixed by genre, it was possible to argue in this setting that activism was a kind of analytic operation, an elaboration of the significance of what is being done in order to generate more of it. Even a sympathetic voice offered that it was a program to train generals and not privates. A dean from another school that also provided artistic training weighed in that this was a model of cross-school collaboration.

Some from within the Tisch School worried about what it meant for their interdisciplinary space to become a departmental program competing for resources like any other. The concerns from various quarters had the effect of focusing the program so that it would remain open to other kinds of interests and purposes to the intersection of art and politics. The result was a partnership among five schools and some two dozen faculty, across which there was a shared interest but little by way of institutional commitment. The program was marked, therefore, by the contention over arts and politics within the university. It offered a modest contribution and a marker of how these might be engaged by affiliating faculty but also by keeping room, even in the required courses, for students from other programs and schools at the university.

In the first few years, students appeared to recruit themselves. Many said they found the program by an Internet search of the terms "art" and "politics," which is to say they were looking for it. Others were drawn to the Tisch School itself or to the work of its full-time instructors, among them Ella Shohat and Karen Finley. Scores of prospective students came in to speak to the chair about the program, and the applicant pool tripled in the first four years. The various filters yielded an inaugural class of selective diversity. Students shared a double displacement, declaring they were the odd ones in whichever course they took. They were interested in law and pop music, worked in a senator's office and did theater, studied international relations and interned in an auction house, hailed from Texas and studied hip-hop poetry in Berlin. Racially and nationally different, they were all women in their mid-twenties. Their conception of activism was not at odds with a commitment to working within or creating arts institutions. One student aimed to create an alternative for-profit arts center to assure that artists would get paid. Another devised a national arts fellowship program. The trajectory of the arts politics program asks that students devise an interventionist project, one that anticipates the conceptual and political problems that one may not have the time to think about when in the midst of forming something. Their projects and presentations operated between genres and included a self-published book of poems, memoirs, and critical writing; a mock auction of Hitler's watercolors; a mapping of museums as favelas; and a performance of a Chinese response to the Tibetan anti-Olympic protests. During the first four years of the program, the class grew from six to twenty-two while maintaining geographical and cultural diversity.

Since students can take nearly half of their coursework outside their home departments and may be in the minority even in their own required courses, they have both moved through the university and consolidated themselves as a cohort. A weekly symposium and a colloquium to discuss their various fieldwork projects are the only exclusive spaces. This opening to the form that work might take inside the university is shaped by the double meaning of arts politics that the program wants students to consider: the politics that make art and the politics that art makes. In other words, there is some tension between what are considered the forces that constitute the spaces of the political in a given cultural context and what makes for the artist's own agency. The relation between economic and aesthetic value—the commodity and the sign—becomes crucial to grasping the inherent political aspect in an artwork without exhausting any given artistic moment or expression. The question of how the politics of a particular work is made legible gets joined with how the artistic practice makes room for itself in the world so as to make certain politics legible. Hence, what appear to be the exceptional moments of controversy, censorship, and celebrity disclose the operations of political processes in the production, reception, and mediated dissemination of the arts. This conceptual framing informs what is to be understood by interventionist work, even if, for a student in a class, this entails writing a term paper. Intervention pertains to how a given moment lives or continues beyond itself, how it is set loose in the world, how it opens itself to further possibility. Intervention, a stepping in—coming between—so as to affect the course of movement in some series of events, carries with it a strategic self-awareness of how one enters and where one takes their potential impact. Rather than assimilating or mastering or being disciplined by a body of knowledge, that body is already in motion and the acts of study redirect what the body can be. Intervention activates the possibilities a given setting presents. The arts activist is thus of a piece with the student activist.

IMMANENT ACTIVISM

If the arts politics program brings activism into the university, the conditions that make students work also yield an activism. At NYU itself, this crystallized in the graduate student strike of 2005–2006. At the heart of the strike was a matter of gaining recognition not simply for a union but for the very character of the activity that students engaged in. The university's position was that the monies paid to teaching and research assistants was financial aid and not salary. By maintaining this distinction, the university leaders sought to frame the relation of students to the university as one of debt to an institution that had granted them a special privilege. The twelve hundred students in the bargaining unit were but a small fraction of the total number of graduate students at NYU—nearly nineteen thousand. Of course, these students were a very large proportion of the doctoral students whose work for the university was key to its research and teaching programs. But this comparison to graduate students in professional fields attached a professional apprenticeship model to academic fields once defined as distinct from those of professional schools.

In a story that has been effectively told, the strike was precipitated by the university's unwillingness to negotiate a contract renewal with GSOC-UAW (Graduate Student Organizing Committee), the bargaining unit that had effectuated a three-year contract between 2001 and 2005. What made the decision to negotiate or not a unilateral one was a change in the composition of the regional panel of the National Labor Relations Board (NLRB) that had previously found in favor of the graduate students in 2000. In a case brought by Brown University, the reconstituted board ruled in July 2004 that the relationship of graduate teachers and researchers to the university was primarily educative rather than economic. This result was applied to NYU, and the university considered itself released from any legal obligation to renew the contract. In August of 2005, NYU gave the union 48 hours on a take-it-or-leave-it offer that would allow it to continue as an association without the benefit of outside binding arbitration. The university argued that its first contract term's twenty-two unfair labor practice filings—all of which it won—represented an onerous condition that interfered with administration prerogatives that put academics ahead of labor matters. Because of the stipulations in labor law, the union was forced to defend its complaint—strictly on labor grounds and without allowing for educational arguments—that union members were being replaced by those outside the bargaining unit at lower salaries. Reducing the number of PhD students was an outcome of unionization, as it has been for other unionized workers.[41]

Beyond the impact on the graduate students, the university administration was concerned to show full-time faculty that a union of academics had no place on campus, even if part-time faculty at NYU had already unionized. When the president held a town hall meeting in July 2005 to announce that there would be no further negotiations with the union, he stated to all in attendance that while he found marking papers to be an unpleasant task, he did not consider teaching to be labor, rather it was a response to a calling. The invocation of religious language suggested that training graduate students to become professors was also not work but a service provided to the future of a profession. The preemption of unionization took the form of a disavowal of labor as such—both for graduate students and for faculty. Both were invited to imagine their relation to the university as one of debt not employment. The student is indebted through financial aid (rather than compensation), and the faculty live in debt to a learning community (rather than a workplace). The graduate students' mobilization was to recast faculty privilege from a peculiar benefit that represented control over their working lives—of which "their" student assistants were an extension—to a position that was a link in a chain of accountability required to report student transgressions to a higher authority capable of taking action.

Breaking the strike and prosecuting the students who remained on the picket line entailed usurping the managerial prerogatives of the faculty to discipline their "own" students, one of the predicates of faculty in the private university being considered managerial labor and therefore ineligible to form a collective bargaining unit. The administration's efforts to transcribe labor as debt produced its own worst fear, an organizational response on the part of faculty. Convened immediately in response to the crackdown on students and surveillance of faculty, a group called Faculty Democracy crafted a series of written responses, support networks, and public appeals that subsequently outlived the graduate student strike and expanded to intervene on a series of questions regarding faculty governance or the lack thereof. Absent the official standing of a union, Faculty Democracy has sought to occupy a space between the formal governance bodies of the university—such as the Faculty Senator's Council, a critical policy voice advocating fair labor practices at NYU start-up campuses overseas—and a convening space for reflection on common faculty experience.

Just as it proved a catalyst for engaging faculty, the effort to deny student's labor activism assures that a feature of current graduate student education is to train them in the practicalities of struggles over academic labor. The tactical success in smashing a union assures that graduate students' own professional socialization will include a struggle with management and an organizational intelligence that transcends their disciplinary and professional training. The central university administration's ongoing anxiety over unionization has led to continued preemptive efforts that open up further contradictions. For example, when the election of Barack Obama posed the prospect of a different ruling from the NLRB on graduate student labor, the NYU administration recrafted its graduate student aid package (what it dubbed Financial Aid Reform, or FAR) to exclude teaching. In this scheme, these students would surrender teaching experience as part of their training but would be eligible to teach as adjuncts, an assignment that would make them part of a recognized collective bargaining group on campus. In fall 2010, GSOC, which never stopped its organizing activities, did gain from the regional NLRB reconsideration of the question of eligibility to engage in collective bargaining. Far from being extinct or quaint, the student activist of today is deeply imbricated in the fiber of the university's labor relations.

Certainly, there is a long history of universities as sites of student activism and political ferment. Considering just the past hundred years, what the university does has increasingly occasioned an activist response, albeit one without a fixed ideological position. If the thirties saw students engaged with existing political formations and the sixties combining a critique of foreign policy with that of the mechanization of knowledge, activism of the past thirty years has incorporated a dimension of academic labor into activist agendas. Indeed, a survey on student activism written as recently as the early nineties made the general assertion that "student political activism tends to be aimed at societal issues and broad political concerns rather than campus questions."[42] Whereas the new positioning of the university within the knowledge industry suggests that campus questions are already entangled in broader political concerns, even if there are myriad ways in which these are named and from which their organization stems. The shift brings together the larger changes in the university with those of students as a distinct social category along the lines that Horowitz and Friedland had imagined some forty years ago. The ways in which activism braids together or refuses what is inside and outside the university speaks to a loss of the autonomy of "student" as a social category that is in line with the changes experienced by the faculty and the institution as such.

What could be said of activism generally would apply to campus expressions—namely, that there has been a dispersion of issues, sites, and dimensions of human experience that are objects of contestation. One clearinghouse that monitors current activity, CampusActivism.org, lists 1,920 groups, 270 networks, and more than 500 resources for activists (as of late 2010). Issues range from academic freedom, Afghanistan, and African poverty to university investments and research, vegetarianism/veganism, and youth rights. There are campaigns—such as the 20 percent by 2010 CT Clean Air campaign, All Diamonds Are Blood Diamonds, and Students for Free Higher Education—that may be based on a single campus or can be national in scope. Networks include Campus Greens or the revitalized Students for a Democratic Society (SDS), which boasts more than one hundred fifty chapters (as of winter 2010 since its relaunch in 2006). Even SDS is able to mobilize around specific issues, as reflected in the antiwar protests across ninety campuses on the fifth anniversary of the Iraq War (March 20, 2008). Campus Activism reflects a coalitional imprint in its mission to "promote the active participation of young people in the formation of a movement to build a society free from poverty, ignorance, war, exploitation, racism, sexism, classism, homophobia, and environmental destruction."[43] Campus groups like Students against Sweatshops link labor and consumer politics on campus and off, and they have been significant in focusing attention on other aspects of university labor practice. Emblematic of the conservative equivalents of these entities is Students for Academic Freedom, which also considers itself a clearinghouse devoted to providing balance for students and protection from professors' radical views. Organized by adults like David Horowitz, who paid students to observe potentially errant professors, the demands for balance suggest that radical views are pervasive and must be immediately countered wherever they appear. Less organizationally than discursively, this right activism imagines an external world run wild within the university that can be corrected only by external intervention. Self-anointed watchdogs operate where internal peer review might once have seemed sufficient to deliver appropriate academic quality. In this respect as well, academic freedom imagines the autonomy of a monologic institution lost to the plurality of voices associated with the appearance of multiculturalism.

Thinking back to the precollege days discussed in Chapter 2, preparation would seem to spell permanent anticipation. The anxieties and pressures of professional instrumentality truck no patience with the eternal present posited by education as its own end. Yet, as with their younger brethren, college students appear no less capable of differentiating demands upon them and strategizing how to array present and future with substantive and instrumental capabilities. The ability to see oneself and think beyond the university does not diminish what one can do within it. The split focus is not a deficit of attention but a dispersion of what to attend to, a selection of attributes that can be leveraged to the most consequential difference, a partiality in the midst of heightened volatility from which courses of activity can be derived. The professional turn carries certain practical demands that students look to in their courses, college, and careers that also impinges upon the faculties of the future. What this sensibility means for the professoriate is taken up in Chapter 4.

4

W(h)ither Academic Freedom?

Revaluing Faculty Work

Immanuel Kant begins a personal exchange with King Frederick William
II of Prussia by offering to give an "account" for "having misused my
philosophy." His aim is to wrest a measure of authority away from state
power so as to render the professoriate a kind of incorporated scholar. "The
University would have a certain autonomy (since only scholars can pass judgment on scholars as such)."[1] This nascent notion of academic freedom based
upon professional expertise would trade rule over the cloistered and restricted
domain of the university for recognition that knowledge must not usurp the
power of the state. Kant endorses the idea of censorship for the general intel-
ligentsia, or "businessmen of learning," who operate outside the constraining
quarters of academic institutions. Within the United States, over the course
of the hundred years since Kant wrote "The Conflict of the Faculties"(1798),
the professionalization of faculty would emerge hand in hand with the modern research university—both of which adopted strains of German influence.
In 1915, the newly formed American Association of University Professors
(AAUP) would argue for tenure as an employment contract on the basis of
professional self-policing of academic freedom. The expansion of higher
education after World War II was entangled with that of the professional-
managerial class, as expressed in the relative prowess and pervasiveness of
tenured faculty at the end of the sixties.

The shift away from tenure over the past forty years has been justified
by many exigencies and explanations, including nothing less than a "new
spirit of capitalism."[2] Certainly, management-driven flexibility is at odds with
permanent employment. Team- and project-based research sounds a lot like

interdisciplinarity in contract labor. Within the meritocratic logic, tenure is linked to the master grammar of academic labor—research, teaching, and service. When research is aligned with knowledge production in contradistinction to teaching as a distribution mechanism for already made knowledge, only knowledge that is productive (i.e., that circulates outside the university) would lead to tenure eligibility. In practice, productivity (even when measured narrowly, as by prolificacy of publication) has expanded consistently since the sixties, with more faculty presenting research portfolios for the sake of promotion and reappointment. In teaching, as in business, productivity takes myriad forms. Teaching load is one, but so too is teacher evaluation, which introduces performance-based norms that insinuate schemes of accountability without control over the curricular means of account. In the case of proprietary schools, the basis for academic freedom is rendered moot. As these become models of privatization across higher education the ability to tie job security to professional autonomy is deeply jeopardized. Finally, the category of service is conventionally placed outside the realm of merit and into a liminal space somewhere between courtesy and obligation. This marginalization of service has a corrosive impact on the aspirations and capacities for faculty governance, as it is divested of meaningful scrutiny, value, and critical elaboration. As professional status weakens as a means to deliver categorical faculty control, the arena of service, or more properly, administrative labor, becomes all the more essential.

WHERE FREEDOM LEADS

For the past hundred years, "academic freedom" has been the term by which faculty rights and responsibilities are specified. While there are a range of views as to what the term means—what it covers and how it operates— "academic freedom" has been widely deployed to establish the conceptual framework by which academic faculty are set apart from other occupations, and it is therefore what establishes the university as a singular institution. Because it has been so central to the identity of the university as a place where rigorous methods of inquiry assure untrammeled pursuit of knowledge, the term has helped solidify a coalition that crosses disparate ideological positions and places in the organizational hierarchy. Academic freedom has two foundations. One is in constitutional protections to expressions of political speech. The legal case history has therefore centered on the appropriateness of particular utterances of professors in classrooms or extramural settings. The other root lies not in individual rights but corporate interest. Here, academic freedom is enshrined around a particular kind of employment relation introduced by the self-organization of professionals. The organization, the AAUP, was itself the response to an exercise of conventional employer rights, that of hiring and firing workers.[3]

In this instance, the cause célèbre was the dismissal of economist Edward A. Ross from Stanford University in 1900, at the behest of an owner of this private corporation, Jane Stanford. Stanford complained to the university's then-president, David Starr Jordan. She was weary of the political stance Ross had taken against Asian immigrant labor conditions and on behalf of free silver—a populist response to the power of creditors who controlled the monetary supply then denominated in gold. The seminal 1915 *Declaration of Principles on Academic Freedom and Academic Tenure* emerged from a joint committee that convened from three professional associations meeting in 1913—economists, political scientists, and sociologists. They reconvened a year later, in December 1914. In January of 1915, the first AAUP meeting was held that promulgated a committee of fifteen faculty—largely social scientists from prominent public and private research universities around the nation (although one of the authors of the document, Arthur O. Lovejoy, was a philosopher, and others came from zoology, education, English, and law). The document drew upon German traditions that applied to teachers and students. It took up the concepts *Lehrfreiheit* (faculty discretion over its topics of inquiry) and *Lernfreiheit* (student selection of courses without administrative interference), so as to identify what should properly belong to faculty: "freedom of inquiry and research; freedom of teaching within the university or college; and freedom of extramural utterance and action." While the first two of these prerogatives was thought sufficiently safeguarded, the last concerning public utterance was the basis for the five cases that the new association was investigating, and it chose to defend such civic intervention on the basis of a model of teaching grounded within the university. As a practical matter, academic freedom would rest upon clarification of "(1) the scope and basis of the power exercised by those bodies having ultimate legal authority in academic affairs; (2) the nature of the academic calling; and (3) the function of the academic institution or university."[4] With respect to this authority, the declaration sets forward a notion of "public trust" against proprietary institutions, which are deemed to uphold a private and propagandistic viewpoint. Trustees cannot "bind the reason or conscience of any professor" but must appeal for authority to the "general public" to maintain a "non-partisan institution of learning."[5] Such institutions have three chief purposes: "to promote inquiry and advance the sum of human knowledge; to provide general instruction to students; and to develop experts for various branches of the public service."[6]

Universities, from this perspective, would take the lead in establishing and realizing the implications of a then still novel distinction between private proprietorship and public trust, between interested ownership and disinterested moral authority. The moral dimensions of this trust infuse the nature of the academic calling. Those who heed this compact eschew the pursuit of economic rewards and, in exchange, gain "the assurance of an honorable and secure position, and of freedom to perform honestly and according to their own consciences the distinctive and important function which the nature of the profession lays upon them." Hence, the professor's own motives would sustain the distinction between the proprietary domain of market-driven self-interest and the moral realm of trust "exempt from pecuniary motive." Those trained and dedicated to the "quest for truth" are subject only to the conclusions that their methods of inquiry lead them to and not to "echoes of the opinions of the lay public, or of the individuals who endow or manage universities."[7] Tenure, while emanating from an employment relation, confers governance of intellectual activity to "fellow experts" who are unmotivated by profit, unswayed by public opinion, and uninterested in managing the institutional features of their working environment. Faculty members are appointees but "not in any proper sense employees" of the university administration.

The model for the discharge of the faculty's professional responsibilities is not that of labor but of judgment, and so tenure follows the model of judges in federal courts—hence the emphasis on appointment rather than hiring. At a time of militant labor organizing and revolutionary political activity, academic freedom for university professors would position itself in an autonomous realm of professional moral authority outside the politics of labor and government. It is interesting that the AAUP itself began as an association of professional associations, an interdisciplinary initiative that reached across existing (if themselves still emergent) disciplinary societies in a way not wholly unlike the congresses and federations that would give labor its organizational might. But in forgoing the status of employee as a basis for limiting the powers of employers, tenure was constructed to avoid this parallel by invoking a higher authority than the market along the lines of the secularization of religious calling. In reaction to the proprietary powers of trustees, who expected their command of the wage relation to control delivery of an intellectual product, the framework of academic freedom insinuated an organizational authority that would temper that of state and capital. This authority, conferred by professional peers, would displace its own field of influence from the instrumentalities of markets and policies to a purely substantive realm of moral claims to truth as a basis for advancing a general societal will that could be measured by the progressive accumulation of knowledge.

This careful parsing of a sphere of influence turned out to be an incredibly influential doctrine—adopted voluntarily by thousands of institutions and professional associations and eventually enshrined in law. Indeed, the first legal case to formalize academic freedom as a right was the Supreme Court hearing of Paul Sweezy's dismissal by the University of New Hampshire in 1957. Ironically, Sweezy's own Marxism was dedicated to understanding the relations of the state and labor under conditions he would describe as "monopoly capital."[8] The AAUP's own formalization of the 1915 principles was published in 1940, the same year that the Smith Act sought to purge labor unions of communist influence. The autonomy imagined for the professional association is both an assertion of a social right and an acceptance of a kind of negative freedom at the institutional level. Politics from this perspective would be limited to utterance based on expert authority and not on assertion of power through organizational capacity. Criticism of government or business must remain an idea, and even then one that is organizationally circumscribed. This is evident at New York University, where the faculty handbook relies upon that 1940 statement to define tenure. It also has a separate clause to define what tenure cannot protect—sedition. What counts as a seditious act or utterance is left to those who, as we shall see, will take it up as an accusation. Academic freedom is above all a regulatory principle for dealing with conflicts among spheres it takes to be both empirically and conceptually separable, even as the specific controversies that occasion its application speak to the ways in which the domains of authority covered by profession, labor, and government are, in actuality, deeply intertwined.

While much has changed in higher education since the 1915 *Declaration of Principles*, the doctrine of academic freedom remains central to the adjudication over what is permissible within the boundaries of professional conduct and university authority. Over the course of nearly one hundred years, the formal doctrine has been implemented in the context of self-policing that has been adopted in other areas of higher education governance, such as accreditation, and tested in the courts so that gradually it came to have some force of law. Yet, as a set of professional norms, academic freedom is at its most potent when it operates tacitly, as underlying assumptions by which faculty imagine what is possible and internalize the constraints that mark any institutional habitus. From its inception, academic freedom has been delimited by the terms of its controversies, which both identify the principles under normalization and disclose the force of the norms as much as by any explicit invocation of precedent. Just as with the launching of the AAUP, how those controversies are understood and conveyed are revealing indicators of both the prospects and limits of faculty authority.

Robert O'Neil, former counsel of the AAUP, has published a careful and highly useful report on the state of thinking in academic freedom called *Academic Freedom in the Wired World*. His aim is to demonstrate the abiding viability of academic freedom as a framework for maintaining faculty rights by taking the measure of both new risks and greater opportunity. His general appraisal is that in contrast to the dark days of the fifties, the political ambiguity of the campus climate today spreads controversy across the political spectrum so as to be depolarizing and results in a "freer and more open level of debate in the twenty-first century."[9] At the same time, after the attacks of September 11, there are new risks to our liberty and security that need to be accepted, as O'Neil reminds us: "Anyone who expects academic life ever to return to the conditions of September 10 is hopelessly naive . . . many of the changes that have occurred must be seen as permanent and accepted as such."[10] These poles of enhanced and diminished freedom are meant to set the norms beyond which individual cases do not merit serious attention or concern. By appreciating that we live in relatively free times and accepting the limits of external constraint, faculty can more readily embrace the parameters of what is now proper and possible. While O'Neil is genuinely concerned about the compromises to the disinterestedness of faculty research from corporate and government demands, he finds the political cases to be "isolated outbursts from individual professors who can fairly readily be dismissed as oddballs, dissidents or marginal players."[11] This line in particular stands out in a book that is notably temperate in tone and judicious in its treatment of individual cases. The urge to dismiss those instances that fall outside the protocols of due process points above all to an investment in the fairness of proceedings as evidence of a kind of institutional rationality.

The burden of O'Neil's argument is to demonstrate that where faculty was dismissed on the grounds of extramural political utterances, these fell outside the boundary of what academic freedom should be expected to protect. In this, O'Neil's position is in line with others of a pragmatic vein (potent in the early conception of the concept), such as Louis Menand and Stanley Fish, who insist that freedom can be exercised only in its specificity, and that it disappears altogether through efforts at blanket coverage.[12] Because this sentiment is so consequential, it is important to look at how O'Neil treats his own limit cases, that of Ward Churchill and Sami Al-Arian, the former dismissed from his tenured appointment in ethnic studies at the University of Colorado for research misconduct, and the latter from his faculty appointment in engineering at University of South Florida in conjunction with a federal indictment. Both proceedings were initiated after outside media attention brought extensive pressure to bear on their respective institutions.

O'Neil is careful to place in his normative center of freedom those who would fit the label of both liberal and conservative. He opens his book with an account of a longstanding Holocaust denier Arthur Butz. Butz teaches engineering at Northwestern University. He published a book in 1976 called *The Hoax of the Twentieth Century* and maintained a Web site that endorsed Iranian President Mahmoud Ahmadinejad's characterization of the Holocaust as a myth. To illustrate the auspicious times in which academic freedom exits, O'Neil recounts the coverage afforded the case by the Fox News television program *The O'Reilly Factor*. O'Neil calls host Bill O'Reilly "a seemingly unlikely champion of free expression." In response to Emory University historian Deborah Lipstadt, who remarks that Butz "shouldn't be near students," O'Reilly demurs. "After eliciting a brief negative response, O'Reilly insists that any such disposition would be 'punishing him.' The basis for that view, in O'Reilly's words, bears attention: 'You [Lipstadt] teach at a university and you know what a university is. That it's a place where all views, even abhorrent views, are tolerated for the sake of freedom of expression. You don't want to inhibit anybody."[13]

O'Reilly is here referring to what is appropriate to the pursuit of truth in the university. With respect to his own approach as a host, the request to avoid behavior that might inhibit others might best be read ironically. O'Neil introduces the telecaster's encounter with Al-Arian, the show's guest on September 26, 2001, by affirming O'Reilly as a champion of academic freedom. "Ironically [Al-Arian's] troubles began with an appearance on the *O'Reilly Factor*." On the show, professor Al-Arian "conceded he made strongly anti-Israel statements." The next morning, the university "was flooded with calls and e-mails from angry alumni and public officials, anxious parents and nervous neighbors, demanding immediate action against Al-Arian." The university barred him from setting foot on campus, suspended him, and dismissed him without a campus hearing within a matter of weeks. "The grievance process understandably ground to a halt the moment the indictment was revealed and Al-Arian was incarcerated awaiting trail." It is curious that a case that fits so closely to AAUP initial concerns that professors be insulated from the ire of public opinion and government would be treated by a scholar of academic freedom as so readily understandable. O'Neil sees the Al-Arian case as exceptional "because of the serious criminal charges that lurked in the wings and eventually resulted in his deportation."[14] Unlike other cases where O'Neil carefully examines the legal circumstances, here he seems to take the accusation by an unlikely champion of academic freedom and its consequences at face value. While O'Reilly may have countenanced freedom for Holocaust deniers, his insinuations toward a guest on his show were instrumental in destroying the life Al-Arian had known. When, subsequent to Al-Arian's appearance on the show, the University of South Florida received death threats against the professor, these were treated as a menace to campus security rather than an endangerment to a member of the faculty. An excerpt of the exchange between O'Reilly and his guest suggests a different vector for O'Neil's irony:

> O'REILLY: In—in 1988, you did a little speaking engagement in Cleveland, and you were quoted as saying, "Jihad is our path. Victory to Islam. Death to Israel. Revolution. Revolution until victory. Rolling to Jerusalem." Did you say that?
>
> AL-ARIAN: Let me just put it into context. When president Bush talked about crusade, we understand what he meant here. The Muslim world thought he is going to carry a cross and go invade the Muslim world and turn them into Christians. We have to understand the context. When you say "Death to Israel," you mean death to occupation, death to apartheid, death to oppression, death to . . .
>
> O'REILLY: But not death to any human being?
>
> AL-ARIAN: No, absolutely not. Absolutely not.

O'Reilly: No.

Al-Arian: Absolutely not.

O'Reilly: All right. So now what we have here is you saying death to Israel. You're bringing a guy over here who gets paid by the good citizens of Florida and then goes back and becomes one of the lieutenants or generals of the Islamic jihad, but you don't know nothing about it. Another guy sets up an interview with Osama bin Laden for ABC, and you don know anything about that.

You know, Doctor, it looks to me like there's something wrong down there at the University of South Florida. Am I getting—am I getting the wrong impression here?

Al-Arian: You're getting completely wrong impression because you can pick and choose and interpret it, you know, different ways.

The fact of the matter is we have been involved in intellectual-type activity. We brought dozens of people. All of them are intellectual type. You're going to get the apple—a bad apple or two, but that—if you focus on them, you get one conclusion.

The fact of the matter is that we've been investigated by the FBI for many years . . .

O'Reilly: Correct.

Al-Arian: . . . and there has been no wrongdoing whatsoever even suggested.

O'Reilly: Well, I don't know about that . . .

Yeah. Well, Doctor, you know, with all due respect—I appreciate you coming on the program, but if I was the CIA, I'd follow you wherever you went. I'd follow you 24 hours . . .

Al-Arian: Well, you don't know me. You don't know me. You do not . . .

O'Reilly: That doesn't matter. With all of this circumstantial evidence . . .

Al-Arian: If you don't know me, you can't judge me by . . .

O'Reilly: I'm not judging you.

Al-Arian: . . . simply . . .

O'Reilly: I'm just saying . . .

Al-Arian: That's exactly what you're saying.

O'Reilly: I'm saying I'd be your shadow, Doctor.

Al-Arian: We've been—we've been looked at, and a judge—a judge has said that we are not a threat to national security.

O'Reilly: All right.

Al-Arian: Even the government itself said we're not.

O'Reilly: OK. All right, Doctor. I'd still shadow you. I'd go to Denny's with you, and I'd go everywhere you went. We appreciate you coming on.[15]

In this exchange, it is hard to see the tolerance for speech or the willingness to separate critical speech acts from violent actions. For Palestinians, as for many others who seek a political solution to Israeli occupation of their lands, the present constitution of the Israeli state is not a viable basis for conflict resolution that would afford to others what Israelis seek for themselves—self-determination, self-representation, economic development. For its part, Israel is not alone in taking action aimed to dismantle government authority deemed hostile to its own survival. Al-Arian's utterances are consistent with this line of thinking. O'Reilly's response is not simply to disagree with a reconfiguration of the Israeli state to permit the emergence of a Palestinian entity (whether separate or binational) but to accuse his guest of illegal actions and treat him as if he is an enemy of state who O'Reilly would personally subject to surveillance. O'Reilly slides easily from invoking the powers of the CIA (whose prosecutorial functions have been extra-juridical) to arrogating that authority to himself, attaching himself to Al-Arian's body as his shadow. O'Reilly's verbal assault does in fact pursue Al-Arian and strip him of any protections of academic freedom, such that subsequent death threats become risks to the university and not a danger to the faculty.

For more than a decade, Al-Arian had been under investigation by the FBI for his work with Palestinian support organizations. The post–September 11 laws that designated such groups terrorist and made association with them prosecutable offenses became the occasion for using the aftermath of the O'Reilly attack to generate an indictment. After months of incarceration, Al-Arian was acquitted by a jury on December 5, 2005, of terrorist charges. However, he was subsequently reindicted on the lesser charges, over which the jury had deadlocked. When Al-Arian finally accepted a plea bargain that would allow him to leave the country, the U.S. Department of Justice violated it by requiring him to testify in other unrelated trials. He refused to testify. For the refusal, he was entrapped between contempt and perjury charges in the face of hostile questions, kept in jail, and has gone on hunger strikes to bring attention to his plight.[16] At this point, it would seem that any issues in the case pertaining to academic freedom have been eclipsed. And yet such an assertion verges on tautology. The University of South Florida treated Al-Arian's extramural political speech as terrorism, for which the campus could provide no sanctuary. Stripping him of his academic position and conspicuously suspending the university's investigative process deprived him of any invocation of such rights, leaving him subject to judicial penalties. Years of FBI surveillance did not have the effect that one night on attack television managed to have in canceling the ambit of academic freedom.

The Al-Arian case points to the limits of an academic freedom that relies on the notion of the university as sanctuary outside the state or market. While universities' initiatives in commerce make the latter quaint, the conviction that a university serves as protector against the demands of state and public opinion—so central to the original formulation of the concept—is far less remarked upon. Ward Churchill's dismissal case by the University of Colorado seeks to invoke an internal review that does the work of a antiterror-type investigation, while separating and preserving the question of academic freedom. The Churchill case shares a media trigger mechanism, including notice on *The O'Reilly Factor*. An essay of Churchill's, "Some People Push Back: On the Justice of Roosting Chickens," written the day after September 11, 2001, drew parallels between the civilian victims targeted in the U.S. bombings of Baghdad in the first gulf war, when command and control centers were treated as military targets, and the World Trade Center workers, who, operating at a site with equivalent functions, "formed a technocratic corps at the very heart of America's global financial empire."[17] He referred to these workers as "little Eichmanns" and characterized the attacks along the lines of what came to be referred to as "blowback."[18]

Several years later, the essay was cited by a student newspaper at Hamilton College, where Churchill was scheduled to speak in spring 2005. Death threats followed and the talk was canceled. Administrators at the University of Colorado pressed Churchill to resign his position as chair of ethnic studies. They claimed to uphold his free speech rights under the First Amendment as they launched a probe into his alleged research misconduct. The investigating committee, composed of two outside and three internal faculty members (but none in Churchill's field), found evidence of plagiarism, falsification of evidence, and miscitation. Colorado President and former Senator Hank Brown asked the board to dismiss Churchill, and he was fired in July 2007 (a decision subsequently overturned by the Denver District Court in April 2009).[19] O'Neil accepts the decoupling of the case from academic freedom saying that "a probing analysis of Churchill's research activity found substantial evidence of misconduct."[20] The committee took as evidence an accusation from John Levelle, a longtime critic of Churchill's. Levelle claimed that a footnote inaccurately attributed a decades-long policy of mistreatment toward Native Americans to a single piece of legislation, the General Allotment Act of 1887. Levelle pointed to the use of a citation to "cloak extreme, unsupportable, propaganda-like claims of fact that support Professor Churchill's legal and political claims with the aura of authentic scholarly research."[21] The committee acknowledged that Levelle's critique was motivated by malice but surmised that the accuser's own credibility matters only if the committee found no misconduct. The committee's report makes inferences about footnotes that some in the field characterize as tantamount to a kind of research misconduct of its own, accepting academic disputes as grounds for dismissal.[22]

As a genre of academic investigation, the report parses peer review with expertise. It readily concedes its absence of expertise while invoking universal methods of scientific inquiry, which are taken to suggest that falsifying any detail of research can invalidate the research as such. Were this procedure applicable to due process for dismissal, it is difficult to know what research would survive such formal scrutiny without the capacity to contextualize the terms of dispute—precisely what disciplinary authority is said to offer. Hence, far from validating the institutional autonomy for sustaining academic freedom from extramural accusation, the Churchill case points to a purported affirmation of this right that eviscerates the right-holder's critical capacity to exercise judgment in ways that would mandate the disinterested and specialized knowledge the university is said to uphold as its own specifying feature.

The Al-Arian and Churchill cases point to the weaknesses—both conjunctural and conceptual—in entrusting to procedural review faculty misconduct related to free speech and directly contentious of government positions and policies. The Churchill case especially triggers the shift in orientation from freedom in political speech to that of professional self-regulation. This distinction has been vigorously advanced by Robert Post, who argues for a return to the principles outlined by the AAUP in 1915 that emphasize professional freedom over individual rights. The goal is to "facilitate the professional self-regulation of the professoriate so that academic freedom safeguards interests that are constituted by the perspective and horizon of the corporate body of the faculty."[23] This legitimates the autonomous authority of faculty whereby "knowledge is advanced through the free application of highly disciplined forms of inquiry, which correspond roughly to what Charles Peirce once called 'the method of science.'"[24] Citing the cases of both Edward A. Ross and Sami Al-Arian as examples, Post insists that universities disclaim responsibility for faculty's extramural speech so that administrations can decide what is appropriate speech on campus.

The Churchill case casts doubt as to the degree to which faculty who are accused of research misconduct can invoke professional norms of expertise to convene a review by peers who have sufficient understanding of their field to adequately contextualize the dispute in question. Nor is it clear that a review can proceed as if invoking scientific method as a transdisciplinary and homogeneous authority for establishing the adequacy of a particular line of inquiry could settle accounts or provide appropriate guidance. Judith Butler has asserted that the notion of progress based on quantitative augmentation of knowledge is suspect and that the idea of an expert class serving the public interest is debatable. She challenges the notion of a priori professional norms that enable academic freedom and therefore are beyond interrogation. Part of the responsibility of academic work is to redefine its own boundaries.

Without subscribing to a "generalized distrust of authority" that "makes serious critical debate into an adolescent complaint, and so misreads and dismisses the terms of the debate in advance," Butler insists that norms are vital and in constant tension.[25] Butler also argues that academics "must always be free from administrative and state constraints on the expression of our political views."[26] The Al-Arian and Churchill cases are significant in this context because they point to the political limitations on controlling precisely the terms under which debate is embraced, and when and whether their views are free from the state. The problem becomes whether arguing on behalf of that freedom constitutes a sufficient condition for reclaiming it. We can wonder whether there is a point at which asserting even a notion of freedom as ethical constraint to recognize divergent perspectives is not strategically adequate to understand what generalizes the distrust of academic authority. We can also worry over how dismissal of debate might be countered in terms other than those requiring more debate (a remedy consistent with First Amendment conceptions of academic freedom). Butler is here responding to the threat to academic freedom authorized by September 11, specifically H.R. 3077, which in response to purported bias among Middle East programs establishes a board to review grants to ensure that funding is consistent with the national interest. The selection criteria would apply not only to government monies but also to Ford and Rockefeller grants, which accept State Department lists of terrorist organizations (of the sort that Sami Al-Arian fell victim to). In the private laundering of government language, reminiscent of the formation of area studies fifty years before, scholars are proscribed from associating with organizations that "promote violence, terrorism, bigotry, or the destruction of any state."[27]

Butler is quick to demonstrate the chilling implications of such prohibitions. Frantz Fanon, George Sorel, Desmond Tutu, Nelson Mandela, surely, also John Locke, for advocating the end of the divine right of kings, and Montesquieu's research on U.S. State Constitutions, would all be candidates for proscription. Extending beyond any specific authors, Butler asks, "What about a tract on nonviolence that admits that under certain conditions violence might be needed to effect democratic change?"[28] She makes her point eloquently that all this restricts our imagination to the states we have and know. Yet what is curiously omitted in looking at the kinds of intellectual positions and organizations around the world whose ideas could not be studied or taught is whether research in support of officially named U.S. government interests and ideas could meet the same criteria. Not just area studies but many fields of inquiry in the arts, social sciences, humanities, and natural sciences have informed, inspired, and been in the service of policies that have promoted violence and bigotry within the United States, as, for example, against Native Americans, and terrorism and regime change against foreign populations and governments.[29]

The self-exception of the United States government from the norms it applies to others is a basic tenet of its exercise of right and might.[30] This could seem to be such an obvious point that it need not be made, but its elision within the discussion of the conjunctural conditions for academic freedom leaves intact the impression that academics, by imaging a separation from the state in the governance of their own affairs, might actually be left alone by the state. Yet Butler names with great precision the trouble that ensues when critics treat state restraint as a condition of their own internal professional work and their public utterances. Under these circumstances—ones we currently face and have faced—the question becomes, is any conception of self-governing norms, however critically reflective they may be, sufficient to advance the conditions for inquiry named by academic freedom? Perhaps more difficultly, is any framework of academic freedom sufficient to think through the challenges to professional norms that these cases and contexts present? Interestingly, at the very moment that area studies were being conceived as disinterested pursuits of state interests that authorized professional autonomy, a no less stalwart supporter of publicly funded advanced education—Dwight David Eisenhower—was also worrying about the consequences of a nation under the incontestable sway of technocrats.[31] In this regard, the history of the generalized distrust of authority may not be so easily separable from the assertion of technical expertise as such.[32]

Split Appointments

Using academic freedom arguments to situate the professional activity of university faculty presumes a generalization from a particular employment relation, that of tenure. One could argue that without some having tenure none can have academic freedom, but given present employment patterns, that merely states the problem. Part-time faculty has increased over the past thirty years. What has been called casualization, to describe the minimal commitment of institution to employee, now increasingly describes full-time appointments as well.[33] Of nearly 3.5 million people employed in higher education, 1.3 million were faculty—slightly more than half of these were employed full time, and the proportion of full-timers with tenure is trending below half. In 1970, when fewer than a half million were employed as faculty, full-timers outnumbered part-timers by more than 3 to 1.[34] Now, for those working part-time, 64 percent report this is "due to personal preference," although in institutions that rely most heavily on part-timers, fewer faculty say that they prefer to be adjuncts. For example, among public four-year institutions, less than a third of the faculty are part-time, and of those, two-thirds say they willingly work fewer hours. Whereas, in public two-year colleges, nearly two-thirds are part-timers and less than 60 percent work part time by choice. Employment and preference also vary by discipline. The professional fields can be the heaviest employers of part-timers, with Protective Services leading the list at nearly 80 percent.[35] By contrast, the increasing commitment of personnel is seen in nonteaching areas, or technical fields, which have now become intrinsic to notions of instructional delivery—technical education already complicates the relation between teachers and teaching, and whether well-packaged instructional materials can speak for themselves.

The greatest employment growth is in nonteaching professional staff—which doubled from 10 percent to 20 percent in the thirty years to 2007.[36] The weakening grasp of faculty on the priorities of the university is also reflected in compensation. Despite the attention given to salaries for academic stars and elite professionals, faculty salaries as a whole have flatlined (although compensation, or pay plus benefits, which reflects rising health care costs, has actually increased). After some modest gains in the eighties and nineties (averaging about 1 percent a year in real terms), faculty salaries now lose ground to inflation. The average salary gap between disciplines is also widening. To take one example, in 1987, salaries (controlled for inflation) for full-time faculty averaged $60,760 in the humanities and $92,900 in the health fields. In 2003, average salaries in the humanities had declined to $59,970, while those in health increased to $98,480.[37] As with the student body, what was once a monoculture has undergone diversification, though not yet proportionate to the population at large. Roughly 45 percent of faculty were white males and 36 percent white females. Just less than one in five faculty is a minority—half the ratio of undergraduates among minority populations (32 percent).[38] Yet even this measure of diversity does not translate proportionately into tenured appointments, which retain a logic of distribution typically described in terms of excellence and not a commitment to diversity.

A basic distinction used to delineate tenurable from nontenurable faculty positions is increasingly crafted between knowledge producers and knowledge transmitters—or researchers who teach and teachers who disseminate what others are said to have discovered. The notion that teaching is a form of transmission, borrowed from Cold War communications theory, posits teachers as bearers and students as receptacles of knowledge, with little attention paid to what is created in the classroom such that a capacity for learning, evaluating, and contextualizing is possible. While the anxiety over the passivity of young minds persists in the face of new technologies, information reception is, in practice, deeply active. Whatever the acquired knowledge of an educated person was thought to be, the framing of teaching as a movement of facts from one location to another downplays what students are able to do with the knowledge they gained, such as aspiring to something as active as research. While the distinction between producing and transmitting may be invidious and conceptually unsupportable, it speaks to how the boundary between professional activity and teaching gets thought about. It also cautions about generalizing from the situation of the research university to academia more broadly in terms of how academic freedom might be deployed to organize and amalgamate the interests and attentions of the professoriate, especially in those cases where what faculty is employed to do falls short of activating professional norms as a condition of employment in the way that the authors discussed above imply.

The bifurcation of appointment structures between the prized and the disposable incorporates a range of job titles that specify research or teaching but do not confer tenure. The bracketing of research from teaching, at a time when more faculty from all manner of appointments are likely to publish work, points to the cover under which nontenure-bearing positions are spreading from adjunct to full-time lines. Research professors, clinical professors, arts professors, professors of practice, lecturers, instructors, and master teachers form a pool of renewable or nonrenewable contract positions that may or may not offer ladder structures for career movement within a given institution. Casualization renders faculty employment similar to other labor relations. But the association of teaching with what is casual suggests that learning itself is part of the ephemera of the university, when increasingly revenue gleaned from the gap between suppressed labor costs and increasing tuition funds the activities and areas designated as research intensive. All this is to say that the distinction between teaching and research is administrative in more than one sense. It allows for ready classification of what merits further investment and it removes the decision over how money will flow to administrative entities. The devaluation of teaching that extends from primary through postsecondary education is not entirely separable from the discrediting of what gets taught. This too speaks to the challenges faculty has faced in affirming the value of its work when operating in a climate of skepticism toward critical endeavors and learning that challenges received tradition.

It is worth recalling one influential report aimed at the revaluation and reintegration of teaching and scholarship: Ernest L. Boyer's *Scholarship Reconsidered*, published by the Carnegie Foundation for the Advancement of Teaching in 1990. The report reflects on a contradiction of post–World War II education—namely, that the advent of a mass university system entailed an enormous expansion of scale in the student body, while demanding research productivity from faculty. Higher education was to provide the labor for the expansion of the knowledge economy in the form of the professional-managerial class but also the intellectual capital by which knowledge could be industrialized. Knowledge labor was to be extensive while knowledge capital intensive. The former justified increasing educational capacity and tuition funding, while the latter implied intensive investment to create centers of production. Research in this regard came to be associated with excellence or measurable outcome of efficacy. The emphasis on research productivity (while public funding receded and all institutions have had to rely on excellence rather than entitlements to function) has meant that the research model has extended across all manner of institutions as a means of valuing faculty activity. Boyer's strategy was twofold. To redistribute this value by extending the metric of research to cover the range of activities that faculty might engage in and to pluralize faculty contributions to recognize diverse abilities and capacities over the course of a career.

Boyer identifies four scholarly functions that professorial work performs: discovery, integration, application, and teaching. The scholarship of discovery pertains to research innovation based upon unique investigation, which, Boyer notes, is unevenly distributed over the course of even the most productive careers. The scholarship of integration entails interpretation that reshapes the boundaries of human knowledge. While interdisciplinarity that presses on those very boundaries is now moving from the margins to the center of academic life, conventionally, a lifetime of learning is required to achieve adequate synthesis. The scholarship of application subjects civic engagement to professional rigor in order to serve the public good, yet such service must be able to incorporate practical knowledge and political demands into its own disinterested approach and self-concept. The scholarship of teaching extends beyond what is already known and available for transmission to the transformation and expansion of knowledge. But for knowledge to count, its efficacy must be demonstrated, and this requires assessment from all who participate in teaching—faculty, students, and peers. If not, Boyer observes, teaching "is like a currency that has value in its own country but can't be converted into other currencies."[39] Learning that is ongoing and lifelong requires continuous, multidimensional assessment. The various forms of research can be integrated into a faculty portfolio—a collection of work that displays development but also an array of investments whose returns can be summed in the aggregate. At the same time, assessment implies convertibility—the means to make differences commensurate with one another. Generalizing the research model affords a kind of gold standard, taking up a range of activities like teaching, interdisciplinarity, and service. These could be considered local, and they could be departicularized and translated for external measurement, on the assumption that the local values lost to convertibility will, like the economic policy models for poor countries, secure development (and not further impoverishment).

Boyer's report aimed to ground research in a metric that was comprehensive and universal. Research requires demonstration; it cannot simply invoke privilege. Assessment entails a shifting calibration of value over time (a career) and across disciplinary space. Measurable gain will be the stuff of excellence. While Boyer's ambition is to affect a revaluation of teaching by extending definitions of research excellence, providing intercommensurability of diverse currencies and values also permits a parsing within each of the categories. The Carnegie Foundation advances teaching by itself serving as currency—both the store and measure of value. It provides crucial research aimed at the valuation of teaching, but it also undertakes the classification by which institutions rank their status—not by determining the ranking per se but by delimiting the classes by which mobility across class might be recognized. The proliferation of research categories and the engagement of all institutions along a classificatory schema informed by research assessment exercises abets the internal differentiation by which rewards, such as tenured appointments, are meted out. By this logic, tenure is not what binds one to an institution in a usurpation of employer prerogative, but it is what marks convertibility or mobility by which hiring away faculty becomes a mark of institutional prestige.

Excellence engenders this sorting out by which some can become what Marc Bousquet refers to as a "waste product" and others the scene of accumulation. Bousquet ingeniously critiques the notion that the academic job system fits with the supply-and-demand logic of a labor market:

> Increasingly, the holders of the doctoral degree are not so much the *products* of the graduate-employee labor system as its *by-products*, insofar as that labor system exists primarily to recruit, train, supervise, and legitimate the employment of nondegreed students and contingent faculty.
>
> This is not to say that the system doesn't produce and employ holders of the Ph.D. in tenurable positions, only that this operation has become secondary to its extraction of teaching labor from persons who are nondegreed or not yet degreed, or whose degrees are now represented as an "overqualification" for their contingent circumstances.[40]

For many, Bousquet observes, the PhD is not the portal to a rewarding life in academia but the terminus known as a teaching career, making the apprenticeship an end in itself. In place of the illusion of graduate study as a dream deferred, casualized academic labor induces a grasp of the larger context for the academic's work. "They know they are not merely treated like waste but, in fact, are the actual shit of the system—being churned inexorably toward the outside: not merely 'disposable' labor (Walzer) but labor that must be disposed of for the system to work."[41] The contingent work inside the university is connected to that beyond it in an organizational "dictatorship of the flexible," an assertion of the dispossessed that can re-create jobs from the piecework of teaching assignments. The aim is an increase in tenured positions that is linked to the casualized knowledge work beyond it.

In addition to disclosing how casualization has become an internal feature of faculty tenure—insofar as the former is the residue of the latter—this analysis makes evident the limits to the reproducibility of tenure as a self-regulating realm of peer governance. It also describes a moment when the humanities start to look like other professional circuits, where training inside the university morphs into technical-managerial fields without determinate content or career structure. In the case of these professional fields, the space outside the university provides the legitimating and judgment operations that the craft model of the professoriate has sought, through academic freedom, to reserve for itself. For faculty in these professional areas, now the overwhelming majority, a PhD might or might not lead to an academic appointment, but it would not be the presumed end of graduate training. While there are certainly professional fields, like accounting or medicine, where academics hold the reins of peer judgment; however, in most professions, from business to the arts, the locus of professional excellence is located outside the university, and the faculty demonstrates its participation in these realms as a measure of its stature and credibility.

This situation reflects my own experience in an art school, where an influential and accomplished coterie of faculty sought rights and protections but eschewed tenure as a means for conferring it. For these faculty members, it was their status as working artists and the recognition from their nonacademic peers that was the most salient reference for their evaluation. In their conception, tenure bound an individual to a particular institution rather than to a professional field. Further, some felt that the creative ensemble upon which conservatory training rests demanded not simply individual achievement but an aesthetic compatibility with other faculty who could share complementary approaches to professional training. In some cases, the heads of these conservatory training programs saw themselves as artistic directors more than department chairs, and faculty members understood this model of leadership from their own professional experiences. Already the film and acting programs could count graduates whose professional prominence exceeded that of those who had instructed them. Yet there were also faculty members without tenure, but with long-term relations to the university, that had received their professions' highest honors, such as Oscar, Tony, Drama Desk, or Grammy awards—or National Medals of the Arts. These faculty members had no interest in being excluded from governance or subject to the decisions of tenured faculty in matters of academic policy. They saw no reason to be subordinate in terms of compensation or support for their professional activities. They sought regularized promotion and reward, due process, and powers of professional adjudication, equivalent to their tenured colleagues.

Devising and implementing this structure entailed securing the support of tenured faculty in the school and university administration. Academic rank, criteria for promotion and reappointment, and attendant perquisites—such as sabbaticals and eligibility for and prioritization in faculty housing—mirrored that of the tenure stream. There were also some key differences. One was an option to stay at a junior rank (there was no mandate for up and out). As opposed to a linear model of development, opening up the clock for promotion fit especially well with those in more technical fields of film production (lighting and sound). And it meshed nicely with those with lower professional profiles, experimental and avant-garde artistic scenes, or longer periods of gestation for creative work. It also fit with those who might maintain a standard that did not follow an expansive tract assumed in the ever-enlarging spheres of influence that follow an academic from local to national to international reputation. These were also term appointments that required an initial review parallel to tenure and subsequent affirmations of maintenance of standards to qualify for reappointment. The judges for the reappointment portfolios would largely be drawn from the professional world in which the faculty operated. Where these worlds were multiple, different professionals would speak to the achievements in disparate domains.

Some tenured faculty was concerned that support for and approval of these appointments would constitute an erosion of tenure, in the sense of reducing the proportion of tenured to nontenured faculty at the school by making future tenured lines less available and by sharing governance with faculty who had not been socialized to the university through the tenure process. Further, the hesitation toward tenure among leading artistic faculty meant that an alliance to push for it was unlikely. After many iterations, the university administration was willing to create these appointments—for which it had to amend its own bylaws—subject to the further stipulation that they would be reserved for faculty at the art school and not available to the large numbers of contract faculty in other schools that sought similar rights and privileges. In doing so, the university recognized a line of authority and assessment that was not indigenous to its own professional structure. Certainly, this was common to many income streams but was now being extended to evaluation. The openness to this worldly judgment broke the seal on professional autonomy contained within academic walls. Professional impact and achievement were external but not subordinated to a market demand, even if the work was applied to the professional activity that provided supplementary remuneration.

FROM SERVICE TO ENGAGEMENT

Incessant measurement without reference to value yields in academia what it generates elsewhere—namely, volatility. The *U.S. News and World Report* rankings of America's Best Colleges switched over to the Carnegie classification scheme in 2006. The criterion with the greatest weight in the ranking is peer assessment (25 percent), in which administrators (presidents, provosts, admissions deans) are asked to rate schools in their classificatory cohort. The designation of quality, which ranges from marginal to distinguished, is tabulated from the average of all ratings received. While a little more than half of the schools respond, the number of ratings received will vary, as many administrators will simply not select schools that do not have national reputations and those they are personally unfamiliar with. Direct knowledge is collapsed with indirect impression. This is followed by faculty resources—largely faculty compensation and class size—and graduation plus freshmen retention rates (at 20 percent each). Selectivity itself, largely test scores and high school standing, weighs 15 percent.[42] There are no measures of mission fulfillment, student satisfaction, teaching abilities, curricular innovation, or other substantive values. Peer rating, hardly a disinterested exercise, stands in for peer review.[43] Yet the common interest in advancing quality in higher education chafes against the zero-sum measures of excellence in a manner that would undermine the solidarity of the peer process. In May 2007, a dozen college presidents called for a boycott of the rankings system, while Reed College has long refused to accede to measures of what it considers wealth and privilege. It, and many—but not all refusniks—get ranked anyway through the culling of information from their Web sites. Even the recent president of top-ranked liberal arts college Williams, Morton Owens Schapiro, admitted he gave most campuses an "I don't know" rating. In defense, *U.S. News and World Report* editor Brian Kelly asserted a need for nonexpert judgment in the service of journalistic representation in the public sphere. "We make judgments all the time. Why did I put George Bush on the cover this week? Do I need a scientific based panel of academic experts to put him on?"[44]

Institutions, while assimilating these protocols of standardizing measurement, also undertake the seeming opposite number—branding, product differentiation, and niche marketing. The tension between movement on a standardized ranking scale and uniqueness demonstrable through generally recognized dimensions of comparison (best party school, most academically inclined, best location, and so on) is negotiated through the strategic planning process. More will be said about this in Chapter 5, but for now, the salient point is to acknowledge the thickness of evaluation from which faculty personnel decisions are derived. The particularities of expertise and the realm of faculty input must be carved out in this generalized climate of ongoing assessment. While the demographic mass of those who attend college continues to expand, the logic of the mass that subtended Boyer's research-driven excellence, the narrative of progress by which improved methods allow all to rise, now meets a countervailing logic of differentiation and dispersion. Recruitment of students and faculty is voiced in terms of best fit. We're not absolutely better; we're better for you.

The model of recruitment, carefully applied to yield selectivity, would seem to pay no mind to those it treats as readily dismissible—whether excess labor that cannot be placed as faculty or surplus pools of students who will never join the incoming class but whose interest lends value to the institution. The assessment process is not simply volatile in the sense that it makes for unstable, shifting hierarchies whose naturalness seems beyond account. It is also volatile in that it demands an excessive production of value—multidimensional, polychronic, heteroglossic. The burden on faculty members, if they are not simply to become the passive objects of measurement, is to engage these protocols of value to redirect what matters at the university, to rejoin judgment and work. Such a move requires a rethinking of the academic freedom contract that imagined a moral space free of politics and labor, where professional autonomy emerges as a place of permanent judgment (modeled as it was on the federal court justice). It also requires a rethinking of the normative categories of evaluation through what is most conventionally its absent term—"service."

Typically, service straddles the extra-intramural divide that characterizes the professional concept of faculty work. If the truth of faculty activity is to be found in knowledge for its own sake, its application via service would constitute a derivative form, as it would be diluted by its very instrumentalization. From this logic, service could never weigh in faculty employment criteria with equivalent value accorded to professional activity. Even within the Boyer framework of discovery and application, the originality that justifies the irreplaceability of faculty implied by tenure's permanence cannot be met in the realm of application. Service is an export of knowledge gained in the private disciplinary realm to the public needs of either the institution or in the opinion formation of civil and political society. The subsequent recognition of civic engagement by the Boyer Commission in 1990 provides an opening to the rigorous codification of service as applied knowledge, but does little to value it as work. Service retains its ecclesiastical garb as a voluntary contribution, a moral duty discharged.

More recently, there have been other initiatives to give greater credit to service learning in student education and to civic engagement in faculty evaluation. Campus Compact is a coalition of more than one thousand college presidents with a commitment to fulfillment of civic purposes in higher education. While focused initially on community and liberal arts colleges as well as state universities, it has recently made an appeal for inclusion of research institutions. Its recent call for a new scholarship points to some of the challenges of definition and negotiation that delineate the terms of engagement:

> For example, does research conducted on behalf of pharmaceutical companies or the military have a public, civic, or community purpose? Some may think not, preferring to draw the line at research with and on behalf of communities, schools, non-government organizations (NGOs), and non-military government agencies in which the benefits flow firstly and directly to the broader public. Others may feel that research leading to drug treatments for "orphan diseases" or to greater national security through biosafety, the detecting of explosive devices, etc., is engaged research. These issues must be thrashed out and resolved, but not necessarily in an "either-or" fashion.[45]

Here, community is expanded to any client or constituency beyond students within the campus. Norms of peer review hold, and methodological rigor is key to assessment of value. The emphasis on action, engagement, and application tend to be agnostic toward the targets, recipients, or partners. The modifiers "civic" and "public" suggest a type of purpose or good but increasingly leave open the questions of whether private monies compensate for lost tax revenues, whether philanthropic endeavors are more efficient and innovative than are government sources, or whether market measures themselves provide more accurate indicators of the worth, sustainability, or ethos of a given endeavor.

The coexistence of these intentions points to the irony that we rely on private funding sources to provide the criteria for and mapping of the parameters of public purpose. The enlarged view of who or what can count as a community embraces business interests as it imports certain features of corporate assessment models, such as best practices, emphasis on outcomes, and rewards for excellence. The rankings and hierarchies associated with the notion of excellence might be at odds with the embracing of a diversity of communities, where judgments that some are better than others is precisely what something like multiculturalism was hoping to counter. Excellence is being used to refer to outcomes of strategic efforts rather than to sorting communities, but the practical impact may be one of rewarding some with funding or other investments while those communities that do not generate results deemed excellent will suffer. And yet the notion that service and engagement proceed by a learnable technique that makes a measurable difference runs deep among those committed to uplift and development. Indeed, the report from Campus Compact concludes with an epigram from Martin Luther King Jr.: "All labor that uplifts humanity has dignity and importance and should be undertaken with painstaking excellence."[46] There is a productive ambiguity in this quote, where labor is paid work and more general effort and excellence is at once an internal commitment and a demonstrable result.

The initiatives to include civic engagement—notably, Imagining America's Tenure Team Initiative—straddle this ambiguity between a strategic understanding that excellence is the coin of the realm for faculty reward systems and that it can be expanded to include diverse criteria. This consortium of schools, unusual in its composition of graduate students, faculty, middle and senior administrators, and artists and civic activists, is a clearinghouse for emerging work and has convened a number of meetings and conferences to articulate the substance of public scholarship. The consortium issued a report that urges recognition of a continuum of work that can be considered civically engaged, from scholarly endeavors that explore a public charge to collaborative research projects that issue from community partnerships. The report aims to rethink initial appointments that make community engagement part of a faculty workload, to promote portfolios that feature a broad range of scholarly work, and to expand who can be considered an expert in the process of peer review. Because the report is providing advice to faculty and administrators in preparation for and evaluation of tenure cases, it aims to establish equivalents by which a permanent appointment can be conferred so that ongoing and stable community relationships can be established. Job security would here pertain to an institution's commitment to its community, rather than a transient exchange characteristic of student involvement or episodic projects that has characterized an institution's own approaches to community and service-learning offices and programs.

Excellence comes to signal both the equality of position and the difference of an abiding link to community to which professional expertise is offered as a resource. As such, there is a basis for affirming the transcendental character of excellence. "The basic motivation for public scholarship is no different from any other kind, except that what varies is who helps frame the question, who wants to generate and then interpret the evidence, and who uses the results—but using the same principles of excellence that we would apply to any other form of scholarship."[47] The initial formulations have not had to address the issue of scarcity that accompanies other uses of excellence to measure conventional research accomplishments. The report is cognizant of the "tension and distress over the unequal positions of tenure-track faculty" and contingent and contract faculty, particularly where the latter may have closer community ties but be ineligible for even modest grants to realize them. It also acknowledges that those institutions with the strongest community commitments have cut back on tenured lines while those that preserve tenure can be the most scholastic—"even though with their many arts and professional schools, research-intensive campuses nurture in their midst some of the most promising models of tenure and promotion policies for publicly engaged faculty."[48] The more difficult link to explore would be the ways in which these models are also the basis for reducing the availability of tenurable lines.

The pressures on service learning pertain to demonstrations of civic interest that have become part of the student admissions portfolio and indicate a place where students can customize themselves beyond the standardized criteria of class ranking and achievement test scores. The concern with service can be placed at a crossroads between a commitment to earlier norms of higher education as preparation for citizenship, a rethinking of the town-gown relation in terms of a host of urban development issues, and a need to enlist faculty members in these matters and respond to their diversifying interests beyond the institution. None of these aspects are necessarily stable or singular. While early twentieth-century versions of citizen education imagined adult and vocational learning for assimilation of recent immigrants into a national labor force, the civic is now conceived most conventionally as a realm distinct from that of a professional career, where breadth of study is to engender a concern with national interests beyond personal professional pursuits. The extramural breadth of community service stands for the well-rounded person, where the precollege student (implicitly in a white suburban enclave) shows evidence of reaching beyond narrow self-interest. This is contrasted to racially and ethnically marked students who are regarded as more predisposed to give back to their communities. The presumption is that the former group of students has no intrinsic tie to its own community and must properly serve another (the "underserved"), while the latter group is defined by a community link it is destined somehow to represent. Similar expectations pertain in hires of minority faculty, where this presumption of a service that represents one's own particular minority community, and diversity as such, is a tacit part of one's appointment.[49]

In a different vein, something more than community is being imagined when the town-gown public relations term reappears in a college or university that is charged to be an engine of local development. Just what counts as an economic motor can slide between local government support for favorable terms of campus expansion or community redevelopment—either of which can have the effect of devastating or displacing extant communities— or research triangle-type models of job creation where tax abatement is used to recruit higher wage industries to deindustrialized municipalities. While a campus might hold itself aloof from contending demands of preservationists, community activists, or displaced workers, engaged scholarship may prove precisely the bridge to renegotiate or reimagine how the considerable wealth-accumulating capacities of the campus might be deployed. Such is the context in which the nature of public scholarship becomes directly significant to how the institution is positioned in terms of economic development, democratic participation, and community service as ineluctably joined domains subjected to criteria of excellence. Faculty members would here be in a position to ask "excellent for what?" in a manner that would invite them to participate in the reshaping of norms of both professional and community development.

Pressing on the terms of excellence and on the ability of the faculty to reshape its engagement of community as a function of its professional commitment points to another stream of meaning for the category of service within the university. This one, like the civically minded conception, rests upon an earlier partition of public and private realms, but in this case, the valences are reversed. "Public" is the arena of waged labor, and "private" refers to the uncompensated activity of the domestic sphere. This double meaning of public and private is well discussed in terms of the split between the political and the economic (polis and oikos) and the later Victorian divide of the waged and unwaged realms of the economic and the domestic. The emergence of a service economy with which the rise of the U.S. university sector is so intertwined pertains most directly to the industrialization of the activity of this domestic sphere and the range of charges that connect social reproduction, consumption, affect, introspection, and the like. This realm of service is fundamentally raced and gendered. It is rooted in the histories of slavery and indentured servitude and in unwaged women's work so foundational to this and other nations that took their advance upon this substantial subsidy. If the extramural dimension of service adheres to the preparation of labor for the professionalized knowledge economy, which includes commodifying the various forms of social work that had occurred within the home—health,

education, welfare—the intramural aspect of service is likewise tied to a gendered and racial formation. This is apparent in terms of who staffs service
positions within the university, who now constitutes the majority of unten-
ured faculty from whom service is most heavily extracted, and who is freed
from service to pursue other ends, such as governance or the political realm of
the university.

Unpacking these various meanings of service argues for a redefinition
of this dimension of faculty activity from a service that allows one to apply
or engage nonscholarly spaces and affinities to one of administrative labor
by which the work of running the university gets done. That some are com-
pensated handsomely for this effort and others not at all forces us to recon-
sider the terms of the tripartite classification of faculty activity. At the same
time that service is devalued as an import and residue of unpaid labor, it has
become all the more valued in the actual running of the university—namely,
with respect to the work of administering the institution. Loss of public support for state institutions and for individual tuition has fed entrepreneurialism
as a capture mechanism for philanthropy and for institutional innovation. The
extramural aspects of civic engagement are not independent of the shift away
from revenue streams tied to teaching. Rather than tenure per se defining who
is able to manage the affairs of the university, the locus of authority shifts to
executively constituted management teams of area heads, chairs, deans, and
provosts—all of whom control access to the information and the deliberative
mechanisms by which decisions are discharged. Faculty governance, where it
continues to hold sway, commands less and less influence over budgetarily
consequential decisions, especially if course and reappointment discretion is
confined to existing or shrinking allocations of funds.

If the apex of faculty governance described in Riesman and Jencks's
academic revolution (discussed in Chapter 1) as a move away from trustee
prerogatives was underwritten by a larger apportionment of government
money for both public and private institutions, the shrinking pools of aid for
campuses has made the regents, boards, and trustees larger players again. This
is evident not just in the push for fund-raising that individual board members are expected to participate in. More broadly, the assumption, whether
tacit or explicit, of these governing bodies is that, in accordance with their
own fiduciary responsibilities, shared governance with faculty is fiscally irre-
sponsible. The fiduciary burdens may extend to what kinds of students will
deliver the highest returns to future university endowments, a subtext in Ward
Connerly's sidestepping of faculty consultation as part of his attack on affirmative action at the University of California.[50] Regents may deem tenure itself
to be inconsistent with required budgetary flexibility. This is clearly a feature
at the University of Minnesota, where, in 1996, the regents hired the law firm
Hogan and Hartson to revise tenure codes (without faculty input) to eliminate peer appeal and academic freedom mandates. The result there was a near

unanimous response from faculty across the rank and ideological spectrum and a bracing unionization drive.[51]

In California and Minnesota, these initiatives also served to galvanize faculty opposition, thereby again raising the profile of the very shared governance it sought to suppress but also underscoring the degree to which maintenance of even traditional domains of faculty input are being recast in terms of university priorities over which faculty members are said to have shrinking claims. Recently, such battles have been joined explicitly around the redirection of tuition fees to capital expenses at the University of California, where the promise of rising student fees has been used to guarantee construction bonds and negotiate interest on loans during a time of wholesale contraction of the university workforce.[52] Coalitions of labor and students are occupying the rooms emptied by the expectation that the regents govern the university as a state-mandated public trust.

The committee operations of faculty do not necessarily impinge upon the institutional directions that universities pursue, unless strategic planning itself is inhabited fully as a participatory mechanism and occasion. For this, however a deeper understanding of the technical arguments and mechanisms of the university is required and this literacy must be seen as an abiding feature of an academic career. Certainly, a portfolio of administrative positions and responsibilities remains an option for faculty unwilling to leave this work to others. The understanding that administering the university is part of academic labor moves faculty in a very different direction than the compact of academic freedom that left the professoriate unencumbered by the grist of its most immediate context. Now that context is elaborated into circuits of knowledge production that flow inside and out of the institution in ways that faculty itself cannot be free from. Academic freedom delivered much for those covered by its compact. The beneficiaries of such freedom have not been able to sustain the covenant to the expanding sectors of the professoriate. A faculty more fully cognizant of what has become of its labor may find more strength in versions of solidarity than in fainter calls for autonomy.[53] Curiously, where the social and interdependent aspects of the faculty's work are most explicit, academic freedom itself offers little cover and service scant reward. The managerial energies behind the entrepreneurial spirit need to be made more explicit. The cloistered quarters of academe may indeed be spawning a proletariat in its midst. But the army of labor—the socially binding work—looks more and more like a generalized condition of management. This requires a closer look at university managerialism, in its concentration among the executive suites, surely, but more consequentially, in its dispersion throughout the halls and groves.

5

The Work of Administration

The shift in value of higher education from a public to a private good centers power and authority on senior administrators, who are taken to be responsible to delimit a particular brand of excellence that will maintain the health of the enterprise. At the same time, faculty governance under the sign of the proletarianization of professions is transcribed into ever more time-consuming administrative duties. The tension between a centripetal management manifest in an increasingly centralized administration and a centrifugal managerialism—evident in the diffusion of accountability protocols among faculty and staff—generates all manner of fault lines as to which kinds of decisions belong to whom and what conditions of partnership advance the university's purpose. The simultaneous centering and dispersion of management speaks to the more general blurring of the boundary between what is inside and outside the university as an organization. The result is a series of mixed metaphors and messages. These confound the instrumental demands for survival and growth and the substantive values from which the sense of exceptionalism rises. The university is all business (like any other) and, at the same time, it has a unique mission, calling, and ethical mooring that bespeaks its ecclesiastical origins (whose Greek root "ecclesia" means "to call out" and refers to the civic assembly). These schisms become more vertiginous as one ascends the administrative heights. The university president is at once chief executive officer and shepherd, fund-raiser and benefactor, rule maker and adjudicator. Yet these roles are seldom left to coexist in a happy plurality. If a fund-raising drive mandates procuring $1 million a day, it is not such a stretch to guess who's coming to dinner or to imagine what whispers will likely fill the presidential ear.

The drive to excellence, which all campuses are subject to, produces assiduous attention to a metric without any determinate content. Movement on a scale of ratings provides its own justification for outcomes-oriented strategic assessment. The rhetoric of strategic planning, responsibility-centered budgeting, benchmarking, and other rationalizing schemes are offered as value-neutral techniques for mobilizing the university community to coalesce through a participatory process. Yet, in practice, distributions are always substantively particularizing in one direction or another—driven broadly by the need to niche and brand in order to achieve a competitive platform while simultaneously dedifferentiating from others by emulating best practices. The swirling doubts regarding the value of education and the believability of faculty self-reports as to performance have been used to justify regimes of accountability, while at the same time, a pursuit of venture philanthropy replaces publicly accountable judgment with private discretion over what is worthy of support.

Equally confounding to cogent leadership is the interaction between the positional advantage of the ratings and the more ineffable measures of reputation that come from news-making acquisitions of faculty, new programs, and signal achievements. These last have the potential to unseat the equilibrating rationality of distribution, and they lend support to initiatives that contribute to the brand as tied to a unique attribute rather than to a mission as a generalizable feature of the institution. The business model is that the best and brightest are not simply marginally better than the mean, but they are logarithmically more productive. The star analyst makes markets while the academic zenith makes a field.[1] Decisions to invest in presidential salaries or those of select faculty are a consequence of this reasoning, but the context is a conversion to a value-added model of the university along the lines of the emphasis in corporate governance on delivering market price to shareholders. Far from being a repository of unchallenged expertise, higher education is open to judgment from all quarters. Unlike the shareholder whose demand for return is said to derive from a tangible investment, the notion of public stakeholders shifts the demand for answerability to any voice capable of making itself heard. Consequently, greater demand is placed on a particular figure of leadership to assume the burdens of representation—to be both the face of the institution and to assert which differences, initiatives, or decisions are to make all the difference.

In this regard, leadership in higher education assumes the form of a kind of arbitrage, the investment activity by which small variations in value (outsized salaries in academia are modest by corporate standards) are leveraged to immediate positional and reputational effect. The arbitrager must be ever vigilant for better opportunities, which may shift investments in midstream or lead to their own departure after achieving some movement within their own portfolio. What is important here is that projects are initiated, not that they are brought to a conclusion. The arbitrager works through constant vigilance over the volatility that the demand for initiative generates. This requires ongoing assessment. Incessant assessment of this sort, before a program or project is completed, has the consequence of focusing ever-increasing attention on productivity. The high performance areas establish the expectations for all others, even if performance is achieved through momentary or short-term investment, such as the hiring of a prominent faculty member who may, like the senior administrator, move on to another opportunity, or the securing of a major gift that can shift focus from university to donor goals. Leveraging of this sort can apply to all manner of university investments, not least of which is the endowment itself. While a handful of schools have amassed endowments that are substantial enough to provide significant per capita returns (so that, for example, need-blind admissions—tender acceptance of students regardless of their ability to pay—are possible), the endowment itself is more likely to serve as collateral by which fund-raising initiatives and capital campaigns are underwritten.[2]

The technical sophistication of these schemes will itself favor boards of trustees over faculty bodies in decision-making processes, while the schemes' impact will enlist faculty in the planning and accounting process. Consequently, much will hinge on the literacy that faculty achieve in the financial and managerial logics to which they are subject and in which they are expected to partake. Despite the language of value neutrality, the culture of assessment and accountability has a politics that sharply poses the dichotomous values between the agents of decision and the evaluative criteria by which judgments are made. The norms and protocols of faculty governance can carry with them the association that they are part of a management team and that all the faculty does is in the service of the enterprise. In contrast, identifying what counts as the labor of administration counters this disavowal of the worth of the faculty's own labor and its capacity to rethink what the university is for. Moreover, the work of administration pertains to how value circulates throughout the university and its surround. Moving that value strategically produces the conditions whereby faculty matter most in the running of the university. Clearly, many management styles, dispositions, and aims run across the range of various kinds of institutions. Further, much has been made of the distinction between management and leadership, or administrative technique and vision, in the attainment of excellence—often to explain the scarcity of the latter as a function of rare individuals.[3] This chapter seeks to identify the logic through which administrative work is derived at the point at which labor and management meet.

THE TIME OF LEADERSHIP

James J. Duderstadt is a Michigan Man all the way. In 1968, after earning a PhD at Cal Tech in three years, he was appointed to the Michigan faculty as an assistant professor of nuclear engineering. He quickly rose through the ranks and became dean of the School of Engineering in 1981 and provost and vice president for Academic Affairs in 1986. With the departure of the incumbent Harold Shapiro to Princeton the next year, he served in an interim capacity before being appointed president in 1988. In 1996, Duderstadt returned to the faculty. Such institutional loyalty and opportunity for internal career advancement is rare now in higher education. Presidents are typically hired from outside, stay a half dozen years, and move on. While faculty positions are filled through peer-driven search processes (even when deans make the hires), presidential searches are typically conducted by professional headhunters, whose own consultant fees are indexed to the level of executive compensation—a factor that favors external candidates. Trustees are charged with selection but often lack the expertise to choose. Duderstadt saw the search process up close and followed it at other institutions. He concludes: "It is ironic, indeed, that universities that put great effort into the very thorough evaluations of faculty candidates for hiring, promotion, tenure, and academic leadership roles tolerate such a cavalier approach to the selection of their leadership at the top. In over two decades of tracking presidential searches through the nation, I must confess that I have yet to see a search conducted with the thoroughness and rigor of a faculty tenure evaluation. . . . [The process] is sadly lacking in rigor, insight, and, at times, even integrity."[4]

The rift between peer-driven expertise and populist criteria linked to the authority of state governments recalls again Kant's split between higher and lower faculties, the former oriented to public service through professional knowledge and the latter committed to inquiry as an end in itself. The process of appointing presidents is skewed toward their external obligations as corporate executives even as the title they claim is "chief academic officer." The president navigates the doubt that support for education should be prioritized over other expenditures. A president must also combat the wariness from within that the managerial prowess required to make the corporation attractive to such funds, sufficiently values what takes place there. Duderstadt offers himself as a kind of counterfactual to the national trend of presidents as takeover artists who remain at the helm long enough to enhance the standing of the university but not so long as to have to deal with the consequences of doing so.

By these lights, the president was following in the footsteps of executive common sense that demanded increases in shareholder value (the market standing of the firm as measured by its rates of return) frequently gained by cutting costs or offloading assets. Duderstadt himself eschews the model of rewarding a president as a CEO, something he regards as opening a psychological gap with the faculty and therefore undercutting leadership effectiveness. His term in office was therefore something of a test case as to whether a university president staying close to home can resist the trends in managerial shortsightedness. Reflecting on his presidency at the University of Michigan, he exudes self-confidence about his mission: "The secret to success is simple: attract the very best people; provide them with the support, encouragement, and opportunity to push the limits of their talents and dreams; then get out of their way."[5]

By the measure of his own substantial ambition, he was indeed successful during his tenure from the mid-eighties to the mid-nineties—another time of trouble for public universities, especially one such as Michigan whose past glory was built on a now decaying industrial base. Duderstadt could count a number of significant victories during his time as president. Michigan became the largest recipient of research monies, it achieved the highest faculty base salaries of any public institution, it launched an admissions policy that doubled the proportion of minority students on campus, and it undertook an extensive expansion of facilities and its endowment—in the process, adding dozens of new structures through a multibillion dollar capital and fund-raising campaign. Without shrinking from legislative battles, Duderstadt recognized that public funding for the university would continue to decline in the years to come as it had in the previous decade, turning it into what he understood as a privately financed public university. Indeed, by 2006, 7 percent of the budget came from the state of Michigan, 10 percent from private gifts, another 16 percent from tuition, 18 percent from research grants, and 49 percent from auxiliary income—this last largely from health care, which pulls in more than thirty times what the athletic program generates.[6] Of a $4.5 billion budget, health care spending outstrips education $1.8 billion to $1.6 billion.[7] Liberal arts and undergraduate education account for 30 percent of the faculty and 15 percent of the budget, while the medical facilities (the largest in the state) account for two-thirds of the university staff.

The ability to shepherd such robust expansion requires a sturdy self-concept, one that Duderstadt elects to voice in the heroic terms of military leadership. "On rare occasions, one encounters presidents who view themselves as change agents. . . . Like generals who lead their troops into battle rather than sending orders from behind the front lines, these leaders recognize that winning the war sometimes requires personal sacrifice."[8] Those willing to take the risk can suffer short tenures despite their success. In this conception of leadership, the agency of change is expended and consumed in the course of achieving goals. In addition to the military metaphor, Duderstadt invokes a patriarchal trope for his position. He considers the job to be shared with his wife, Anne, who serves not simply as unpaid labor for myriad social functions, but as one of the ur-parents of the institution. "In a very real sense, the president and spouse are the dad and mom of the extended university family."[9] They are not simply heads of residential in loco parentis for students, but guardians of faculty as well. Like students, faculty have limited independence and depend on the president's ability to keep the disruptive effects of the world beyond the university at bay. "They also seek protection from the forces that rage outside the university's ivy-covered walls: politics, greed, anti-intellectualism, and mediocrity that would threaten the most important academic values of the university."[10] In both the military and patriarchal metaphors, enemies surround the university, and the president must take personal responsibility to maintain adequate separation.

While combating these dangers gives a sense of isolation, the president cannot lead alone. The challenge is to understand what can be relinquished to others. Ideally, university governance can be shared if each constituency accepts its appropriate role: faculty presides over academic matters, the administration manages the institution, and the board oversees fiduciary and public accountability. In practice, these boundaries are not respected. From the presidential perch, institutional complexity and the self-interest of constituents render shared governance unfeasible. "The political variability of an elected board, its inability to agree on many politically controversial issues, and its tendency to circle the wagons and protect even the most outrageous behavior of its occasionally maverick members can erode the board's credibility. University administrators are always concerned that the regents not only will fail to support them but actually might attack them publicly on one agenda or another that advances a political purpose—a not infrequent occurrence."[11] A board of this sort may simultaneously curtail budgetary expansion to alleviate the tax burden of the university while seeking to keep tuition low as a benefit to affluent constituencies (in 2006, the average household income for students at UM was $120,000—nearly four times the median earnings in the state of Michigan).

Anemic faculty governance discourages participation from prominent faculty and leaves the door open to a situation where a "cabal of discontented faculty members in a particular department would engineer a coup to take over the faculty senate in an effort to push their personal agendas."[12] From this perspective, the president is uniquely poised to provide focus and the unifying vision to advance university autonomy as a form of institutional self-interest that enhances the capacity of the institution to develop its own course. Because the president's position and authority derive from that of the institution itself, while others identify with constituencies beyond its walls, the president is best placed to know and defend what the institution can and should be. Rising through the ranks, being an internal candidate, and returning to the faculty, are each important to this claim of fidelity. Shared governance is in alignment with this perspective when presidents can convince deans to encourage appropriate selection for faculty representatives, and key alumni can promote candidates to the trusteelike board of regents.

Articulation and coordination of decision making melds governance with vision. Determining the path by which the institution moves forward is the keystone of what in the business world is termed "strategy." When public institutions lose operating support from the state legislatures that also set limits on their tuition revenue, "strategy" stands for the discretionary income that must be raised and the institutional attractiveness where money is seen as well spent. Beyond aggregate measures, success is seen in the identification of crucial achievable differences. Change becomes the medium through which an inadequate present becomes a desirable future. The president must convince all constituencies to "accept that change is inevitable"[13] and at the same time, delegate to a few the responsibility for delivering the version of change under consideration so as to "empower our best people to drive the evolution or revolution—of the university."[14] Change in this formulation is at once a fixed necessity (an inevitability) and a choice of direction (a revolution). If the aim was to build "the risk-taking culture necessary for the university to explore entirely new paradigms"—that is, total transformation—the means would be leveraging highly selective investments and attention. For Duderstadt, "much of the momentum of academic institutions is driven by a few truly exceptional, visionary, and exciting appointments—what I called 'essential singularities' (drawing on my mathematical background)—that set the pace for academic programs."[15] These hires would be impelled by potential opportunity, not existing institutional need. There would be no disciplinary mandate but rather a recruitment of competitive proposals and candidates across the institution. Minority faculty would be recruited through the same technique.

Singularities in math and physics are points where infinite value or density is assumed. The effects are not direct but are the consequence or derivative of a particular operation or function; hence, a singularity is "a point at which the derivative of a given function of a complex variable does not exist but every neighborhood of which contains points for which the derivative does exist." In astronomy, a singularity is "a point or region of infinite mass density at which space and time are infinitely distorted by gravitational forces and which is held to be the final state of matter falling into a black hole."[16] An essential singularity is described as exhibiting "extreme behavior," where a given neighborhood or region takes on "every complex value" derived from the function, or it is described as how much change is imaginable from a given point. Intriguingly, this mathematical trope is one moment where Duderstadt's own disciplinary content becomes manifest in an otherwise formalist managerial schema.

Not simply a "how to get the most bang for the buck" quandary, the conviction here is that a properly applied investment (hire) can generate an infinitude of difference in the whole neighborhood where it is applied. The idea of an essential singularity rationalizes the pursuit of star hires in terms of peer impact rather than adopting the logic of the borrowed prestige of raiding other institutions. The singularity also translates to faculty the leadership impact the president is thought to have. If the impact is to be pacesetting, then it is unclear how other faculty members proceed to "keep up" with the special hire, particularly if their characteristics, interests, or resources are sequestered within their own appointment benefits. This would seem very different from the approach that builds collaborative intensities from which something like schools of thought are created that push disciplinary horizons, and in contrast to program building, which requires assembling key interlocutors. Believing that the singularity generates abundance and not scarcity, that it has infinite capacity to lift boats and not sink some, suggests an approach where all faculty members are convinced that they too are "change agents" in moving to the future. This is where corporate strategy is most focused, on convincing all employees that they too will be leaders and not simply beneficiaries of leadership.

In order to mobilize the university community to this perspective, Duderstadt turned not to engineering but to management—specifically, Michigan professor C. K. Prahalad—to lead seminars for faculty and administrators "through the same strategic process that he had conducted for the executive leadership of many of the major corporations in the world."[17] Prahalad's work has been in the areas of corporate strategy (how companies win) and business in developing economies. His book with Gary Hamel, *Competing for the Future*, treats the field of business strategy as in crisis, stuck on short-term market gain through downsizing (firing) and reengineering (getting those who remain to do more) that mires companies in a presentist approach.[18] Future profits will be won by those firms that drive the revolution in competencies and opportunity. The future is now, and strategy entails forgetting the past, maximizing the rate of new market learning, and deploying preemptive investment in core competencies. To shift the managerial frame and achieve the animating dream that distinguishes strong leadership, organizations need to adapt by learning to forget. The dream, vision, or future is itself an instrument of the present, one that labels opposition as passé and contrary claims to what the future might be as an unwillingness to change and as resistance to embracing what lies ahead. Since the success of a given strategy can be known only in retrospect, the future orientation is a promissory note that asks all to give up their contrary and contending claims on what could be, and for those whose projects are not selected or whose basic programs are not supported, to accept that they are justly relegated to extinction.

The cover for this academic Darwinism is a form of putative decentralization called responsibility center management (RCM).[19] Accordingly, budgets are devolved to individual units (which can be newly created research centers or traditional departments) which act as independent revenue generators that can keep income and reinvest it in their operations—or wither if they are unable to stay in the black. RCM operationalizes a principle of meritocratic management by making allocation rules and decision-making lines transparent, and rewarding effective planning and strategy over claims to intrinsic worth of the educational activity. Unit managers rather than faculty are held to account and granted discretion, concentrating authority in super-unit executive bodies (of chairs, deans, and so on). Duderstadt, who was committed to implementing RCM in order to privilege the activities of "faculty and staff with strong entrepreneurial interests and skills,"[20] also recognized that this success limited advances in faculty governance and campus consensus. He came to see that faculty bodies need "executive not merely advisory authority."[21]

As is common to heroic narratives, there is a tragic aspect to this one as well. Inhabiting the future in the present can make the end come soon. Michigan achieved its fund-raising goals ahead of schedule, yet programmed success can operate as its own kind of planned obsolescence. Presidents "become increasingly aware of just how much of their time is spent doing things they do not really like to do, such as stroking potential donors for gifts, lobbying politicians, pampering governing board members, and flying the flag at numerous events—football games, building dedications, political rallies—that eventually become rather boring."[22] He also understood that "fighting battles you know you are likely to lose is frustrating" but also necessary. Even the exceptional commitment and loyalty that Duderstadt displayed could not save him from institutional anthropophagy. Success has a way of eating its own. If leadership is so celebrated, what renders it so unsustainable? Strategy assumes constant reinvention and imagination of what has yet to come. Institutional loyalty can name a committed interest that is sacrificed through its expression. The president stands as the ultimate singularity, standing for a change that can be derived only from his presence but that creates a position that must be vacated, allowing leadership to reappear within the institution. The role of presidents as change agents engenders a volatility that they themselves cannot survive.

In a study of a number of research institutions, Gary Rhoades suggests that these antinomies are more endemic than incidental. While typically, faculty members are labeled special interests that distract from institutional focus and vision, Rhoades finds that the multiple pressures and messages that managers must contend with can in practice have a greater effect. Strategic planning that redistributes funds according to centers for excellence, or departments that receive the highest ratings in competitive assessment exercises, can starve the surrounding environments, generate zero-sum cannibalism for students, pit deans against one another, and generate an underground economy of private appeals for reallocation that violate the publicly stated norms of transparency by which budgetary distributions are made. "Yet central managers do too little by way of ensuring *managerial* focus. Focused on academic fragmentation, they overlook managerial fragmentation."[23]

High turnover at the top further complicates these problems as the new regime disinvests from the priorities associated with the previous administration. Faculty left out are demoralized when treated as undeserving of university resources, and good faith efforts to participate in schemes that are canceled or forgotten upon completion fosters cynicism as to the efficacy of calls to change. Painting faculty with the brush of fragmentation leaves administrators nowhere to turn but outside for innovation and incapable of recognizing the capacity for initiative in their midst. The devaluing of the durable presence associated with tenure—which offers the deeper resource from which intellectual innovation takes place—stands in striking contrast to the image of improvement stemming from a transient relation to the institution that goes by the name of leadership. This is not to say that college presidents, provosts, and deans should stay in their jobs indefinitely, but that the forces now driving pervasive turnover place senior leadership in an antagonistic relation to what they would view as an indigenous ability to steer and stay the course.

The tragic aspect of managerialism extends beyond the high personal costs its exerts on institutional leaders and the volatility it visits upon institutions. The industrialization of higher education introduces a scale of competition that opens the door to rationalizing measurement schemes that are charged with delivering success through innovation without being able to anchor the imperative for change in demonstrable improvement. New schemes are fated to die at the moment they would have been expected to yield their successes, and their promise of solving what was inadequate in the framework they replace fades upon implementation. Imported from business on the model of a product cycle that must be completed if new demand is to be generated, these administrative novelties will consistently clash with the educational time frame of deferred value. The aspiration to treat education as fully rationalizable along the lines of commodity production is as long as that of scientific management itself. In 1910, the Carnegie Foundation for the Advancement of Teaching commissioned a study by mechanical engineer Morris Llewellyn Cooke. The resulting *Academic and Industrial Efficiency* launched a hundred-year campaign against academic exceptionalism—touted by Thorstein Veblen—that what is good for and works in business can be transcribed perfectly to higher education.[24]

The first fifty years of this managerial offensive resulted in the separation between education and administration. The omnipotent president, whose vision drove the institution, would yield to the professional manager, who demanded greater efficiency. The last half-century has witnessed the advent of an academic administrative science that would claim to substitute politics for analysis by switching backroom whims for spreadsheets in the plain light of day. The pursuit of these goals amounts to what Robert Birnbaum calls "management fads in higher education," incessant turnovers of not simply leaders but techniques of reorganization, as new paradigms fail to live up to their promise.[25] As Birnbaum points out so persistently, evidence-based management has succeeded in generating mountains of data but precious little proof that the successive schemes, or fads, as he calls them, work. The Planning-programming-budgeting system developed by the Rand Corporation and promoted by the Lyndon B. Johnson administration was developed to assess which new weapons systems might deliver the most bang for their buck. Yet the use of computer-inputted data could not clarify which investments in higher education delivered the highest returns. After being introduced with great fanfare and government support in the sixties, this rubric had largely disappeared by the mid-seventies. It was replaced by the business model of strategic planning that fostered interorganizational competition for resources.

Benchmarking, as discussed in Chapter 1, came next and featured best practices and performance indicators to distribute funds, despite uncertainty as to whether it makes more sense to cut or reinvest in poorly performing programs. Based upon Xerox Corporation's response to its lost market share in the 1980s, benchmarking "is the process of continuously comparing and measuring an organization with business leaders anywhere in the world to gain information which will help the organization take action to improve its performance."[26] Rather than thinking of education as an investment whose realization is deferred over the course of a lifetime, continuous assessment responds to a purported crisis of value with an immediate and tangible result. In each of these cases, formal rationality threatens to overtake judgment, replacing context-based understanding with an innovative metric that is evidence of the new leader's bona fide standing as a change agent, which in turn allows that leader to gain influence with little opposition.

Historically, management schemes have been advanced to enlist the participation of employees to a corporate end, yet even supporters of strategic planning observe that "it is the lack of participation and the resulting distrust and power struggles that lead to the failure of the strategic planning process in many colleges and universities."[27] Paradoxically, if presidents can't enforce bottom-up mobilization from on high, the plan is unlikely to succeed. Moreover, the mandate for change is typically positioned as an externality. Where there is greater competition, higher education must adapt.[28] Change, even transformation, is the order of the day. Education management consultants caution about the ironies of managerialism for which they want leaders to be prepared by "scaling down the number and frequency of policy initiatives designed to eradicate ambiguity. . . . The irony here is that school staff are being urged to be 'transformational,' implying the achievement of radical change, under conditions that actually constrain their opportunities for achieving change."[29] Change has no academic content, but it requires an internal response. The formalism of the exercise can generate an opening to faculty to assert programmatic innovation that allows the institution to achieve its own evidence that it is repositioning itself to meet these pressures and demands. The otherwise circular planning process is opened at the point where participation is effectively applied.

Despite his repeated demonstration of their inadequacy, Birnbaum is sanguine that for all their foibles and failures, management schemes offer up prospects for change that can be taken advantage of if only balance can be found. "Judgment without data can be arbitrary; data without judgment can be sterile."[30] Part of his confidence stems from his conviction that organizationally, business and universities are fundamentally different:

> Institutions of higher education (except in the proprietary sector) have no owners and cannot distribute profits, so there is less pressure to operate efficiently. They function in a "trust market," in which people do not know exactly what they are buying and may not discover its value for years. Their participants and managers tend to be motivated by idealism rather than by profits. All "customers" are subsidized, the product is sold at less than the cost to produce it, and the value of the product is enhanced by the quality of the people who purchase it. Compared to business firms, colleges and universities have multiple and conflicting goals and intangible outcomes. "Employees" may be more committed to professional groups outside the corporation than to their own managers, may think of themselves more as principals than agents, and may themselves have roles in management (including selection of the chief executive), as well as permanent appointments over which managers have no discretion.[31]

Certainly there is much to recognize in higher education in this portrait, but it is as much normative as actual, and the departures from expectation are becoming increasingly salient. Universities are turning profits for some. Students are encountering enormous debt, which affects outcomes efficiency and shades the appraisal of what counts as long-term value. Fewer faculty can claim the autonomy and managerial prerogatives mentioned. On the flip side, many businesses, especially those claiming the mantle of the new economy, would recognize their internal culture and ambitions in this picture from human capital models of product enhancement, the difficulty in measuring efficiency for intangible products, be-your-own-boss approaches to employment, conflicting goals, and talent-retention compromising managerial authority. Perhaps the greatest confluence of logics between universities and business lies in the anxiety over what means need to be implemented in order to deliver improvement. This amounts to a shared sense of time, where the future is brought into the present and the present shifts to the immediacy of coming to a decision.

The time of administrative labor stands in contrast to the contemplative duration of academic reflection. Meetings are scheduled for an hour or less, memos are composed on short-order time, topic and focus are continually shifting, moments of decision and points to take away must be stated at the conclusion. To engage the meeting at hand and bring those in attendance to decision, all that preceded must be suspended and the immediate gathering treated as the only job to be done. Preparation for what comes next requires an active letting go of what preceded. The emotional drain of whatever conflict was precipitated in the previous hour must be forgotten, the synapses washed clean for the next procedure. The new constituents are treated as if they are the only ones who matter, the only meeting all day. Full-time administrators live in this time zone. Faculty, students, other constituents come to visit. From the perspective of leadership, the future will have an episodic quality, each moment erasing itself in a long march to success. Managerial time, in this optic, is lived tautologically; its answer lies in the question of where to go next. Change procures its own values, eclipsing consideration of what it might be for. And yet, despite all this leveling formalization, the conviction is sustained that the next decision, the proximate moment of change, might make all the difference in the world.

Making Room at the Top

Leadership can be said to matter most when an institution that is in physical and fiscal duress moves to a place of prominence. New York University stands, in this regard, as the counterpart to Michigan in the realm of private universities. In 1973, with deindustrialization and fiscal strain taking its toll on New York City and its key institutions—much as in the state of Michigan, NYU sold its campus in the Bronx to the municipal government to fend off bankruptcy. Regrouping around its decaying Manhattan campus, NYU underwent a strategic reorientation, from a commuter school for area residents to a residential college with a national draw. During the eighties, a billion dollar capital campaign, under then-president John Brademas, funded the dormitories to house this new student population. The school continued to recover under President L. Jay Oliva, subsidized by tuition dollars from a proliferation of new programs and teaching performed by low paid adjuncts. As with the branding campaigns of New York City itself ("I ♥ NY"), which saw its real estate fortunes soar, the university underwent a dramatic makeover under the fiduciary eye of the city's re-energized realty moguls.

By 2002, when John Sexton assumed the presidency, deferred maintenance, debt, redundancy (specifically ownership of two medical schools), demands of facilities exceeding capacity, and an accreditation review that warned of dangerously low full-time faculty ratios—still hung over the campus. Faithful to his roots as a New Yorker, Sexton has had a double career, first as a professor of religion at Saint Francis College in Brooklyn, then as law professor, dean, and president at NYU. He taught at Saint Francis between 1966 and 1975, after which he earned his PhD in religion from Fordham in 1978 and, the next year, his JD from Harvard. After law school, he clerked for two years with Supreme Court Justice Warren Burger—before joining the NYU Law School and becoming its dean seven years later in 1988. Sexton likes to speak of his origins as a working-class Catholic kid from Brooklyn with an entrepreneurial spirit and humble academic origins to connect his own transformation to his institutional aims.

Feistiness and grit fit NYU's tale of reinvention. Thirty years after its near-death and self-designated miraculous recovery, it was deemed by *The Princeton Review* as the "#1 Dream School" (first choice for students when factors such as price and selectivity are not considered, a position it held between 2003–2007) and led the nation in number of applicants for undergraduate admission (more than 37,000 in the 2007–2008 academic year).[32] Tuition remains a budget driver, with the highest per-student loan debt at graduation and, for private universities, among the lowest percentage of met-student need. These factors have earned the school *Princeton Review*'s number one designation for students dissatisfied with financial aid.[33] While the university has many fine faculty and programs, by the measure of various rankings, it is not in the top flight of research institutions—or at least not breaking past the top thirty among the various compiled lists.[34] The less populist Center for Measuring University Performance at Arizona State University asserts that "the fundamental requirement for research university success is money" measured primarily by endowment size and grants received.[35]

Given the qualitative assertions of momentum, influence, or the significance of idea making, little credence might be given to such aggregate quantitative measures but for the leadership's own claims to affect a "category change" in its designation and recognition. At his installation as president, John Sexton declared that under his charge he sought, for NYU, "a transformation in the years ahead from a leading university to one that will be among a handful of 'leadership universities,' those few that execute their core mission with such manifest excellence that they become the models others emulate. Our purpose, in short, is to create at NYU one of the first exemplars of what universities will be in this new century."[36]

This ambition for upward mobility is based upon a claim to innovation that others emulate, rather than an acceptance of received sorting criteria. Transformation would hence be an effect of success, something the university can generate for export and not simply a means to achieve a strategic end or relative repositioning. Mobility is also part of NYU's own foundational story as a school of opportunity for nonelite students, one that has tangible manifestations as well as conceptual claims for what university leadership can be. In keeping with the notion of essential singularity, some departments received extraordinary attention, which brought them to the front of the line. Philosophy, for example, was in receivership in the seventies and became the number one ranked program after hiring a cluster of prominent analytic philosophers.[37] While the department had once been known for a broadly accessible social and political philosophy, the move to a more technical aspect of the field focused the gain on citational indices, where a few journals can command extensive influence that in turn affects ratings. In addition, analytic philosophy shares intellectual assumptions with rational choice models with similar positionings in economics (which rose to twelfth place in the citation index) as well as to prevailing currents in political science.[38] While no specific claims were made that the ideas promoted in these specific versions of philosophy and economics were best suited to the global vision NYU sought to advance, there was a substantial fit in both form and content. Compared to facilities- and equipment-intensive sciences and engineering fields, these investments bore relatively low costs for high returns of tangible gain that could then be claimed for the university as a whole. This success then seeded a $2.5 billion dollar drive to expand the physical plant by adding six million square feet to the campus, acquiring an engineering school (Polytechnic University), and expanding overseas (a campus in Abu Dhabi).

The University of Michigan account points to a stronger meaning of privatization than implied in what was called a privately funded, publicly committed institution. "Private" refers not simply to revenue streams but to the advent of a proprietary self-interest in advancement through accumulation of various kinds of assets that demarcate excellence. New York University calls itself "a private university in the public service." NYU President John Sexton is bent on a strategic mission to redefine public service by placing the university itself at the heart of urban development and vitality. His prognosis is of a city undergoing another sectoral shift from an emphasis on finance, insurance, and real estate (FIRE) to an economy driven by intellectual, cultural, and educational activity (ICE). If FIRE led to the city and university's revival, ICE will ensure the preeminence of both—if their fates can again be effectively intertwined. The future he sees places the university itself at the core of the city's needs; hence, public service is redefined from vocations that apply expertise to civic duty to maintaining the generative, expansive quality of urban space itself:

A strategy for New York of the 21st century must focus on the ICE sector—on the life of the mind that makes New York a hub that cannot be replicated in cyberspace; on the creativity that will retain commerce and those who engage in it; and on educational institutions that generate pathbreaking and profitable research.

What is vital to the success of New York over time is the soul of the city. To nurture that soul, we must turn to the many centers of learning and invention in New York that sustain intellectual and artistic life. These centers will enrich not only those within the academy's walls, but all who are drawn to the life of the mind and the imagination. I have no doubt that our capacity to secure New York as the intellectual and cultural capital of the world will be central to New York's continued global preeminence.[39]

In addition to managing this transformation of its environment, the university is the repository of tradition, a feature that sets it apart from the corporation. "Universities are quite distinct kinds of organizations, unique in several ways. For example, they ordinarily will buffer their cores from the demands of society at large making only symbolic adaptations. This capacity explains in part their staying power; they are the carriers of tradition. Quite unlike the typical business firm, which could not buffer itself in the same way and survive the competitive rigors of the marketplace, they endure."[40] Yet the present is characterized by what Sexton terms "hyperchange." He declares that "the way our great centers of creativity and learning operate in that domain are undergoing fundamental transformation as we witness the continuing collapse of traditional boundaries—in time, in space, in disciplines and in culture." The fact that knowledge now drives societal transformation places the university in dynamic tension with its own traditions: "universities are in a race not with each other but with their own distinct vision and ideals, and are called to rethink the scope and reach of how they discover, test, convey and preserve knowledge—applying to their study of institutional self the same principles of continuous, rigorous examination and inquiry that guide academic research and dialogue."[41]

For Sexton, the threat to research universities lies primarily within. They may become complacent, take their value and excellence for granted, and fail to subject themselves to rigorous inquiry. They may also disconnect research and teaching and leave undergraduate education to part-time faculty and undergraduates. He admits that at NYU, use of part-timers "goes beyond what it should" and that their "conditions of work" need to be addressed. But he also surmises that the institution could not afford tenure for all. Some full-time faculty will focus on teaching and have renewable contracts. On the other side of the spectrum, he is concerned about tenured faculty in the thrall of a celebrity culture, "stimulating an economy of rewards and recognition which tends to push faculty members to seek financial compensation and psychic satisfaction outside their university."[42]

Alternately, he wants such faculty to consider the "domestic advantage" of engaging scholars of diverse disciplines and viewpoints on their home turf, of encouraging participation in residential life, admissions, alumni. Permanent faculty will treat the campus as home; "they will embrace this notion of the common enterprise university as grounded in part in the collective faculty responsibility and ownership of the institution which provides and nurtures the base from which they conduct their activities." Faculty members are "principal architects" who exercise through their governance genuine "ownership of an increasingly complex entity." Faculty will need to play a role in adapting to "economic discipline" and assimilating to "difficult trade-offs"—this in the face of declining public support and soaring costs for state-of-the-art facilities stocked with gadgetry. And the half-life of investments continues to diminish with each advance ("a light microscope costs $10,000 and lasts a lifetime; a confocal microscope can cost well into the six figures and is outdated within ten years"). In the context of excellence-driven internal scarcities, ownership means "a willingness occasionally to sacrifice for the collective good."[43]

The tenured faculty model is the "fiduciary obligation" that all faculty members must abide as they set aside self-interest in the form of salary and benefits, additional tenure-track lines, and the like. Governing the common enterprise entails managing their own desires. Tenured faculty members, so entrusted, "recognize that the future depends on asking what is right for the whole institution and not just for themselves as we share and distribute the university's 'commons,' its financial resources." In exchange for this sacrifice, faculty may join a moral economy, which Sexton constructs as a foresworn oath:

> I understand and expect that the university I join will provide for me the sacred space—of place and mind—in which I will be free with no restraint of thought or orthodoxy to pursue a life of inquiry and exploration and to share the fruits of that life with colleagues, students and all who are interested. In return, and as part of that life, I commit my talents and my time to my university community as a sanctuary for knowledge creation and a center for the learning of a new generation.[44]

If community governs this moral economy, markets serve to differentiate salaries. While free agency inflates salaries and prompts disloyalty, the university should not "foreswear totally attention to disciplinary markets or that it should adopt utterly egalitarian compensation." Markets have the double advantage, first in that they "aggregate judgments of the relative importance of someone's contribution. Second, actually allowing the external market to set compensation—to have it value faculty—is less disruptive than a process of ongoing ad hoc internal evaluation." That is to say a process whereby faculty might invoke its collectivity to negotiate just or appropriate salary levels would be disruptive to the communal spirit by which the university is governed. So too would such internal negotiations disrupt the appropriate allocation of responsibility within the university between those who create knowledge and those who transmit it. While great researchers are obliged to embrace the calling of teaching (albeit in suitable contexts where students are "ready" for them), the majority of faculty will be devoted to transmission without benefit of the full citizenship that rules the commons. All faculty will not, for example, be eligible for tenure—which according to this scheme gets decoupled from academic freedom. Instead, the university itself, in its role as guardian of the disinterested pursuit of knowledge, is the keeper of rights of inquiry and teaching, which it protects and extends to all. Rather, tenure conveys a "firm commitment to the university and its core activities" (contractually mandated research and teaching); it bequeaths the status of an elder, a shepherd in the community, and is "entrusted only to those whose lives manifest such integration."[45]

And yet it is the employment relation and not the intrinsic quality of faculty members that defines whether or not they are paid for the new knowledge they may generate. By accepting this employment relation, they have agreed to the characterization of their being as not integrating these functions for the institution. Tenure "shifts some of the risks associated with creativity from the creative actor to the university. . . . [W]ithout tenure, the professor would be vulnerable to existing scholarly tastes and the preferences of colleagues. This is not a matter of academic freedom, but of the freedom of intellectual choice, autonomy and creativity." By absorbing such risks, the institution de-instrumentalizes the knowledge that the professor can pursue and differentiates the time of creativity from the continuous schedule of teaching. "While teaching must be consistent in its rhythm, the creativity and genius at the highest level does not reveal itself at regular intervals. Even a genius may experience a hiatus of years before following one insight with another."[46]

While the university is not detached from the world, "the free, unbridled and ideologically unconstrained discourse in which claims of knowledge are examined, confirmed, deepened or replaced" render it a sacred space or sanctuary. The university's distinct temporality must be protected from the world that would subject thought to the ever quickening and foreshortening rhythms of mechanical productivity and cultural deficits in attention and reflection.[47] Pure research, profound reflection, and nuanced dialogue can also serve the public mission of the university. These provide depth and complexity to an otherwise simplified and foreshortened popular discourse found on talk shows and in news coverage. This function is exercised by bringing controversial figures to campus and exposing them to rigorous inquiry. Sexton cites as an example an invitation he extended as Law School dean to Cuban Justice Minister Carlos Amat under severe protest from Miami-based Cuban expatriates. The president held a dinner and invited Cuban Americans who refused to break bread with the minister and subjected him to "intense questioning," while chants of protest were audible outside. Yet, when such protests hamper the operations of the university, they threaten the sanctuary not simply in its day-to-day operations but in its claim to be able to sustain terms of inquiry through self-governance. Especially in the context of the war on terror, government is having greater impact on which students and faculty can come to the university, what can be taught and researched, on access of military recruitment, on what levels of surveillance and scrutiny are appropriate. "It is troubling, however, that increasingly government itself is exercising its enormous power to exert pressure on the nature and content of the dialogue on campus—and of the research that is the predicate to that dialogue."[48]

Of concern as well are the internal threats to dialogue and debate that occur when members of the university community assume "doctrinaire viewpoints" and engage in "ideological conversation." Lost to dialogue is the capacity for active listening. "The danger in academe is the development of a parallel tendency not to listen with a generous ear to methodological, political or religious 'others,' just to name a few." In order to protect and preserve this domain, where all viewpoints can be subjected to the most profound engagement and scrutiny, it is crucial that a president not assume the bully pulpit and become, as did former Harvard president Charles Eliot (about whom Sexton wrote his dissertation), a first citizen. If external and internal threats would conspire to foreclose dialogue, the president must embody a nonpartisanship by which he remains above the fray. "I believe it is essential for the university's leader to refrain generally from expressing views publicly on any issue that is not centrally related to the core mission of the institution; to do otherwise would compromise the moral authority of the presidency in the forum and undermine the credibility of the leader's commitment to the role as guardian of that dialogic space."[49]

Restricting public speech to issues that pertain directly to the governance of the university preserves presidential autonomy, so too does avoiding consideration of the university's own finances with respect to extant social and ethical concerns. Just as the president's own political views must remain private, so too should the private matter of the university, its endowment, be shielded from political speech. "I believe it is an error (at least generally) to make the University's endowment an instrument for political expression, for doing so raises the same problems as presidential pronouncements." While the university Senate or other deliberative bodies might generate a different position that the president could then endorse, he preserves his position as outside of politics. This neutrality allows him to intervene with due authority when a different consensus is reached. It also permits him to stand in judgment where individual professors or events may stray from the tenor of balance required to sustain the sanctuary's dialogic capacity. Sexton admits that "it is conceivable that the president might perceive an affirmative duty to intervene in order to assure a balance and diversity of the conversation." Leadership in this account must personify civic dialogue at the same time that it looks over each expression countering extremism through direct intervention.[50]

While the university is enterprising with respect to the emergent knowledge economy, Sexton's pastoral role emanates from a sense of loss as to the effects of culture on the majority of the population, subject to the very prevalence of mediated imagery that issues from ICE. In an address to the Catholic University of Leuven, his theological voicing is more clearly discernable. He locates the circumstance of the university in what his Fordham adviser, Ewert Cousins, termed a "Second Axial Age," a rare turning point in human history with the potential of delivering a new convergence. Looking at his cultural surround, he detects a

> more pervasive dogmatism, one born of the increasing allergy of many citizens to the hard intellectual work of dealing with complexity and nuance. In my view, the resulting appetite for simple answers is nourished in a feedback loop involving the media and civic leaders, and breeds a discourse by slogan (equally untestable in civil dialogue) and a powerful civic dogmatism.
>
> The confluence of these elements of dogmatism is combining with the political reality of a divided America to undermine the style and substance of civic discourse. It is my thesis both that the research university is perhaps the last real hope we have to reverse this trend and that, if our universities fail to provide an antidote to dogmatism, they themselves will become victims of it.[51]

The dogmatism that Sexton experienced in the Catholic Church during the fifties, before Vatican II, has now become manifest in civil society, driven by the very information revolution that has weakened respect for professional norms and the authority of expert knowledge. The Internet, "even as it empowers and informs vast numbers of citizens, it also is a tool for misinformation and false attacks, polluting the dialogue with an apparent 'knowledge' base undisciplined by traditional standards of accuracy in public communication. Bloggers are their own editors and many make little effort to verify what they post." This information surplus begets an accountability deficit that overloads our sorting capacity and results in "a kind of nihilism about knowledge which leads almost inexorably to an equation of fact and opinion and the reduction of argumentation to assertion." These assertions are made in the mode of a millenarian shift that is itself more faith based than evidentiary and that elevates the transformational imperative from a self-interested positional gain in rankings to a culture-saving institutional exceptionalism. Despite this dire and sweeping cultural condemnation, Sexton finds in the existing complexity of political positions, those who might vote for George W. Bush simply because he appeals to them, even as they reject certain of his economic policies that are at odds with their sense of fairness, like an increase in the minimum wage. Sexton applies the same antiessentialist reasoning to the place of religion, which should not determine viewpoints in the university but has a place there and in the public sphere as a respected affiliation. In the end, complexity is a moral position and the university its church, whose practice and place serve "to offer a rebuke and an alternative to the coliseum culture." The concern about popular mediated-culture leaching complexity from public discourse is reminiscent of a long line of cultural conservatives who worry about a larger scale civilizational decline.[52]

Sexton himself does make a particularly poignant foray into the coliseum culture, an appearance on *The Colbert Report*, December 6, 2006. The segment opens with Stephen Colbert introducing the president by proclaiming, "President Sexton, thanks for being on the show. You represent everything I hate." Sexton replies, "I'm here to defend knowledge and wisdom." He says to his host that "a magnificent mind is limiting itself" and that he wants Colbert to "be all you can be." Colbert refers to him as a real New York intellectual, beard and all, and asks if stroking the beard makes him feel smart. Sexton indicates that, yes, it is very nice, and Colbert says, "I can do that too, beard please." Out comes a bearded associate who places his face next to Colbert's and, while Sexton replies, "I'm here to call you to your true self," the comedian caresses the beard of his adjacent staff member. Colbert then names the complaint that is to be aired on the show: "You've got a problem with our culture, you say it's been reduced." "There's a terrible disease abreast in the land and you're contributing to it," Sexton replies, and says that Colbert is wasting his mind by simplifying the world's enormity to shallow slogans. Colbert sticks closely to the caricature and gleefully provides him with "That's America; love it or leave it," and "Where's the beef, Sexton?" Sexton seeks to draw him into complexity by reminding Colbert of his high school debate experience and how they prepared columns, each one deepening the argument. Colbert offers that he debated to travel in a van and drink beer. Sexton, he says, is trying to solve a problem that does not exist and therefore gets no points in the debate. Sexton asks that they do some debate "cross" and wonders how Colbert's going with his gut could cure any disease. Colbert asserts that sticking with his gut has rid the country of maladies such as "wishy-washiness, waffling and flip-floppery," so he takes a position and never changes it.

Sexton, seated at a table set amid a seasonal crèche—with Jesus, the wise men, and sheep—intones, "It's exactly that kind of dogmatic thinking that shuts out the gift that God gave us." Sexton concludes his argument by declaring that of the eighty-five institutions that have survived intact for five hundred years, seventy are universities, "and that's why learning and universities are important." He then leans forward and says, "On that round," and checks off an invisible box in the air, clucks his tongue, and proclaims victory over the comedian. Colbert reaches under his desk, saying, "OK, you've made your argument, now let's talk about your book," and introduces Sexton's law textbook—the standard in the field—*Civil Procedure: Cases and Materials*, 7th ed., as if he's going to do a Charlie Rose interview, but there the segment ends in a din of audience laughter.[53]

A parallax view of this encounter might allow each to come away with what they sought: Sexton speaking truth in the den of iniquity and Colbert poking fun at intellectual self-seriousness. Yet the comedian's mastery of his medium, his technical proficiency in rendering intellectual seriousness playful, is no less a kind of professional expertise than the invocation of academic traditions. Certainly, the fact of institutional persistence does not answer the question of relevance. The representation of the university within a moral economy with theological purpose pertains to only one aspect of Sexton's own brief for relevance. It is not as if pointing to the centrality of knowledge to contemporary commerce would yield the ground to cultural critique. Absent the dialectic between innovation and tradition that Sexton explores in his writing, the public positioning of education, as legitimized by its own autonomy, literally becomes the butt of jokes. Whereas Colbert's skill was to direct the humor of the lampoon at himself, Sexton was left declaring himself the winner in a debate with rules he could not regulate. The dogmatic sphere of popular culture, with its slogans and sound bites, belies a complexity of reference and interpretation beyond a declaration of the will to truth and intrinsic value of knowledge. This exchange references more than a dilemma as to how to make the case for complexity using a medium of assertion.

Of all the privileges that can be lampooned, that of knowledge for its own sake comes easily when knowledge itself is so thoroughly instrumentalized. The defense is not of the role of critique but of tradition generating truths that yield progress, allowing popular humor to become the skeptic. It may not be reasonable to expect these arguments to prevail in a six-minute comedy sketch, but the privilege invoked by the managerial hierarchies Sexton seeks to naturalize have met with hearty suspicion within the university as well. That a contemporary administration would marshal and prioritize resources is unsurprising. That it would seek rhetorical consensus in place of governance is far more interesting. The appeal to vision as a substitute for the kinds of participation that community norms rely upon winds up generating the very skepticism of moral ends that leave unchecked the market mechanisms that have been put in place for goal attainment. The unraveling of the moral and political economy is no less a problem now than it was at the time of Adam Smith, but in this narrative, the gap between the two is to be filled with managerial finesse. The sacredness of university space, the selectivity in who can fully shepherd it, and the dissociation of management from labor are all to be achieved by placing administrative responsibilities in the moral domain outside the question of compensation and employment, and beyond the purview of how managerial activities are inscribed in the university's own shifting division of labor.

While this move to emphasize moral over economic aspects of university aims omits much of the managerial work that faculty undertake, it also reflects the redistribution of labor from the professoriate to other categories of labor at the university. While core teaching may be displaced from tenured to contingent faculty, increasingly, learning is technologically driven and delivered by professional staff members who lack academic freedom, have no claims to the intellectual property they may themselves produce, and gain no benefit from the protections of peer review. While faculty are declining as a percentage of total campus personnel (now less than a third), professional staff, or what Gary Rhoades refers to as the managerial professional, are the fastest growing category of employees. "Yet managerial professionals are more than an increasing administrative cost. They are increasingly involved in key activities from assessing quality and ensuring accountability to providing student and consumer services to facilitating the production of instruction and research to engaging in entrepreneurial activities."[54] The move to learner-centered education shifts focus from faculty to new technologies, such as Blackboard (a proprietary instructional management tool accessed online) and Educause (a professional association that promotes information technology), which are maintained and taught through these experts. In contrast to the flexibility of contingent faculty, the capital-intensive investments marshaled by these staffers for organizational infrastructure become durable features of an economic circuit of instructional distribution and consumption. The silence with respect to this growing cadre of labor is meant to stand for its allegiance to central managerial lines of authority outside of any departmental structures.

LEADING INDICATORS

These twin tales of public and private university leadership certainly point toward areas of convergence. The transformational mandate that assigns authority to the leader is actively linked to the half-life of leadership. The change agent selects a handful of initiatives meant to ripple outward for maximum effect while putting in place systems of evaluation that treat all units as subject to the same prospects of reward for contribution. The resulting volatility drives the leadership life cycle. The metrics of administration calibrated in hour-long sessions where consensus is formed and equivalent time allocations for written memorialization of decision reference a universe of change challenged to identify what ideational content will fill its time. The meeting promises life-giving possibility and the memorandum is a memorial to its closure. The benefit of managerial formalisms in the university is that they do not prescribe (and claim not to proscribe) what can be thought—even as they produce their own internal evidence that rationalization generates an untenable uniformity of expression at odds with the academic enterprise.

The openness to all ideas is repeatedly betrayed by the investment in a few said to make all the difference. Meeting times are set in hours uniformly distributed as units of value across campus. Managerialism is a temporal rationalizer, advancing a common currency and clear hierarchy of what time spent with whom is worth. In contrast to this temporal dispersion, the spatial compensation is to concentrate the privilege to be exempted from these time demands to a select few, the tenured faculty, whose presence stands in for the eternal standing of the knowledge-producing institution. In this division of labor, the few are entrusted with vision, while the many must keep the faith.

Not only does such a division beg the question of what knowledge is for, at a time when it is positioned by the leadership idea as an instrumental value (the ICE economy); it also covers the increasing applications of managerial knowledge mobilized to operate the university as such. Leadership in this idea does not simply steer but unleashes, authorizes, and disperses administrative labor, while seeking to govern the hierarchies of value by which it will be rewarded and taken into consideration in determining institutional aims and processes.

If leadership is to demonstrate its value by externally measurable output rather than capacity-building inputs (as rubrics such as benchmarking would have it), then governance will need to look more like something to be executed than shared. Restructuring the division of deliberative labor serves as an announcement of new norms based on consultation or notice and comment of leadership mandates, rather than cogeneration, deliberation, and consent. Joan Wallace Scott observed restructuring as a kind of presidential self-fashioning:

> The restructuring process has both caused and depended upon a devaluation of faculty status: the faculty's capacity to govern itself and to participate in university decision making has had to be compromised for the corporate model to succeed. The faculty is depicted as—and probably is—the biggest obstacle to the new bureaucratic-commercializing model of the university. One conservative university president expressed the wish that the twenty-first century would be "the century of management," while the twentieth (happily over) had been "the century of the faculty."[55]

While doubtless a wishful simplification, this sorting of faculty as labor and administration as management into a past and future of governance, respectively, is meant to facilitate a seizure of the present that grants moral high ground to the voice of initiative and innovation.

It would be tempting to dismiss these two accounts of public and private stewardship of successful strategic mobility as exceptional to elite universities—even as all manner of institutions suffer the implosion of the distinction between government-sponsored, nonprofit, and proprietary schools. The sense in which success breeds success, or at least attracts more of the money said to be its measure, is doubtless restricted to a few exceptional cases. This arithmetic of scarcity is typically what underwrites fables of mass mobility even as the math itself would suggest that most will not meet the test. The management industry operates by making rules that anyone can follow out of these exceptions, even while the culture of leadership imagines that those who come out on top had it in their natures to begin with. Instead, studies in leadership disclose the nature of the confidence in the difference that such talents make. Even a study of "pragmatic" presidencies among rural community colleges devoted to regional development asserts, "Where there is no aura or mystique, there is no *presidency* as such."[56] Hence, it is less the practices of those designated the best that are emulated than the practice of emulation, the conviction that leaders somehow need to be led.

For all this, there is an abiding irony in the focus on leadership as it has been imported from business schools to the business of running schools. As Rakesh Khurana observes in his study of the business school's own self-hollowing professional turn:

> From a scholarly perspective, then, leadership as a body of knowledge, after decades of scholarly attention under the social science research lens that the Ford Foundation viewed as so eminently promising, remains without either a widely accepted theoretical framework or a cumulative empirical understanding leading to a usable body of knowledge. Moreover, the probability that leadership studies will make significant strides in developing a fundamental knowledge base is fairly low. The reality is that inside universities and research-based business schools, leadership research has relatively low status.[57]

On closer inspection it would make sense that the obsession with formal excellence would extend to leadership at the very moment when the concept is emptied of content. The leader would be charged with compensating for the larger skepticism as to what education is for, with resolving ambiguities of value with prodigious fund-raising, by substituting a comprehensive answer with a few exemplary instances of undeniable worth.

Surely, anything as complex as running a university will require extensive solicitation of advice and learning. The steep learning curve is mirrored by the often rapid descent into exhaustion, making it difficult to discern what an appropriate stay at the pinnacle might be. But the very question of leadership tends to cast eyes toward the skies when a downward cast would be more appropriate for due humility and focus. The leader's dilemma crystallizes a problem felt throughout the institution. What is easiest to overlook are the capacities that the institution generates for understanding how it operates and where it should go, for identifying values and weighing priorities. The recognition of this capacity may prove elusive among those leaders most focused on institutional success. But for those who labor with administration, seeing how their own work of leadership counts will be more important still. Extending the time and space of decision against the protocols of its foreclosure is in many ways already resident in the office work of faculty, staff, and students. The knowledge of operation needs to be derived from this experience. This is not a question of whether administrative hierarchies and coordinating functions, selectivity of information, and specialization of knowledge need exist in complex organizations, but of what the substance of participation means when managerialism would ask that it be invoked only formally as means of self-advancement. University leadership holds a mirror more broadly to new management than it does to itself. Through that looking glass comes back not only a gap between excellence and its performance but also the question of what it means to make a claim on the generalized capacities of knowledge production. This shift from who governs to what it might yield leads back to the question of what can be made through university work and of how the managerial moment in faculty's own creative energies might be best educationally realized. This turn is explored next as conditions of interdisciplinarity.

6

Conditions of Interdisciplinarity

Interdisciplinarity appears in so many guises and hails from so many quarters that it might seem to be the organizing universal within the university. From on high or at the margins, the formulation covers innovation—whether through administrative consolidation or critical initiative. Ambiguity as to its intentions jostles with ambivalence toward its end. To move inside the work of interdisciplinarity and disclose where its greatest possibilities lie requires breaking from the either/or logic of co-optation and rupture, futile assimilation and celebratory congratulation. Interdisciplinary conditions, the intellectual and institutional circumstances that shape academic work as we know it, are pervasive but not unitary—every utterance of the term betrays a certain parochialism. While the speaker might often be located in a Western research university, the rarefied address is too often taken as representative of some generic academic home.

Given its proliferation, the conditions of interdisciplinarity are at once general and particular—mandated from above and driven from below—everywhere recognizable and differently situated. It is perhaps wisest to hold on to the tension between work that emerges within a given institutional setting and the range of intellectual projects that transcend location. While there are any number of dimensions that establish a given interdisciplinary moment, the accretion of historical factors can be arrayed into formations that vary occupationally, institutionally, organizationally, geopolitically, and epistemologically. This highly differentiated space is not simply a backdrop upon which to map an instance of academic labor. Rather, the work undertaken entails an active shuttling between spaces, a series of lateral moves that demand attention to how expertise travels and what is left behind as we move from the places of disciplinary formation to those disparate events of reception. With the refashioning of what is inside and outside the university—what has been referred to here as the professional turn—the sidesteps and shuffles that interdisciplinarity effects take on, lending added significance to the larger trafficking in knowledge.

As a term for administering and organizing academic knowledge, "interdisciplinarity" emerges early in the twentieth century. Yet the tension between discordant and transitive specialization is as old as Western philosophy. Aristotle held that philosophy alone could integrate and transcend otherwise self-interested specialized fields. The medieval university began studies with the foundational trivium (logic, rhetoric, grammar) before advancing to the professionally grounded quadrivium (arithmetic, geometry, astronomy, music). For Kant, unlike professional knowledge, reason transcends disciplinary division, and philosophy is contentless with respect to field and can therefore govern itself in the pursuit of truth. Vico's new science privileges the humanities, which constructs its own knowledge domains against scientific specialization derived from nature. But when philosophy itself is no longer presumed to be transcendent, when the culture and interest of procedural forms are no longer considered contentless, when scientific method is not a measure independent of the world but a feature of a kind of world, the relation between what cuts across fields and what disperses them requires active theorization.

As Joe Moran observes, the simultaneous reference to joining together and keeping apart is an intrinsic ambiguity of interdisciplinarity, evident in the double valence of the prefix itself (e.g., intercourse and interval) and the juxtaposition of an open exchange and fixed place. "It can suggest forging connections across the various disciplines; but it can also mean establishing a kind of undisciplined space in the interstices between disciplines, or even attempting to transcend disciplinary boundaries altogether."[1] Moran sides with Roland Barthes in the view that interdisciplinarity marks the place where the solidarity of the old disciplines break down. Terms like "postdisciplinarity," "antidisciplinarity," and "transdisciplinarity," represent efforts to resolve the contradiction that would take away the inherent flexibility and indeterminacy. "Multidisciplinarity" is seen as a concept based upon proximity (voluntary or imposed) between fields, without a consequent integration. Mieke Bal treats interdisciplinarity as the more generative term, associated with propagation of emergent knowledge as opposed to the diffusion of existing forms, which she associates with multidisciplinarity.[2]

The current proliferation of interdisciplinarity in the university suggests that the tension referenced by the term is not simply horizontal, as between integration and dispersal, but vertical, as an assimilation of administrative requisites. The conviction that all knowledge forms can be linked together by ordered classification and set to work together recalls philosopher Theodor Adorno's formulation that "whoever speaks of culture speaks of administration as well."[3] But Adorno does not leave the matter with a pronouncement of a deadening bureaucratic hierarchy that assimilates all critical impulse. Administrative expertise also carves out a critical limit that "opens a perspective for the protection of cultural matters from the realm of control by the market." To do so, "administration which wishes to do its part must renounce itself; it needs the ignominious figure of the expert."[4] The advocacy for such critical administrative work is not a position typically associated with the Frankfurt School. Rather, Adorno's insistence here that not all of administrative labor can be captured becomes crucial to our approaches to interdisciplinarity. The fact that it bears the stamp of administrative approval does not cancel the transformative opportunities it may present. Realizing these nascent political potentialities requires a fuller recognition of how administrative forces operate on the epistemological field of emergent knowledge.

In what follows, I take interdisciplinarity itself to be not only the consequence of recognizable limits in the disciplines but also their foundational grounds. After all, disciplines do not emerge by themselves; they arise and consolidate themselves by enclosing several outside entities. Treating interdisciplinarity as foundational may seem contrary to the spirit with which it is commonly used as an escape from those very kinds of generative grounds. This reversal, however, also allows a momentary resolution of the myriad challenges to the purported hegemony of disciplines and the assimilative powers of interdisciplinarity as such. More than simple disavowal of foundations, claiming their authority while maintaining a kind of contingency over their formation provides a strategic difference for interdisciplinarity.[5] But before moving too readily to this new normative state, it is important to pause over a whole range of contrary possibilities for how knowledge making might be qualified—including the conventional grammar of disciplines, divisions, and schools into which academic work is clustered. The groupings of humanities, social sciences, and natural sciences are commonly treated as pregiven and internally consistent arrangements securely separate from the applied professional fields, which occupy the greater swath of campus real estate. These assumptions are examined in the light of shifting social and historical contexts that prove to have significance for how knowledge moves in and out of the university and articulates a range of organizational prospects.

If the violence of the hyphen cautioned about matters of identity, the prefix seems to stand in similar position regarding epistemological concerns. I want to consider two related and very appealing arguments that address the contradiction between the integrative and the differentiating moves of knowledge formation—one of which comes from a proposal for transdisciplinarity and the other of which issues from an invitation to rethink a discipline's public mission and attendant civic practices. At stake is not simply the semantic investment in the superiority of one prefix over another, for it is clear from the disparate proposals to revise disciplinary knowledge that many aims are shared. Rather, what is at stake in these revisions is how difference is to be governed and how knowledge formations are to incorporate the self-criticism that would allow for both worldly engagement and transformation, such that knowledge making does not cede the institutional and organizational ground that is its condition of possibility and efficacy. If interdisciplinarity is inescapable, it also makes legible forces that prevail upon and emanate from what is gathered through the university.

DISCIPLINE'S INTERDISCIPLINARITY

The twin demands for flexibility in resources and the relevant application of the purposes behind many epistemological initiatives have sought to answer the university's legitimation crisis. By asserting a more public mandate and justification, the university defends its interests as its own to govern. Both the constituent elements and methods of mixing disparate expertise are on display in collaborative project-driven team approaches. The center rather than the department is the typical administrative unit, and a claim for a new object of study that names emerging epistemological conditions provides an integrative plane. By way of example, one team of scholars from the University of Salzburg Center for Advanced Studies and Research in Information and Communication Technologies and Society (ICT&S) has proposed a transdisciplinary approach that would overcome the longstanding problems of C. P. Snow's two cultures—humanistic and scientific. By coming together around a global object of study (in this case, the advent of an information society), discrete disciplines can forge a durable collaboration that both solves problems and alters their own self-concept. "Transdisciplinarity is an integrative but not a holistic concept. Disciplinary isolations are therefore suspended on a higher methodological level, as transdisciplinarity goes beyond specialization but without substituting disciplines."[6]

Such collaborative structures are meant to keep transdisciplinary endeavors publicly accessible. Crossing academic boundaries solves real world problems by arriving at solutions that include various stakeholders, such as government, business, and civil society. In this reckoning, the structure of society itself parallels the various disciplinary domains that compose a transdisciplinary project, such that networking technologies would be designed to "inhere the potential of providing the glue" for a globally sustainable information society.[7] Malfunctions to the sociosphere, technosphere, and ecosphere derive from and can be remedied through information, each of which offers a value (harmony, humane efficiency, political freedom, cultural equality, economic solidarity) rooted in a particular disciplinary knowledge that is brought into concert with others.[8] Hence, exclusion from one sphere means that the values of others go unrealized—nonquality in the cultural sphere results in lack of influence; absence of freedom yields powerlessness; noncompliance with solidarity exacts expropriation—all of which leads to imbalance or domination. The transdisciplinary research field promotes values contrary to domination by including stakeholders in the research design; advances technology for cooperation, as in open source software; and offers a critical science that makes transparent what is implicit.

Doubtless this schema has much to recommend it for approaches to what are now termed public-private partnerships that universities are asked to undertake. It is skeptical toward technological determinism without eschewing technology, respectful of the contributions of each partner while asking that the perspective of the marginalized be the point of departure, hopeful about the integration of "is" and "ought" (what it terms the "not yet"), and positive about the public applications of specialized knowledge. It operates to critically engage the mandate for branding ("a unique 'Salzburg' approach") by which institutional resources are allocated. What remains a challenge however is thinking through the administrative or technocratic principle by which integration (the "trans-" in question) is to be achieved. The formal equivalence of stakeholders (government, business, community) assumes a pluralistic interest that can be balanced through effective procedure. Yet, both for those excluded from claiming a stake and for those whose stake is at odds with the interest in harmony by which they would enter an unsustainable compromise, the confidence in the integrative power of a disinterested administrative principle can repay considerable damage to already marginalized participants. The question, in other words, of what disciplines transdisciplinary integration, of what techniques are assimilated to informational rationalization, of what tames foundational critique of tenets or methods, is foreclosed when informatic problem and disciplinary solution are so tightly mirrored in one another. In this case, transdisciplinarity would posit an administrative solution whose problem it was unable to discover.

While the work of the Salzburg ICT&S Center seeks to make a publicly engaged transdisciplinary endeavor the focal point of a university, another publicly minded project has sought nothing less than the transformation of a discipline's purpose as an affirmation of its rightful place. Michael Burawoy's stint as president of the American Sociological Association (ASA) is exemplary of what visionary leadership can do to mobilize a field toward an activist sensibility. Burawoy's election in 2003 came after a controversy several years before in which he resigned in protest over procedures for selecting the editors of the discipline's banner journal, the *American Sociological Review*. Underlining the dispute was a broader concern about the representation of methodological and cultural diversity in the field. Burawoy, who as a radical graduate student had considered how to put an end to sociology, gave a presidential address some thirty years later, in 2004, rallying the discipline around the project of public sociology, a call to focus the field on the questions of what and for whom its knowledge was produced. More than a fleeting conference thematic, his argument launched an enduring conversation about the discipline's mission.[9] The rhetoric he employed to mobilize the myriad inclinations of the field was sublimely capacious, making room for sociologies of every disposition, finding a contribution for each within an expanding disciplinary tent. At the same time, by specifying sociology's ambit as advancing the perspective of civil society and the defense of the social, he offered both differentiation from and affinity with allied fields of economics and political science that would view the world from the vantage of market and state, respectively.[10]

In Burawoy's formulation, the discipline itself is comprised of four interlocking fields, each the complement of the other. Professional sociology "provides true and tested methods," for insight into the nature and dynamics of the civil order. Public sociology bridges the gap between sociology's ethos and its world. It embraces both traditional—or established—and organic or emergent publics across a spectrum of conservative and transformative social demands. Policy sociology solves clients' problems (where the government, nongovernmental organization, or movement organization acts as patron). Finally, critical sociology "examines the foundations" of the profession with an eye toward revising underlying assumptions of the work's means and end.[11] Burawoy himself notes the "uncanny resemblance" between these functions and those articulated by Talcott Parsons (the grand theorist of sociology whose seminal book, *The Structure of Social Action*, conceived sociology as a field constituted from kindred disciplines)[12] that make up any social system. "If critical sociology corresponds to latency function based upon value commitments, and public sociology corresponds to integration, where influence is the medium of exchange, then policy sociology corresponds to goal attainment, and professional sociology with its economy of credentials corresponds to adaptation."[13] While the structure of the field is here presented synchronically as a kind of homology for that of its object, both profession and society also share an historical dynamic and narrative of progress. Sociology, after a first incarnation in the nineteenth century as a utopian project, and subsequent development as a science in the twentieth century, "now, in its third wave, it harnesses that science to its earlier moral concerns in order to give vitality to public sociology."[14] Public sociology is, in this view, a plateau that harmonizes aim and method, fact and value, through a kind of professional evolution.

Hence, as a disciplinary grammar, Burawoy offers both a synchronic and diachronic mapping that centers the field less around its interest in defending the social as its object of analysis and more in the methodological, sovereignty by which its authority is derived. If the function of criticism is to test the truth of methods, the scientific core of the field would be more likely to be preserved (adapted) than challenged. Criticism would remain faithful to disciplinary identity in the form of common values; the public would align the private professional ethos with its world, while policy measured instrumental worth. If synchronically, the professional sphere affords adaptation to external threat for change, historically, science (here defined as method) provides disciplinary life or vitality to external commitments. From both perspectives— from the internal spatial order of the field and from its temporal evolution— the traditional disciplinary core is preserved as functional differentiation and adaptive change swirl around it.

It might seem ironic that the discipline would be defined by its methods rather than by its object of analysis (the social or society) given that Burawoy himself is an ethnographer, and qualitative methods are largely marginal to the field (a feature of the editorial controversy that he joined over the banner journal's reach). As Patricia Clough has pointed out, however, the traffic between ethnography and quantitative methods based upon survey research constitutes sociology's own foundational narrative as a shuttle between private and public, authentic observation and objective display, which she grasps in gendered terms.[15] Evelyn Nakano Glenn, a sociologist who teaches ethnic and women's studies at Berkeley (who also served as ASA president in 2009), writing in direct response to Burawoy's piece, picks up on the question of boundary maintenance. She observes, "The process of defining and mapping a discipline parallels the process of defining and mapping citizenship. Both involve matters of recognition and membership, that is, who belongs. What makes someone entitled to call herself a sociologist? Both involve boundary drawing and exclusion, that is, what is and what is not included in sociology."[16] The excluded others included the subaltern disciplines of anthropology, geography, psychology, and area, ethnic, and gender studies, but also organic public sociology done outside the field in interdisciplinary spaces, which has a colonial relation in the hierarchies of a division of labor so described. Nakano Glenn concludes, "When I see the resilience of traditional and outmoded theories and points of view, when I see recurring patterns of inequality, and when I see the continual outsourcing of people and progressive ideas to subaltern programs and departments, I believe we have missed and continue to miss an opportunity to truly and meaningfully incorporate public sociology into the center of sociology."[17] This question of alliance and affiliation, unmoored from fidelity to method, would seem to make public sociology most coherent through recognition of the mediating forces of interdisciplinarity rather than as one dimension in a machinery of boundary maintenance.

Curiously, in both the transdisciplinary brief and in the apologia for disciplinarity, science stands for the unreflective and ungovernable principle of administration, the silent partner that naturalizes an epistemological division of labor. In the case of Salzburg's ICT&S, transdisciplinarity asks how an administrative principle can allow the global object to stay critical, whereas public sociology asks how a public informs knowledge production. Both formulations rest upon sustaining science as the core function that assigns either an internal or external disciplinary division of labor, which is maintained by leaving unchallenged the boundaries as such. Intriguingly, Burawoy's four-field system for sociology also maps onto Ernest Boyer's taxonomy for civically engaged or public scholarship. Recall that Boyer too was concerned about the ways in which professional norms were becoming unmoored from educational priorities such that undergraduate publics were omitted from the research university's consideration of what would be considered of value. His solution was to translate all faculty labor into modes of research.

Accordingly, for Boyer's research square, scholarship of discovery is anchored to the professional quadrant—that of integration to the public—application and policy are linked, and the scholarship of teaching is identified with the preferred dialogic process by which critique is actually exercised. Within this last dimension, learning communities participate with experts—this is what makes organic sociologists produce reflexive knowledge, as end oriented and consensus based. Indeed, Burawoy sees students as sociology's first public and takes heart in the strengthening number of undergraduate majors as a sign of the field's strength. Boyer and Burawoy share a confidence that research-driven professional norms can reinstate the balance between technical and substantive reason that will sustain autonomy against externally contrived measures of accountability. Ironically, much of the grief that Burawoy encounters from peers in his determined efforts to advance public sociology in the field comes from those concerned that activism will dilute sociology's efficacy as worldly values infuse the neutrality provided by methodological rigor.

If Burawoy's political intuition is correct, then upholding the methodological boundaries around private or pure science would be the way to mobilize sociology by maintaining its disciplinary identity. From this perspective, specifying the work that a discipline can do avoids the colonization of scholarly work to a unifying imperative to serve a state logic, as is the case with neoliberalism. Yet, there is another conception of a kind of public sociology where analytic methods are derived from the project of discerning the agency needed to constitute society as such. This interdisciplinarity at the core of sociology's means leads to a different ordering of the field. As Michael E. Brown, a sociologist who is deeply conversant with analytic approaches beyond the field, puts it, a fully self-critical disposition leads one to "insist, still against odds, that sociology is a discipline constituting adjacent disciplines, a critical practice, a reflection upon the relationship between society and history, and part of the prospect for a realization of the society as yet only promised."[18] In Brown's terms, the professional is dedicated to its affinity with adjacent fields. The critical is already part of professional practice. Public pertains to the agency that can be divined in the production of society. Policy attaches to a promissory form of social affairs. Of course, Brown's formulation is a brief on behalf of a discipline without the problem that Burawoy faced in an administrative adjudication of its boundaries. Nonetheless, it is not clear what would constitute for Burawoy the theory of that field-mapping endeavor beyond postulating a place for all within a professionally tended division of labor, one which we have seen is in any case not without its exclusions.

But something like science does stand as an authorizing claim for disciplinary coherence even where the term cannot adequately account for its own internal dynamics, presumptions, and orientation to nondisciplinary intellectual dispositions. The confidence that quantification of all human values along the lines of something like a price has been the transdisciplinary methodological core that unifies all social inquiry in the name of policy outcomes. Managerial techniques, like benchmarking, posit a readily translatable method from business as a transcendent discipline beyond disciplinary reach. And yet, this model of the calculating, quantifying rational actor prevails within sociological methodology as well. In this respect, sociology is borrowing its science from economics, which in turn rests upon a conception of "scientific method floating free of all social instantiation," as Philip Mirowski so astutely observed.[19]

Paradoxically, the treatment of science as an internally homogeneous approach that is intrinsically efficient or effortless not only metaphorizes science in a manner that cancels its own internal operations and work but is the consequence of a particular interdisciplinary alignment of science studies that underwrites economics itself. Mirowski detects a cross-field alignment "between a self-confident economics, the pedagogical methodological self-image promulgated within the formal natural sciences, and a righteously prescriptive philosophy of science."[20] As its political economy of funding changed from public investment in pure science to the regime of privatization, which privileged application and outcome, there was a concomitant epistemological shift from accounts of large scale social processes to deliverable mathematical models. The resistance of economics to self-theorization was justified as a celebration of the truth of laissez-faire ideology in a discipline that had little tolerance for the free-play of approaches or methodological dissidence.

Hence, not only is the monologic science said to lie at the heart of discipline actually interdisciplinary at its core; this interdisciplinarity is conjunctural, contingent, and in certain respects opportunistic to what it sees as its external conditions of possibility. As Mario Biagioli has pointed out, recognizing the internal heterogeneity of the sciences permits alignments and alliances with certain of the humanities as well.[21] Positing science as a stable core from which the profession moves toward public dialogue also begs the question of what knowledge base or methodological insight a given community introduces to research. Accordingly, the public, those who stand in the place of society, would be more than partners in a dialogue between those with expertise and those without it. In neither disciplinary specialization nor the putative generalist knowledge of society are the questions of how to study a given problem preordained. The abiding contribution of feminist and postcolonial science studies has been to move from an identification of interest in a given standpoint to exploring what entrance into the body of scientific work as already raced and gendered does to how that knowledge is made. As Patricia Clough has argued, this is the matter or ontology of technoscience.[22] Science research in addition to its own excavation of the interdisciplinarity that constitutes what is called science at any given moment has also persistently identified the potent metaphors that enable the recognition of what disciplines do. In economics, the belief in a free market of ideas serves to resist reflexivity on the metadisciplinary dimensions of the field and polices dissident views of economic agency and explanation as hostile to the spirit of economic science.[23]

Such consideration of the interdisciplinary foundations of disciplines would also add a useful caution about treating interdisciplinarity as an a priori force for good in the academic world, or as something necessarily transgressive or transformative.[24] Barthes's forceful claim that "interdisciplinarity consists in creating a new object that belongs to no one"[25] needs to be reassessed in relation to new proprietary demands on objects of all sorts. Institutional constraints may indeed demand that an interdisciplinary formation claim authorship for ideas, effects, and innovation and account for them or compete for resources precisely in the way that departments or budgetary responsibility centers would. At the same time, the fact that interdisciplinary initiatives would be subject to conventional measures of justification or legitimation does not necessarily negate their capacity to engender critical difference in the sites and discussions where they intervene. Julie Thompson Klein is surely correct that, despite ongoing gaps between project and practice, proposal and realization, encouragement and support, conceptual expansiveness and methodological rigor, interdisciplinarity lies in the future of scholarly endeavor.[26] But one should hasten to add that interdisciplinarity also constitutes the active past of disciplinary work—as a necessary foundation to its own intellectual formation.

The preceding discussion makes clear that disciplines did not emerge from themselves. The capacity to construct epistemological and institutional boundaries that delimit fields of inquiry requires explanation. Ellen Messer-Davidow, David Shumway, and David Sylvan observe that "new disciplines are assembled from bits and pieces of other disciplines."[27] Disciplinary formations extend back two centuries, and departmental expressions of them have been around less than a hundred years. Ironically, despite the relatively recent marriage of institutional form and epistemological content, academic departments appear fully naturalized. Their prolific status seems to us now to produce the idea of progress that would seem to enshrine them with permanence. But disciplinary formation is not a straightforward process of combining stable parts to compose a new whole, as quickly becomes evident in a few examples.

In their examination of the emergence of accounting, Keith Hoskins and Richard Macve contrast the standard reckoning of the field as a combination of theoretical frameworks from economics and social psychology to the applied science of auditing. They craft a more complex history where accounting is invented five hundred years before it achieves power, and well into the nineteenth century it lacks disciplinary or professional status as evidenced by the way in which bookkeepers were treated as menial laborers. With the predominance of the business enterprise, however, accountability and managerialism position accounting for a disciplinary breakthrough that will help to construct the world in which economics and psychology are invented. Techniques of calculation are meant to adjudicate the objective demands for success with the anxiety of imminent loss. "Your desire is to be number one; your fear is that you are nothing but a zero."[28] Rather than being derived, accounting provides a conceptual supplement that permeates the theoretical core of the purported host disciplines.

This inversion of order between what is considered theoretical and what is taken to be applied unseats the linear conception of progress by which the story of disciplinary advance is told. Emergent disciplines turn to other fields for specific kinds of authorization. Accordingly, Evelyn Fox Keller suggests that physics provided the social authority for molecular biology, where life could be defined as a mathematical code located in the gene, and biology would be converted from an observational to an experimental science whose interventions in the world would provide "effective mastery."[29] For the development of physics itself, Andrew Pickering counters the "disciplinary essentialism" that pervades thinking about science and argues that the material and social are "coproduced" in particular historical conjunctures. This was made apparent in the way in which the military enfolded or adapted itself to the atom bomb and radar in response to the designs and programs that theoretical researchers provided.[30] Such critical histories of science expose the ways in which disciplinary self-concepts serve to structure the relation of scientific investigation to economic and institutional contexts. The sites and labor of knowledge production disclose how the coherence of the epistemological object is achieved—always amid a struggle for resources—and which expressions of knowledge will receive legitimation. The selective advantage that would favor which versions of interdisciplinarity will win out go to the managerially adept. As Timothy Lenoir, reflecting on the course of disciplinary development, remarks, "Science has not functioned without administrators."[31]

Interdisciplinary Formations: Market, State, and Class

Interdisciplinary knowledge is articulated in what Mary Louise Pratt has called, in a different context, a "contact zone," where the global and universal are reinscribed for a particular otherness that closely resembles disciplinary authority.[32] The circulation back into the university, long a feature of professional programs, poses an interesting challenge to the historically occidentalist claims of education as an end in itself by which the liberal arts have positioned themselves.[33] This boundary blurring between the university and other domains of knowledge production linked to sociopolitical formations of market, state, and class affects the form that interdisciplinarity takes. The humanities, reaching back to Cicero's *humanitas*, had a normative function to dispose the educated toward what would be considered proper civic behavior, grounded in Greek and Latin ideals of paideia, or intensive learning.[34] Questioning the transcendental status of these interdisciplinary roots, insisting on the potent link between interpretation and self-understanding, and holding open a space where immediate instrumentalities of the marketplace would be kept in abeyance in the service of long-term reflection and speculation, the humanities have, at times, positioned themselves as the defenders of a strong boundary between what lies within and outside the university. This position has been eloquently defended by Mary Poovey, who invites a reinvestment in the human as a strategy for both refusal and self-preservation. As she puts it:

> The only way we can evaluate the effects of market penetration into the university in terms other than the market's own is to assert some basis for evaluation that repudiates market logic and refuses market language. In order to assert an alternative basis for evaluation, we must establish a normative definition of this alternative that is just as tautological as the logic of the market. For the purposes of discussion, I want to call this normative alternative 'the humanities.' I do so not because disciplines in the humanities necessarily or inevitably perform the function of critique, but because, as the sector of the university least amenable to commodification, the humanities may be the only site where such an alternative might survive.[35]

The alternative amounts to asserting the existence of nonquantifiable "goods in themselves," which means to "risk something that poststructuralism has taught me to abhor: I have to essentialize 'the human.'"[36] Poovey's strategy is to specify a unique normative function for the humanities. "The function of the humanities in the university is to preserve, nurture, analyze, interrogate, and interpret this living body of cultural materials. . . . In order to realize this norm, humanities disciplines would have to endorse a model of knowledge that does not emphasize utility, accumulation or progress."[37] Because "the humanities have no market worth" their "lack of economic potential may be the only asset capable of insulating us from market logic."[38]

Poovey's arguments help us think strategically about the positioning of the humanities within the university. What is typically grounds for defensiveness—namely, that the humanities have not been at the forefront of fresh revenue streams for the resource-hungry institution—are here made a virtue. Both the lack of economic potential and the irreducibility of the living body of cultural materials to the economic logics of quantification and accumulation provide the humanities with their distinct rationale for continued support. Poovey's situational essentialism recalls Gayatri Spivak's notion of strategic essentialism.[39] Both intend to consolidate a position of value so that further political engagement can take place. If the humanities emerge here as a distinct asset, it is not without conceptual cost that is particularly relevant to interdisciplinary work. For, if culture is enclosed and encapsulated against something outside it called the economic, or conversely, if the economic is something outside of the living body referenced by culture, the ambit of what the humanities might be able to preserve is greatly diminished. This loss would establish a brief for an interdisciplinary project to which Poovey herself has contributed mightily— namely, the culturalization of economic logics.[40]

In a different way, it is hard to sustain the claim that the humanities as an institutional formation are somehow less caught up in university business models. Humanities core curriculum requirements have themselves provided templates for casualization, outsourcing, contingent graduate student labor, and a variety of other schemes by which norms of accumulation have been installed in the university irrespective of the putative content of the field. The lower infrastructure costs as compared to the natural sciences, with their laboratories, equipment, and materials, has established an important cross-subsidy between humanities and sciences that renders the disciplinary discount of the former crucial to the market viability of the latter.[41] A strategy of resistance that takes as stable the delineation between instrumental and substantive reason, between the administrative form and content of knowledge, may not be able to track the critical difference that knowledge might actually make to the organization of the university.

While the humanities can (and must) be conceived as an intellectual project, they are never free of their institutional instantiation, which renders them an administrative category as well. Why the humanities are better placed strategically to resist market logics than they are critiques of the market found across all disciplines is a matter of political discovery and not definitional fiat. Certainly, the knowledge required to critique what markets are doing inside and outside of higher education summon an interdisciplinary energy that is not served by an acceptance of the Trinitarian partition of knowledge into humanities, social sciences, and natural sciences. While this classification may serve internal economies, such as the distribution of undergraduate credits required for graduation, these architectural principles are not robust enough to organize the alliances or provide the knowledges that are most urgent for the very circumstances that Poovey so aptly identifies as the common predicament of the university.

If the humanities themselves cannot provide a sufficient bulwark against commodification, it may be that they themselves have become unmoored from their foundational purpose of the sort that Poovey describes, or that any interdisciplinary initiative simply gets co-opted by the content-leaching actions of the university's administrative machinery. Such are the forceful arguments that Bill Readings offers in his diagnosis of the university of excellence. Excellence for Readings is a compulsive comparison without reference to the interior substance that fleshes out knowledge, "a unit of value internal to a system, the elemental unit of a virtual scale."[42] Excellence reduces the aims of all endeavors to the outcomes of external evaluations as measured by quantitative ranking. The idea of living in a ruin is that we no longer inhabit a continuous history of progress. Contrary to what Poovey describes, the loss of progress does not preserve culture but rather displaces the cultural in favor of excellence. "Once the notion of national identity loses its political relevance, the notion of culture becomes effectively unthinkable."[43] An interdisciplinary project like cultural studies becomes symptomatic of this loss. One irony of Readings's account is that the ruining of the university that forces it outside of its privileged relation to historical continuity itself rests upon a kind of historicizing narrative. Once upon a time, national culture was intact and the humanities anchored its identity. The university was the key edifice of this constructive endeavor. The rise to predominance of the transnational corporation is the principal force behind the erosion of national culture. The university itself is consequently converted into this form.

Readings certainly provides a report from the front, where the din of excellence and accountability threatened to wipe out all other conceptions of what the university might be. Without a doubt, excellence continues to make a lot of noise. Readings also offers an oppositional politics within the university, saying, "The question of value becomes more significant than ever, and it is by raising value as a question of judgment that the discourse of excellence can be resisted."[44] If the university is to become a site of obligation and ethical practice, it must answer to the question of justice not truth. It remains open to dispute, including to matters of accountability that cannot be reduced to accounting. He invites university presidents to spend more time reading faculty evaluations rather than pursuing measures of excellence. Readings's analysis is prescient, but over a dozen years on, excellence is hard to disguise as the rhetoric of fund-raising, a course that consumes the time of presidents and many others. But this is not a change in the function of the president but rather in the demographics of the student and donor population from which funds are drawn.

Diversity signals an abstract market to which a campus must establish a product niche, bringing a corporate identity to the scene of a former community constituency (on the basis of religion, gender, race, geography). And yet, by centering the transformation of the university in the humanities, other operations of the university are elided. The university becomes transnational, and its mission shifts from cultural identity to excellence in a way that preserves the insularity between what is inside and outside the university. The pressures for the reproduction of certain kinds of labor have long been reflected in the university curriculum, as has the intricate relationship with the business establishment. Whether or not there was a time when national culture was intact and effectively reproduced through a disciplinary structure, narrating the university as if this were its hegemonic ideal greatly simplifies the very political economy and class relations that Readings wants us to attend to in the present incarnation of the institution. The rise of professional schools have been just as much a feature of the emergence of the modern university and these have been quintessentially formations of transnational capital flows. The advent of professional geography, so effectively documented by Neil Smith, has been essential to the imperial sweep of the university in the world.[45] Ultimately, positing the nation against which the university rises and falls circumscribes other imaginings of the work available to us that might make interdisciplinarity serviceable to more than formal schemata of self-replication.

Once we recognize that the humanities are more effective when pluralized than when they stand consolidated as a singular institutional or epistemological formation, it becomes possible to rethink the boundaries of what is considered inside and outside the university. In his potent revisionist account of the relation between business and the humanities, Christopher Newfield has accomplished exactly this reconsideration. Newfield has been critical of what he terms Readings's "moralistic antimanagerialism," whereby, "the default result of avoiding administrative agency was, unfortunately, the rule of the market itself."[46] He grasps well the imbrication of both commerce and culture and the university with the economy. This dense thicket of interrelations between the humanities and managerialism provides a historical foundation and a basis for political intervention. As he puts it:

> I was thus not searching for literary and cultural study that existed outside of capitalist economics. I also thought that commerce as such was not only inevitable but also good, since it was at bottom a central form of human exchange and of mutual aid. I was morally opposed to core elements of capitalist commerce: its enormous inequalities, its exploitation of so much labor, its consistent conflicts with democracy, all of which seemed to be getting worse. At the same time, capitalism's large organizations and orchestrated workforces wrought daily miracles of invention, production, and distribution. The forces of innovation and transformation that I loved in the humanities appeared in different and often captive and yet impressive forms in the modern corporation. Both locations—the corporation and the university— sponsored the true wonder of sociable, even socialized creativity.[47]

The parallel and intersecting logics allow the humanities—properly conceived—to play a key role in the reconfiguring of the relation between the economy and its organizations, of which the university itself is a key expression. The hybrid form can be understood as managerial humanism. "Within this culture, generations of university staff and students learned to stress self-development and to see the economic system as functionally prior to their individual activity and uninfluenced by it."[48] The sociological expression of this phenomenon was the rise of the professional-managerial class (PMC), which (as discussed in Chapter 1) treated administrative labor as a kind of craft legitimized by the credential of expert academic training. Humanism itself, according to Newfield is uninflected ethically and politically—it can just as readily subvert as advance emancipatory possibilities. As such, he emphasizes the tradition and trajectory of radical humanism. "The radical humanist regarded managerial systems as the product of collaborative labor rather than as predetermined social system, one that could be remade if necessary. The radical humanist insisted that the PMC recognize and use its own agency within expert systems as it emerges from its everyday work."[49]

As with the market and the nation, as deployed in the accounts of Poovey and Readings, the PMC is a social formation that exerts pressures on the university. Yet in Newfield's account, this class formation is made possible by and drives the expansion of higher education. Also, he understands well that what was initially a vessel promised of class mobility becomes a medium of social stratification. According to Newfield, by 1980, "Professional and managerial practices no longer seemed to seek meaningful independence from markets and finance. The PMC had virtually ceased to exist as a separate interest in society. Its upper strata formed a classic bourgeoisie, while those downstairs managed employees. . . . The research university was as important as business and government in engineering these compromises."[50] The braiding of professional autonomy and disciplinary expertise both preserved values of freedom and cast them as recidivist with respect to contemporary economic development. The middle class came to both distrust and preserve its craft impulses even as it lost the privilege associated with these perquisites of professional entitlement. "Modernity, through the university, became the condition in which the middle classes were convinced that non-instrumental thought and work have been exhausted. Economic determinism and other symptoms of modernity arose from the PMC's loss of belief in the historical agency of all members of a culture, themselves included, which in turn flowed from the dissociation of craft and management, of art and the social processes of organizations."[51]

At this point, it is worth reprising some earlier arguments and placing them in the context of this critical look at interdisciplinarity so as to connect administrative and academic labor. By refashioning the middle class along self-managerial lines, the university abetted a broader social transformation toward a political economy of risk that accompanied the predominance of finance in organizing business and culture. The social compact being refigured by the Reagan revolt augured a shift from defined benefit entitlements and social security to the defined contribution approach, which meant personal financial investment through tax deferred savings and mutual funds. The corporate emphasis on shareholder value or boosting market price as against overall growth in capacity was a cognate of the shift from Keynesian to monetarist economic policy. The Keynesian program used citizenship-driven benefits of increasing wages and government expenditure to assure steady economic growth. Monetarism shifts the policy emphasis to minimizing inflation, which is anathema to participation in financial markets—for it erodes the predictable gains of long-term investments and undermines calculation of market tendencies. While the Keynesian compact privileges the consumptionist notions of belonging to an American Dream that underwrote middle-class ascendancy, the monetarist policy program focuses on the investor's willingness to undertake risk. Rather than being inside or outside the security of the middle class, populations are sorted between the risk-capable and the at-risk, and those able to manage credit and debt for personal gain and those unable to do the same who are treated as a threat to national competitiveness.

Signaled in the 1983 report "A Nation At Risk" (discussed in Chapter 2), the idea that individual performance and productivity rather than civic participation was the means and end of education provided the ideological foundations for the transformation of a college education from a public to a private good. Defunding of grants and aid in favor of greater debt loads was presented as a more rational allocation of resources if a degree correlated with lifetime value-added income capacity. Those denied security became a menace to society best policed along federalized lines of war. The war on crime, drugs, youth, culture, art not only metaphorized an enemy within but also normalized the at-risk as best combated along the lines of a military campaign prosecuted by federal institutions. The war on terror is but the most recent legacy of these policy shifts from mass security to risk management. Rather than saving for a future that will deliver a utopian dreamscape free from toil, the embrace of risk brings the future into the present in an anticipatory or preemptive mode. This is the policy attitude of adjusting interest rates to combat prospective inflation and of the forward deterrence exhibited by recent military interventions by the United States, in Afghanistan and Iraq.[52]

The financial logic being described here does not curtail the demographic expansion of the PMC or other entailments of middle-class life, like home ownership and a college education. While these key indicators of belonging to the PMC continue to rise, its utopian promise of freedom and its historic project of expert autonomy run aground. Through such organizational vehicles as health maintenance organizations and internal auditors (of the sort made notorious by Arthur Andersen's office inside the headquarters of Enron), the professions have lost ownership over their conditions of practice and have become proletarianized. Yet the professional orientation in higher education combines the increasing prevalence of professional degrees as compared to those in the liberal arts with the professional orientation of many liberal arts fields themselves. The professional turn that brings the outside of the university within has also propelled the reorganization of academic labor from the supreme security system—tenure—to a risk model of casualized part-time and now full-time faculty appointments. Real-world experience is embraced against a putative parochialism of the exclusive academic résumé as if the professor is always applying for his or her own job.

Academic entrepreneurialism accommodates changes in patent law that makes universities factories for intellectual property, which convert forays in shareholder value into Readings-like quests for excellence. Administrative mandates create a managerial bulge whereby leanness lapses into obesity.[53] The culture wars view critical intellectuals as placing national cultural literacy at risk, calling into question the interest served by this national account. Interdisciplinarity is assigned suspicion of a specialization without securing method to a domain of analysis—before its evidence can be heard that academic expertise lacks credibility. Ironically, the very postmodernism said to be the province of the accused is a tactic of accusation that authorizes doubt regarding the legitimacy of self-policing professionals. The Hippocratic oaths of the professionals to do no harm are replaced with a demand that shareholder benefit be demonstrated in every academic utterance, or else intellectuals will be lambasted for a nefarious speech act that has them possessed by demon seeds.

Interdisciplinarity figures this double crisis of professional labor and disciplinary authority in a manner consonant with the larger economy of risk. The infinitely flexible, cutting-edge jack- or jane-of-all-trades can be readily placed on the marquee of the entrepreneurial university to be refreshed in concert with the new season. But interdisciplinarity offers another model of academic labor—a collaborative one that has the potential to reorient work when the new university disavows the labor that it relies upon. What is conventionally offered to faculty members as their fulfillment of the university's higher monastic calling by means of service is more properly understood as administration. As argued in Chapter 4, that service is both devalued for material concerns like merit pay and elevated as sheer ideological faith in the rightness of the enterprise speaks to the mischievous role it plays in diverting strategic reflection on the work involved in directing the course of university life. The contribution of interdisciplinarity, in turn, can be to identify what the entanglements of risk hold for academic labor. The volatility visited upon academic life is not only destructive of relative security and freedom; it also embodies approaches to the mutual indebtedness by which risk circulates and expands. Leveraging the flows, alliances, and movements of inside and outside positions, interdisciplinarity becomes a kind of arbitrage, an investment in small fluctuations in value to greater effect.

The financialization of society in general and the university in particular has proceeded too far to stand apart from the entanglements of risk. To seek unsullied ground as a defense against baleful developments invites a kind of passivity. Doubtless, while the reconciliation of labor along the lines of ascendant capital formations induces its own forms of nausea, there is also some prospect for significant political responses if we rethink value along the lines of the derivative, which counts as capital's own most generative investments. For capital, the derivative is a means of generating commensurability among entities that are different from one another so that risks are both dispersed and brought to market. Presently denominated at more than one quadrillion dollars in promissory notes and contracts, the profusion of derivatives enlarge the scope of mutual indebtedness and the volatility by which a move at one point ripples elsewhere.[54] The subprime meltdown of 2007, and the subsequent credit crunch of 2008 and 2009, displays the fragility of these terms of participation and the impact of the industrialization of consumer debt on the capacity of students to secure loans and pay for college, especially as lenders like Citibank get out of the business altogether.

The object of fear and loathing in the aftermath of the financial mess, the derivative—or more specifically, its logic of association through attributes—provides an analytic lens by which to understand social relations more broadly. As financial instruments for trading in risks, derivatives take myriad forms but are effectively contracts that allow for exchange at certain terms and particular moments, like an agreement to trade currency at a fixed rate on a certain date (a future) or the opportunity to swap a contract to buy stock at different prices keyed to disparate market conditions (a swaption). The principle of parsing out certain attributes shared by a range of otherwise disparate entities, and taking this dimension of association to create a distinct value and place it into circulation, discloses a derivative logic in a range of practices and settings. For example, the approach to baseball player selection based upon statistical analysis of bases gained rather than intuitive feel for player talent provides Michael Lewis with his allegorical account of the derivative as the logic behind Oakland As manager Billy Beane's ability to outperform teams with significantly larger payrolls.[55]

Interdisciplinarity, for example, is also a currency whose value is derived, whose combinations are open, and whose effects can circulate extensively through relatively modest investments. The mutual indebtedness borne by interdisciplinarity carries no guarantee of desirable outcome. At their most retrograde, interdisciplinary demands can isolate scholars of color, postcoloniality, and heteronormativity to perform compensatory acts of representation for the institution's lack of commitment to diversity. That one person is profiled into a range of settings through the intersecting identifications of the individual's work can also present impossible conditions of labor by which appointments are split and committee work multiplied.[56] Yet the derivative logic of interdisciplinarity also offers a very different way of valuing academic labor and thinking about how epistemological and institutional formations intersect according to various organizational strategies. In order to amplify the strategic possibilities of interdisciplinarity, it is important to think against the grain of the foundational histories of academic fields—to read intersecting influences at the origins and through the institutional transformations of knowledge work.

In the history of interdisciplinarity—like so many other histories—social forms and forces get introduced but nothing ever seems to fully disappear. For that reason, it may be more useful to imagine waves that continue to break upon a shore of the present rather than rely on a more conventional concept of periodization by which a singular tendency ends and another comes into view. That said, we can consider three interdisciplinary waves—departmentalizing, empire building, and arbitrage—all of which leave their residue on the present, in terms of occupational, disciplinary, and organizational formations. As well, we can respond to and internalize various social forms (nation, market, class). Sketching the matrix of these possibilities restates the arguments already presented, but now in an activist key, with the hopes of setting our work to work. Hopefully, the "we" being invoked here is affiliational and not presumptive. So too the history being referenced is far from universal but starts within the idea of the research university, which invented itself as a disciplinary architecture (again, even in the United States, these number but a tiny fraction of all colleges and universities) in order to imagine what departures are possible from there. Finally, it should be said that interdisciplinarity is something of an anticipatory mode of knowledge making. Specific intellectual alliances, emergent approaches to study, newly identified needs for objects of study, and particular constraints placed upon what knowledge is treated as legitimate are all detectable in interdisciplinary formations. The argument that disciplines form from a coalition of disparate influences and resources allows interdisciplinarity to become a generative condition before it is named as such. While typically treated as a response to concerns of overspecialization, interdisciplinarity is no less specific and no less capable of locating how a self-generalizing educated subject might be expressed. If the common application of the term is traced to the twenties and thirties, its logic, as has been argued above, is already present in the anterior formation of the disciplines themselves.[57]

FIRST WAVE: DEPARTMENTALIZING INTERDISCIPLINARITY

The first wave of interdisciplinarity we associate with the late-nineteenth-century creation of modern disciplines and a corresponding architecture of departments and representation by professional associations. The hierarchy of academic appointments was introduced along with partition by specialization. As Christopher J. Lucas explains:

> To this "vertical" arrangement of rankings was added the "horizontal" dimension of departmentalization. As an administrative expedient for organizing an otherwise unwieldy number of academic specialists within a single governance framework, the institution of an academic department was both necessary and probably inevitable. But as experience made abundantly obvious, the proliferation of quasi-independent bureaucratic structures tended to divide an already-fragmented academic community. Their chief effect, it seemed to many observers, was to release petty jealousies, to foster competition for favor and resources, to increase the importance of attention to public relations, and to set in motion an unseemly scrambling for students among rival satrapies. "Turf" battles and "empire-building" became the norm, not the exception.[58]

While all the disciplines as we know them have their creation myths, the argument here is that they are formed out of mixtures from other fields— philology and history for modern languages and literature, parsings of political economy and philosophy for sociology, and the blending of astronomy, optics, mechanics, and geometry into what would become physics. Departmentalization is the institutional expression of the disciplinary formation that swept through but also gave shape to major research-based campuses for some twenty years, between 1890 and 1910. The newly designated entities bore the internal traces of these fissured foundations. As Laurence Veysey described this state of affairs, many important departments were "intramural battlegrounds":

> Thus philosophy (which included psychology) was torn between Hegelian idealism and devotion to research in the scientific manner. Departments of English were split between partisans of culture and devotees of philological research. Sociology, itself in the process of breaking away from economics during the nineties, had endless trouble defining its relationship both to social utility and to empirical research. Economics was divided between upholders of the old classical theories, whose deductive approach usually accorded well with mental discipline, and believers in utility, research, or a combination of the two. Sometimes a battle within such a department seemed thoroughly won by one side, only to receive new challenges a few years later. History switched from initial predilections toward literary culture to a strong emphasis on research, then found itself meeting the

utilitarian challenge of James Henry Robinson and others. In philosophy, physiological psychology (representing the thrust of scientific research) had just begun to score significantly against idealism when a new faction devoted to utility (i.e. the pragmatists) arrived on the scene.[59]

While the influence of the German research university on the U.S. variant is often cited, departmentalization was a key departure from the German *ordinarius*, who was considered a single disciplinary representative with sovereign authority over research and teaching. Instead, the department was an organizational unit of difference among peers of the same rank, those who attained full professor.[60] But even the settling of organization into departmental fiefdoms did not erase the interdisciplinary affinities within and across them. This was one impetus behind the creation of divisions, as one history of higher education observes, "the forces of compartmentalization did not spend themselves till the twentieth century, and even then they only slackened long enough to organize departments into divisions in order to recognize the growing importance of interdisciplinary studies."[61] These tendrils of affiliation provided organizational structures that were also sustained for the relation between graduate programs in arts and sciences and those in professional schools. Disciplines were expected to provide universal mastery of a field through transcendent theoretical claims and the specialized application authorized via a kind of technical labor. The result was a cross-fertilization between a site of theory and practice that grounded the research university and its pragmatic reach into emerging professional fields as self-regulating occupations.

The alignment between epistemological and institutional trajectories in this first wave allowed the university to achieve a certain work of national formation. It presented naturalized boundaries for the containment of difference that appeared to correspond to some preordained division of labor, just as people would find their appropriate expression in proper national division. As David Shumway explains with respect to the genealogy of American civilization, "It is only after World War I that American nationalism comes to replace Anglo-Saxonism as the dominant ethnocentrism within the literary. The war and the Wilsonian propaganda that had accompanied it had the effect of forging an identity between 'America' and 'democracy.' Instead of being a form of solidarity among the people, nationalism now becomes much more an ideology aligned with government and the ruling class. It is perhaps not surprising that the idea of a distinct American literature began to be deployed by the cultural elite immediately after the war."[62] The new field, hence, enshrined the tension between the linguistic grounding for ethnonationalism and the philological foundation for the evolutionism associated with democratic rule as a fulfillment of human destiny.

Interdisciplinary projects, like the invention of the category of race, drew from biology and statistics, sociology and philosophy, and literature and visual arts in ways that forged a sturdy bond between disciplinary and national boundary, between a unique technique of knowing or methodology, and a distinctive ethnocultural belonging.[63] Just as the models for higher education in the United States hybridized German and British national forms, the civic mission of the university promised to acculturate the national citizen through disciplinary knowledge. This national narrative was the idiom by which business and professional class interests could be expressed, although certainly without exhausting what capital and labor could claim for the university.

Disciplines underwent uneven development through a range of pressures and responses that enhanced the capacities for state legitimation and authority. At times, they responded to external demands and at others they created a market for a particular kind of expertise. As Mark Nemec puts it,

> By developing and nurturing expertise, the university did not simply produce trained personnel for government employment. It also defined national standards and expectations for a widening array of disciplines, fields and professions. These efforts were often driven by coordination among the leading universities. Such coordination meant that national systemization of knowledge did not necessarily include the federal government. In some policy domains, such as forestry, the federal government was intimately involved in defining expertise. Universities worked as active partners of the national state in developing standards and expectations. In other domains, such as education, the federal government was only marginally involved in defining expertise.[64]

The conditions for mixing and isolating fields during departmentalization were as overdetermined by intra- as extra-institutional forces that constructed a play of knowledges.

The political operation of a disciplinary field allows it to be disbursed across a range of professions. Illustrative here is the case of social work, a field that begins as missionary and charity activity in the middle of the nineteenth century. The New York Charity Organization founded a school in 1898 that would eventually become the Columbia University School of Social Work. "Physicians, psychologists, counselors of all kinds—even nurses, agricultural agents, home economists—can act as social workers because social work is a kind of power, a way of seeing things, that traverses every kind of institution or profession, linking them, making them converge and function in a new way."[65] Before the consolidation of a single professional association—the National Association of Social Workers, in 1955—there were seven distinct organizations devoted to social workers. The profession emerged through alternating forces of dispersion and consolidation, of attentions developed as adjuncts to other fields and organized into a credentialing association.

Legal education began at Harvard in 1829 with the appointment of U.S. Supreme Court Associate Justice Joseph Story and provided a pedagogy that was to predominate for the remainder of the century and beyond (notably, with the founding of the University of Chicago Law School and appointment of Harvard's Joseph Beale as its first Dean). Contrary to the intentions that it be established as an academic field of study, Story effectively formed "an associated trade school without standards for admission or examinations for admission or graduation."[66] The case approach based upon incorporation of the extant legal field left the training without a theoretical doctrine that would delimit its boundaries beyond what would pass as law at any particular moment in the courts. One practical consequence was the inductive and precedent-based grammar enshrined in the case method. The advent of selective admissions, rigorous exams, and standards would leave intact the practical field as providing the admixture of disciplinary elements that would comprise the profession. University-based legal training came to predominate the profession as lawyers were pushed by their business clients to master the technical details that would avert subsequent court challenges, rather than provide strict attention to trial performance. The former skill set gave weight to the academic performance of research and writing. This response to client demand meant that "the present contours of legal education . . . are not so much the product of systematic and sustained discussion of how best to teach young men and women legal techniques and professional values but instead are the result of piecemeal adjustment to changing academic and professional concerns."[67] Legal training thus became professionalized across the university, private law firm, and courts, and it developed a pedagogy that could attend to the conflicting demands and dynamics of each of these sites.

The engineering school at Yale had its roots in the introduction of professorships in agricultural and practical chemistry in 1846 and the establishment of the Sheffield Scientific School fifteen years later. But scientific training, far from its present hegemony, was seen by Yale College as vocational and inferior. As one of the Sheffield governors decried, "A year does not pass without our seeing that the work which we are trying to perform is quite imperfectly understood by the graduates and friends of Yale College, by many writers on the higher education, and by parents and teachers who are called upon to select for young men their advanced courses of study."[68] The first engineering school had been founded decades before at the U.S. Military Academy in 1812. It had professorships in mathematics, natural and experimental philosophy, and engineering, and it had faculty members who went on to help start similar endeavors at Harvard and Yale.[69] Rensselaer was the first freestanding engineering school, established in 1824, and required students to attend chemistry lectures on "metalloids, metals, soils, manures, mineral waters, and animal and vegetable matter."[70] The mix of domains in need of engineering would seem to be the chief external factor for its foundational interdisciplinarity. Industrialization expanded the range of objects that could be engineered into existence, the understanding of which would need to select from an eclectic mix of subjects.

If engineering has its etymological roots in genius, planning and contrivance, it achieved an elasticity of method by which anything might be made. But the chemistry of which it was the practical application was caught in its own identity mix, as Bernadette Bensaude-Vincent and Isabelle Stengers pointedly state, "by turns servant, mistress, or rival of its fellows, physics and biology."[71] They warn for the sciences more broadly, "By adopting a particular distribution of disciplines too quickly, we risk overlooking fundamental problems, which are often the most interesting to ponder. The historian of science, by accepting the contemporary framework of disciplinary boundaries, tends to take for granted a structure that was pieced together with considerable effort in the past."[72] Nor, once in place, did these boundaries remain stable. Chemistry's self-concept shifted with the materials it privileged (from soda, chlorine, sulfuric acid, and nitrogen in the first half of the nineteenth century to carbon in the second) and the industrial links it forged. But subsequently, its scientific primacy was reshuffled through other fields and business pursuits. "Just as chemical science saw its territory dismembered little by little and its identity menaced, so the chemical industry in the twentieth century has tended to be dispersed to other sectors and to bend to their needs."[73]

The disciplinary logic that would enshrine knowledge as an end in itself would hence continually be undermined by the epistemological and institutional social formations that would make and unmake the fields of study as we know them. The first wave of interdisciplinarity authorized the departmentalized university governed by a professionalized peerage that could not control the forces outside it in a manner reminiscent of the constitution of the nation state itself. Academic disciples were citizens with little command over the foreign policy that might seal their fates and bring their reigns to a close. But once formed, the departmental territory—like the bounded nations whose form they replicated—would be more durable than its founding occasion. Citizenship might be defined as much by locational address as by substantive knowledge of what made a given institutional territory cohere. Other waves would press on the integrity of boundaries and suggest other loyalties than those first professional disciples. Despite the vestiture of medieval gowns and regalia, faculty would be hailed by other processionals even as the grammar of peerage established through the initial hierarchies persevered. So it is that other logics of interdisciplinarity can be introduced while all the trappings of disciplinary fidelity remain. Under the guise of an iterative process of professional socialization, other affiliations were in formation, which would add to the trajectories of faculty work.

SECOND WAVE: INTERDISCIPLINARITY
AND EMPIRE BUILDING

The second wave of interdisciplinarity emerges with the massive state intervention in higher education from tuition subsidies like the GI Bill and the 1958 National Security Act, and the public investments in campus construction. The sudden expansion of scale that the United States had won in its global mastery after World War II crafted a conjuncture between interdisciplinary formations that could manage the newly wrought imperium, Keynesian demand-side stimulus for knowledge production, and mass production of students and faculty. The enhancement and disciplining of labor in large corporations buttressed by government support that underwrote the prosperity of the American Century is commonly known as Fordism.[74] The term focuses on the coordination of mass production and consumption (through cumulative knowledge, wages and credit). Yet this Fordist massification also had its opposite number in its very namesake the heroic entrepreneur, the lone individual with an idea that shapes a field and gives rise to a way of life. The academic entrepreneur was the exalted subject of this second wave interdisciplinarity, the one who crafted new areas, institutions, and publications. Designated "empire builders," they brokered the resources by which universities could make their mark and their market.

The climate for enterprising academics was hastened by the demands of corporate entrepreneurs who viewed disciplinary training as overspecialized and incapable of meeting their market needs. Rustom Roy recounts the emergence of materials science, an amalgam of physicists, metallurgists, and electrical engineers through a government block grant of $20 million for fifteen years to a handful of prominent research universities:

> It was Dr. Guy Suits, who was then vice president for research of the General Electric Company together with Dr. W.O. Baker, then vice president of Bell Telephone Laboratories, and several of their colleagues who urged the federal government to a major new intervention on the campuses, as the universities were falling far behind, not only in the amount of training they could do but in the very nature of the research, and training of their students to meet the nation's needs. Physicists were not being adequately trained (within physics departments) to meet the kind of demand that Bell Telephone or GE envisioned. Neither the nature of the intellectual environment nor the research equipment was adequate. In response to this identified need of society, the federal government, through the Department of Defense (as it happened) injected very large sums of money into a few university laboratories, triggering a major impact on the academic (and government) world.[75]

In this account, interdisciplinarity is the means by which science goes large to create a series of isomorphisms between business and society, government and military industrialism, universities and empire building, research and market demands. For the industry captains doing the envisioning, public monies are reasonably apportioned to structure research ventures to meet their proprietary needs cast in terms of societal requisites.

Postwar disciplinarity was itself underwritten by transdisciplinary protocols such as positivism, which, as George Steinmetz notes, generated "patterns of imitation and repulsion, the introjection and rejection of theories and practices from outside disciplines, the dynamics of self-definition and redrawing of disciplinary boundaries via constructions of disciplinary Others."[76] Michael Dutton suggests that the moniker "interdisciplinarity" imposed a kind of containment strategy on area studies, relegating it to a translation service incapable of generating its own theoretical framework. "As a geographically defined area of study rather than a theoretically driven discipline, area studies had long argued that it was interdisciplinary. But, as it looked over its shoulder at the hard social sciences, it was stalked by the fear that it had no discipline at all. The social sciences has for years made this claim about area studies, and the latter's response, in arguing for a more 'area-centric knowledge,' only reinforced the suspicion that area studies was indeed a field dominated by descriptive 'social translators.'"[77] Development discourse that proclaimed convergence between recently liberated colonial states and the metropolitan centers who claimed to be all grown up offered a biological analogy to geopolitical dynamics. Follow in your parents' footsteps and you'll turn out just fine. This teleology was organized by an epistemological exchange. Embrace systems models and analytic methods, behaviorism and cognitive science, and the other will achieve the status of a knowable object through the likes of area and ethnic studies. As Christopher Simpson observes:

> In American universities, development studies programs that accompanied and legitimated ideological offensives typically presented themselves as mildly innovative, interdisciplinary subsets of traditional disciplines, on the one hand, or as area studies centers and international studies programs, on the other. The former attempted to deduce rules for introduction of capitalist modernity as a general phenomenon; the later focused on the exploration and management of challenges within particular geographic or cultural groups viewed as special problems. Thus, Russian and Soviet studies emerged as the first full scale area studies programs in the U.S. (Founded at Harvard, Columbia, and MIT and underwritten largely by the U.S. Air Force, the CIA, and cooperative foundations), followed by Asian studies and Middle Eastern studies. In time these new disciplines were joined by country- and culture-specific specialities, which attempted to sort out

the gross, and in many respects misleading divisions that had been created by dividing the world up into these "areas" in the first place.[78]

The heroes of this salvage operation will be the knowledge entrepreneurs—those who master a field, make it their own by coming to know all that can be known about it. The government foundation archipelago was generous toward those willing and able to step up and create a new interdisciplinary unit. Bruce Cumings chronicles the politics of interdisciplinarity in the creation of Asian studies, first as the Far Eastern Association in 1943, subsequently reconstituted as the Association of Asian Studies in 1956. As he explains the initial formation:

> In that period the area programs instantly confronted the existing boundaries of the social sciences and humanities; this often made for interesting intellectual confrontation. William Nelson Fenton, a leading scholar of the Iroquois and was present at the creation of area studies, and in 1947 he wrote that area programs "faced fierce resistance from the 'imperialism of departments' since they challenged the fragmentation of the human sciences by disciplinary departments, each endowed with a particular methodology and a specific intellectual subject matter." But those were not the power lines that counted. The state was less interested in the feudal domains of academe than in filling the vacuum of knowledge about a vast hegemonic and counter-hegemonic global space, however, and it was the capillary lines of state power that shaped area programs.[79]

Clearly, the politicization of the academy from these sources of patronage met its opposite number in the antiwar protests, which linked the campus military operations to foreign policy. Some Cold War programs, like MIT's Center for International Studies, became unsustainable in this climate of campus opposition.

In this second wave, conditions for interdisciplinarity emerged not simply from the university's interpellation of the corporate state but from the internal omissions, infidelities, and failures of the disciplines themselves. Ellen Messer-Davidow has produced a piercing account of the gender divide within conventional departmental culture and socialization that emitted other prospects for knowledge formation:

> The disciplines, I have been arguing, inserted their disciples into normative schemes of practice and thereby produced good subjects who would work all right by themselves. Paradoxically, however, the same preliminary strategies of demarcating and ordering their discourse that enabled the disciplines to produce good subjects also caused them

to produce bad ones. All students who enter the university are discursive migrants: they emigrate from their customary social and school discourses into the unfamiliar and difficult discourse of an academic discipline. Once there, they have to learn the intellectual order (the language, content, and skills), the professional order (the character and conduct of practitioners), and the pedagogical order (the learning protocols). Given the complexity and normativity of disciplinary discourse, any student can flounder and experience the effects—the bewilderment of a student who can't grasp the language, the frustration of a student who commits to the intellectual goals but can't achieve competence in the means, and the isolation of a student who masters the intellectual discourse but rejects the professional conduct. One way or another, these feelings destabilize the self, producing doubt that leads to the student's disengagement or determination that fuels his persistence.[80]

Messer-Davidow traces feminism as a kind of bad subject that is made good through institutionalization that reinscribes a kind of disciplinary authority severed from the social activism that had been the initial impetus for the field. The enormous scholarly productivity unleashed by women's studies breaks open disciplinary boundaries as feminist critique appears across virtually all academic domains. At the same time, the proliferation of academic work is not immune to the hierarchies of reward and the currencies of exchange that allow for influential professors to broker programs, faculty lines and other institutional resources in the manner of the area studies entrepreneur.

The negotiation of what is inside and outside the university does bear a difference in these social movement based endeavors even as they gain institutional recognition, in terms of who or what can make a claim to the ends of knowledge that community-based interdisciplinarity engenders. Writing about the formation of Asian American studies at the close of the sixties (when Berkeley formed a department of ethnic studies in response to a 1969 student strike), Sucheng Chan speaks of the "invisible work" that "included functioning in various community organizations, engaging in intense political debates and internal struggles, organizing and attending mass demonstrations, and doing things with and for students outside the classroom."[81] She too recounts a history where institutional advances in the field have made those very practices internally invisible and invites contemporary scholars not to "jettison the very tools we have used to get to where we are today."[82] Community activism was also instrumental in the formation of Chicano studies. El Plan de Santa Barbara, which emerged from the League for United Latin American Citizens aided the formation of a student vanguard expressed as El Movimiento Estudiantil Chican@ de Aztlán (MEChA), which developed civic participation-based curricula in which higher education figured as a public good.[83]

In this, the PMC professoriate makes proprietary claims for a kind of restricted trade in their own knowledge production that set up the deregulation of intellectual property for financial gain. While departmentalization is still the campus gold standard, interdisciplinary programs can thrive through external funding and what is too-often unself-consciously referred to as empire building. The combination of knowledges, the value of external funding, the celebration of academics ability to be at the center of this whole-scale production is termed a revolution in a manner referencing not the Bolshevik, but the industrial form.[84] Federal tax policies encouraged private giving to non-profit universities, the university itself became part of the military industrial complex, mass higher education reached its apotheosis with the multiversity, and academic labor embarked upon a steady unionization. All of these factors pointed to the industrialization of the university's own institutional forms, including its own growth driven imperatives.

The massive public sector expansion carried with it a whole series of administrative controls such that a 1959 study worried, "By means of riders to appropriation acts, legislatures can now exert close control over certain phases of university policy even where universities enjoy constitutional autonomy."[85] While the professional associations are at the apex of their power when campus growth-driven demand puts a premium on expanded credentialization, so too are the great combines of industrial unionism, which reach a height of membership in the fifties and peak militancy in the seventies. Although it maintains a craft identity, the ascendancy of the professional class across all manner of occupations constitutes a socialization of managerial labor and industrialization of the knowledge economy that drives an extensive unionization of academic labor in the public sector. Exclusive of the research universities that predate this massive expansion of higher education, 89 percent of faculty in the public sector are unionized—eight times the rate of unionization of the private sector economy.[86]

THIRD WAVE: INTERDISCIPLINARY ARBITRAGE

In the third wave of interdisciplinarity, characterized by what has been called here the professional turn in the midst of a risk economy, the figure of the arbitrager takes on special significance. Once again, neither professional specialization nor the academic entrepreneur have gone away, any more than departments and interdisciplinary programs have fallen by the wayside. Instead, they operate according to different logics. While themselves of longer-standing, post-professional, continuing and adult education programs beckon a return to the university as the defined benefits of professional careers no longer deliver the path to security and advancement they once promised. The lateral or downward mobility still requires retraining and educational extension, but the university must compete for attention with other suitors.

Paradoxically, the very forces that expand education beyond the conventional college years also break the hold that Universities have on higher education. Frank T. Rhodes, president of Cornell University from 1977 to 1995, justifies university-industry partnerships as a function of the changing market in and for educational services:

> The centuries-old monopoly on education enjoyed by universities is over, a casualty to new means of learning (information technology [IT] and the Internet) and new providers (especially corporate America and for-profit vendors). . . . The traditional pattern of learning—by college age students enrolled on a full-time basis in a residential, rigidly sequential program—is already being replaced by on-demand, anytime, and often on-line learning from an increasingly competitive "knowledge business." Skills acquired as needed for changing careers and changing job demands by cost-conscious knowledge shoppers of every age.[87]

This affinity with the labor market and need for continual retooling as careers come and go is also understood in terms of interdisciplinarity and a rubric of engaged scholarship. According to one account, lifelong learning will effect a shift in the research endeavor. "The new ingredient will be the pedagogy of active scholarship" and "new fields of knowledge will typically be cross-disciplinary, further reshaping the specialities of graduate study."[88] While universities emerge as "learning commons" for labor generally, their own labor will be rationalized by strategic planning and management and the "use of technology to lower labor costs."[89]

In the most general terms, this laboring commons references the largest growth area for student enrollments, especially among those demographics previously unable to afford or qualify for college entrance. These populations are increasingly targeted by proprietary institutions. With nearly half a million students (as of 2010) the largest of these, University of Phoenix, has drawn controversy for tying recruiters' salaries to enrollment and misleading students regarding financial aid (the school, which receives more than $3 billion in federal aid, is the largest recipient of federal aid in the nation) and the transferability of course credits. The incentives to enroll at any cost are subsequently borne by students, whose default rates (at 11 percent) are double their counterparts at public institutions, and whose graduation rates are substantially below national averages.[90] One company, Straighterline.com, leads with affordability on a kind of smorgasbord model in its advertisements to "start college for $99" per month for all the courses you can take, with an additional price tag of $39 per course.[91] More than three and a half million students attend for-profit schools, which account for 2,732 of the 6,551 total number of colleges and universities.[92] With a drop-off in the number of both public and nonprofit institutions, the for-profit sector is capturing growth in market share for an expanding student population today the way that state institutions did forty years ago.[93] But as with other formerly public goods, access to a market and parcelized bits of credit substitutes for the kind of comprehensive inclusion and immersion once signaled by the promise of universal higher education.

Wage volatility and professional class decomposition mean that education becomes the medium for sustaining lateral (or downward) mobility in the labor force as the recent and prior recessions have made clear. It is the place where labor goes to retool after having gained a suddenly useless bounty of otherwise treasured real-world experience. In the United States, more than one hundred million students are enrolled in these adult or continuing education programs, which catalogue every conceivable teachable human activity and efface the boundary between work and leisure, professional self-development and personal enrichment, career counseling, and self-help.[94] The largest occupational category, professional and managerial labor in particular, requires ongoing infusions of education. A credential hardly sets such labor for life, but rather, education is the medium through which the PMC circulates. At any given time, those returning to class for their work outnumber matriculated students purportedly preparing for a career. For work-related courses, those with graduate and professional degrees (especially in business, health, and computer science) engage in the greatest level of participation, with more than 60 percent enrolled in 2005, as compared to slightly more than half of those with baccalaureate degrees and only 7.3 percent of those without a high school or equivalent degree.[95] That education and labor have become internal to one another could be said to be their most general condition of arbitrage, where the continuous disruptions to what counts as professional expertise generate a volatility that is met with adjunct bits of learning, which in turn destabilize the monopoly of knowledge that professional domains can claim.

For academic labor as such, at the other end of precarity, contingency, and casualization, stand not only the tenured professional and star faculty but also the license-seeking, proprietary interest that treats the university as a host medium, as a venture that can assemble its team for a particular opportunity. Whereas disciplinarity had been defined in termed of its autonomous or private technical interests, interdisciplinarity (or multidisciplinarity as in the case of the Salzburg ICT&S project discussed at the beginning of this chapter) in this third wave, operates under the sign of various meanings of public. While the ends of academic research have, over the past century been understood to ultimately serve commercial purposes, the means were to be governed by self-regulating methods that could be seen as the property of the disciplines own administrative capacities. Current interdisciplinarity constructed across sectors may relinquish such methodological property to various conceptions of public as a consortium of resources and demands—as for example, either the stakeholders, patrons, or investors who occasion the project and sustain its labor; or in the case of public sociology, an interest that lies beyond the university that a research project might serve; or in the case of proprietary institutions taking students' borrowing powers from the public coffers, a use of tax monies for profitable ends; or finally, as a critical faculty that a particular project or program seeks to engender through interdisciplinary collaboration between students and various community constituencies.[96]

Worthy of note in this regard are graduate degree programs that exist off the return or reentry of professional labor into the academy. This is a sign of the decentering of the university in relation to industrial knowledge production but also of the circulation between knowledge production inside and outside the university. The advent of project-based science projects and post-professional certificate programs establish a range of interests in the return to the university from outside it, rather than simply positioning credentialization at the center of a unidirectional dispersion of knowledge. While graduate and professional programs number in the tens of thousands, certificate programs are a smaller niche, numbering some several hundred.[97] But there is also an opening to a range of more critical initiatives, such as the interdisciplinary arts and sciences graduate program in cultural studies at the University of Washington, Bothell, which develops community-based partnerships, or the Centre for Cultural Research at the University of Western Sydney, which also takes an intersectoral approach that melds cultural industries, urban development, and community development with research capacities, or the PhD and graduate certificate program Alliance for Social, Political, Ethical, and Cultural Thought at Virginia Tech that combines courses from the colleges of liberal arts, architecture, and business.

The vast supermarket of educational opportunity is met by the niche of the post-professional program in a manner that sets the instructors of record in motion as arbitragers. Within the university, they take these typically small programs to advertise the innovative worldliness of the institution. However, they also open any number of alliances between universities and other industrial sectors to which the moment of critical reflection and elaboration may matter greatly to the drift of industry. The post-professional program is specialized along the lines of a derivative. Less a stable piece of a fixed whole, an occupation presorted for a determinate division of labor, the assemblage of intellectual attributes from a range of fields and dispositions reflects students' need to be able to simultaneously map and make the field in which they would find themselves. Students are prepared for labor and the predicament of having to work when nothing as orderly or prescribed as a career defines their futures. Such programs, therefore, are occasioned by a generalized volatility in the market that makes recombination of knowledges to hedge against specific imaginable risks.

But this specialization marks a pervasive condition—the prospect of speaking through expertise from any location that can have more generalizable effects. Artists, scholars of the Middle East, students of American labor find themselves elevated like the terrorist from a concrete and delimited capacity to a well nigh universal potency of the sort associated with the voice of the state (recall here the cases of Sami Al-Arian and Ward Churchill). The critical capacity to affect a different perspective, issuing from a seemingly marginal space of interdisciplinarity, suddenly, is made the cause of an unbearable disruption to a self-asserted national consensus. Neither the permanent responsibility of the public intellectual to deliver truth to power, nor the ephemeral attentions of the news cycle account for this force of volatility staged when this will to judgment is released. The demand that knowledge manage itself, slip from its professional vocation to an omnipotent capacity to doubt what discretionary judgment can do (whether prosecuting war, dispersing tax dollars to banks, withholding health care) uneasily slides into an anxiety over the maintenance of rule and order. The organizational cognate of this voice is the political party, the voicing of a comprehensive situation of political affairs that takes the form of a critical intervention. While the conventional political party is by measures of preference and loyalty in decline, the party function to extend a politics from a particular platform, to release a claim to knowledge from the shackles of expertise such that it becomes an affair of state, now has the potential to emerge from any quarter.

Tracing the paths of these intersecting waves of interdisciplinarity not only yields an array of subjects—the departmental specialist, the empire-building entrepreneur, the team/project-making arbitrager—but also allows for a way of thinking of these academic subject positions in relation to an array of agencies that have tangible organizational expressions. Braiding together different forms of administrative work that issues from each wave of interdisciplinary knowledge making yields an amalgamation of the major organizational forms of the past century: the craft or professional association, the industrial union, and the political party. By means of a spirited commitment to administrative labor, these three organizational registers can (and do) get traversed in a manner that offers a new instantiation of interdisciplinarity itself. The professional association also refers to faculty and university governance, to the committee work that affords the long march through the institutions, and to the administrative posts that mediate and ameliorate certain demands of faculty. Without a doubt, new interdisciplinary entities come to life through sustained practical application of what the university teaches faculty about how it is run. The industrial form makes a virtue of the relation between the university inside and outside, and transforms marketization from a passive or defensive pliant to a strategic intervention in the socialization of labor. Finally, the party form perhaps most alien to autonomy-loving academics, who may not always notice how and when they speak to comprehensive issues of power that invoke the state, permits a set of claims to be launched that extend beyond any epistemological or institutional site.

This triumvirate of affiliations is for some already in our midst. It treats nation, class, and market as media through which we already circulate, and it turns the poster children of capital into knights of labor. Accordingly, the professional turn would become more than a torment on the rack of performance-driven assessment but could serve to torque the impact of critical faculties. This is a tall order for interdisciplinarity but one that makes all the difference in the world out of what is already to hand. It requires only a re-elaboration of the work we do as we go, an approach which recognizes that knowledge making also crafts the institutional spaces in which it operates and opens organizational pathways it can travel along. Qualifying the conditions of interdisciplinarity has hopefully made it possible to actively link epistemological and organizational prospects. Chapter 7 rearticulates these organizational potentialities or registers and links these initiatives of intellectual commitment to the practical competencies academics can call upon through their experience of administrative labor.

7

Registering Organization

The dream of autonomy is that you can do what you want when you want: lingering over the perfectly crafted cappuccino and conversation with a colleague, reading well into the night, briskly writing in the morning and attending an intimate seminar in the afternoon, flying overseas as an invited lecturer, engaging in an incisive phone consultation. The idyllic professor's life is the epitome of the inner-directed existence. It is a tour through the intellectual division of labor once associated with the utopian itself—a data miner in the morning, a philosopher in the afternoon. Taking the same credit, sharing the same occupation, the adjunct's flexibility is, by conventional measure, driven from without. A dip in demand in someone else's classroom can cancel access to one's own. Perpetually replaceable, forcibly interchangeable, instruction is separated off from knowledge production. The teacher at the front of the classroom models labor for others, ever at the ready to appear when called upon. A spirit without specialization, or at least without control over the conditions of expertise, it is the division of labor to which the contingent is mere adjunct.

The nightmare of the social factory is that there is no escaping the dull discipline of work. But contemporary knowledge making seems to have enfolded these two states of being. The perquisites of tenure notwithstanding, the good professor works around the clock, each email message rendering the world just a little smaller and closer to hand. No need to go into the office, work is wherever you happen to be, and the next grant, report, or book beckons to be written. The wearily casualized academic day laborer works just as hard at making work available. The next layoff around the corner, there was never an office to begin with. The "last good job in America," as Stanley Aronowitz so invitingly put it, starts to resemble the worst.[1] Work is everywhere, and no amount of productivity is sufficient to tame it. Professional self-management has difficulty extricating itself from pedestrian total management.

Were it not merely cynical, this dystopian collision of privilege and precarity would present a closed circle of solipsism, the solitary career track as all-absorbing or wholly exclusionary. The life of the mind is a drafty Platonic cave inhabited by research and teaching. While given in uneven measure, the shuttle between them avoids the third term by which mental labor suffuses a particular kind of institutional space. Omitted from consideration is the factor often most difficult for academics to embrace as equally constitutive of their existential condition—organization. The dreary emptiness of meetings, the vacuous iteration of memos, and the dull tempo of management render service as most commonly imagined a form of bondage to be avoided at all costs. While full-time faculty may sigh at the prospect of another meeting, adjuncts will take this absence as their only just compensation: "At least I don't have to go." In either case, administrative work may be expunged from faculty's self-concept, but it is not so easy to avoid. Disavowing it may allow faculty members to imagine their freedom from institutional demands but does little to shape the demands they need actually attend to.

Managerialism leads a double life at the university. What is derisively referred to as "the administration" seems to amass (or acquiesce to) greater powers by the day. At the same time, more toil is expended by faculty doing the work of running the place. By formal measure full-timers spend more than 12 percent of their time doing administrative tasks as compared to 2 percent for part-timers.[2] At an average for all full-time faculty of 53.3 hours, this week continues to lengthen and is generally considerably longer than that of other workers in the United States (who, in turn, labor longer than their counterparts in Europe), and when the category of service is added to administration, more than one-fifth of this time is spent in administrative labor.[3] Yet, if administration is considered so repugnant, it also holds the fate of many. While the personality that thrives on pushing paper is notoriously the butt of jokes, the sociality of such work, its terms of mediation, cooperation, dispersion, are largely overlooked. If the faculty portraits sketched above are no more than caricature, and long hours are spent in administration, why is such work so typically dismissed and diminished? Is this a kind of compensatory democracy, the maintenance of an illusion that there are no bosses among those elected to the peerage? Does academia engender a culture where such authority is minimized by self-effacing ridicule that invites others to join in?

In the end, is it that no one wants to do administrative labor and it is left to the few or the leadership—or is it the case that there is ample expenditure throughout the layered institution but that it goes undervalued and unrecognized? If the former is the case, then greater exhortation is in order. Faculty should be browbeaten into accepting greater bureaucratic burdens on behalf of their own self-interest, or they should stir from their slumber and march on the presidential suites. But the very people issuing such a call might themselves sound entirely presidential, an Olympian voice dismissive of all but its own address. Arise from your misery and seize the day (or at least the furniture). On the other hand, the proletarianization of faculty and industrialization of knowledge could be said to have traded in autonomy for interdependence, which is most legible in administrative work, and spread management far and wide. Accordingly, a very different tack might be pursued to extricate some political insight from these circumstances. In light of these structural shifts, it would not be adequate to simply bemoan the absence of political will. While the allergies to organizational efforts are certainly understandable, such self-appraisals discount a central feature of academic labor as it is currently constituted. Alternately, the interdependence and associational principles manifest in our work are already present in the tasks we perform to organize our lives together. Rather than beginning with a deficit of personality, power, resources, historical opportunity, or institutional leverage, in which all is already lost and the ashes rise from the phoenix, making the most of what is to hand requires an analytic framework that begins with the immanence, and not eccentricity, of the organizational capacities faculty can call upon to make the difference it seeks.

When measured by survey, the long workweek gets aggregated into the conventional trinity of categories. Accordingly, teaching and research are free from creativity-depleting administrative tasks. When all the activities that comprise faculty work are considered, the administrative dimension of all labor cuts across everything that gets done. In an effort to ground the work expended against the narrow measure of classroom time, the American Association of University Professors devised a list of the various kinds of undertakings that make for polycentric faculty efforts. Each of these commitments—while identified as student, professional, or community centered—requires the labor of coordinating, processing, regulating, collaborating, incorporating, and reporting—in short, the range of engagements that infuse the administrative. The list of activities is as follows:

STUDENT-CENTERED WORK
- Updating a course to incorporate new research findings, or creating a new course.
- Helping students with subject matter in person, by e-mail, or by way of an electronic bulletin board.
- Developing a class Web site to further student involvement in a course, or advising students about how to use technology in the field.
- Working with colleagues to modify the curriculum to keep up with changes in the discipline.

- Advising students about their choice of major or mentoring graduate students.
- Coaching students who want to go beyond the required coursework in a class.
- Counseling students about personal problems, learning difficulties, or life choices.
- Writing letters of recommendation to help students enter graduate programs or secure jobs or internships.
- Keeping in touch with alumni to assist with employment searches or career changes.
- Reading student research papers, undergraduate honors theses, or doctoral dissertations.
- Directing or serving on a student's master's or doctoral committee.
- Establishing a foreign study program or supervising students overseas.
- Sponsoring a student literary journal or overseeing a drama club.

DISCIPLINARY- (OR PROFESSIONAL-) CENTERED WORK
- Serving on a committee interviewing candidates for new faculty positions.
- Evaluating a colleague's work for promotion or tenure.
- Participating in a departmental self-study.
- Reviewing potential library resources and advising on acquisitions.
- Writing a recommendation for a colleague for a fellowship or award.
- Serving on a university committee that writes policies for academic programs, student, scholarships, or financial aid.
- Applying for a grant for the department, or helping to raise money for the university.
- Participating in the activities of a professional association to advance standards and research in the field.
- Giving a scholarly presentation at a disciplinary society meeting.
- Editing a professional journal to help disseminate new knowledge in the field.
- Reviewing articles and books submitted to journals and publishers and advising about whether to publish them.

COMMUNITY-CENTERED WORK
- Giving a presentation to a business or school group, often at no expense to the group.
- Providing professional advice to local, state, or national government.
- Providing professional advice to associations, businesses, or community groups.
- Answering phone calls from citizens and offering professional expertise.

- Helping to keep the public informed about issues by talking to the media.
- Serving on the boards of local, state, or national group.[4]

It is not simply that each of these implies meetings and paperwork in their own right. The extensiveness of the list suggests an administrative competence in total time management, of days packed with a diversity of activities, and events scheduled far into the future—that speaks of a thoroughly planned and plannable existence. At the same time, as demonstrative as these lists are in suggesting the availability of every moment for further work, the activities center around the traditional domains of faculty governance rather than university matters, proprietary aspects of research, or the most instrumental features of revenue intake (admissions) and expense (hiring). Doubtless, such limits express in part the dilemma of maintaining the partition between labor and managerial employees for the purposes of collective bargaining.

The nonrecognition of administrative labor begins but does not end with the service designation. Service to the institution, the profession, and the world nestle within the ecclesiastical calling of ministering. Yet lumping so much into the category of service suffers the fate of being unwaged or undervalued and of sorting those worthy of attention (leaders, stars, public intellectuals) from those who form the audiences, give attention, and deliberate in unseen confidentiality. If research follows a calculus of merit, and teaching is rendered through an arithmetic of credit, service eludes easy valuation based upon a similar metric. Hours spent in meetings and on memos and deliberation are just as countable as those spent otherwise. But the weight of these events is what is at issue. Significance of service, weight of contribution, and salience of venue lend themselves to the kinds of measurement error that comprises the subjective dimension of all merit exercises. It would seem that the obstacles to making service count are political, not technical. Focusing on the value of administrative work raises directly the question of control and of how decisions are made, by what principles, and by which agents. One way of placing oneself in a hierarchy is on the basis of who one can say no to. But such positional advantage cannot account for the work that gets done.

Conservation of organizational authority resides in secreting the logic of the hierarchy while making transparent the fact of it. Making plain who is responsible for what effectively conceals what and who generates that responsibility in the first place. Administrative accountability tied to actual compensation would not vitiate hierarchy per se, but it requires a division of labor to disclose its logic of self-rationalization. No doubt this is part of what is at issue in the distinction between faculty and university governance. Faculty members may be uneasy at the thought of sitting in chambers with staff and senior administrators if this diminishes their hold on academic matters. But if command of the curriculum or departmental control is a narrowing slice of institutional life, it is the faculty's own place within the university that may be increasingly compromised if it is unable to engage the intersection of administrative domains and concerns. Certainly, if appointments that provide for continuous employment are shrinking for faculty, and technical staff is insinuated more directly in instruction, if hires are driven by opportunity targets and not staffing plans, it follows that realms of faculty discretion will be shrinking at a rapid rate. Pushing for fuller self-recognition of administrative labor suggests a rethinking of the basic contract that had established faculty autonomy a century ago, when faculty were free to teach and research while finance and planning were left to campus lords.

One straightforward response to unwaged service work would be to shift compensation formulas to reflect proportional commitment of effort. Make the time count. Where successful, such initiatives would introduce more equitable approaches for distribution of monetary reward, but such gains would likely come at the expense of recognition for teaching and research. Especially where what is at stake is an annual merit increment, the results are likely to be modest, indeed, especially if an axiom of salary reform is to contain the pool of funds available for faculty pay. Documentation of the minutiae of labor expenditure can invite a kind of auto-Taylorization, that trades individual tasks for a command of the context in which they are assigned or the end to which they are put. While undoubtedly deserved, waging administration more effectively will not necessarily inspire the kind of self-critical knowledge that would promote consideration of what is to be run, not simply done—of how work allocation shapes the profession, the institution, the industry, and the society that generate the various instances of knowledge production.

The chasm between individual effort expended on particular tasks and a strategic sense of what all this work is for cannot be filled simply by making market mechanisms for compensation more transparent. If faculty members themselves do not recognize the value of administrative work, they may accede to its value transfer, even if they do so at their own peril. One can certainly imagine a management scheme where faculty selects compensation criteria from a menu of choices and opts out of the administrative tasks. In some measure, this takes place when appointments are divided among research, teaching, and administrative positions. In each case, governance rights are minimized because the employment is limited by term rather than being continuous. Research and clinical professors, professors of practice or teaching, and administrative directors are just some of the titles that fit with these schemes. Recently minted PhDs may find themselves with initial appointments not on a tenure track but as assistant directors of centers, or assistant deans, even as a host of professional credentialing programs train their students for these kinds of positions. Administrative labor might be less mystifying than collegiality as a basis for dismissal in those cases where service is deemed inadequate. But even a clear calculus for weighing this work would still add to the burden of expectation for continued employment.

One term that has come to stand for the entire reach of knowledge making as a critical capacity is "general intellect." In the words of the Italian political theorist Paolo Virno, "The 'general intellect' includes formal and informal knowledge, imagination, ethical tendencies, mentalities and 'language games.'" Virno cautions:

> The peculiar public character of the intellect indirectly manifests itself in the state through the hypertrophic growth of the administrative apparatus. The heart of the state is no longer the political parliamentary system but the administration. The latter represents an authoritarian concretion of the general intellect, the point of fusion between knowledge and command and the reversed image of social cooperation. This indicates a new threshold, beyond the long debated growing relevance of bureaucracy in the 'political body' and the priority given to decrees over laws. We are no longer confronted with well-known processes of rationalisation of the state; on the contrary, we now need to oppose the accomplished statalisation of the intellect.

Rendering knowledge into a formal scheme of production not only spreads administration but also engenders labor relations that, because they come already mediated through language and culture, cannot be contained by an apportionment within the division of labor: "The labouring action of the general intellect presupposes the common participation to the 'life of the mind,' the preliminary sharing of generic communicative and cognitive skills. The sharing of the 'general intellect' becomes the actual foundation of all praxis."[5]

This separation of colonizing administration and freely shared intellect has animated autonomist politics that may occupy institutional sites without being caught up in their command and control structures. For those whose lives have been made precarious by institutions, those denied institutional access, or those apportioned to institutional waste there may seem few other options than pursuing this line of flight. Within the university, the barricade between continuous and contingent positions might itself be challenged and the intelligence of administrative competency divined. Hence, another strategy that engaged faculty members, who also reside in those structures, may explore is how this fundamental sharing, or common participation, can also be applied within the administrative operations they find themselves within. For a general intellect to infuse institutional aims, more would need to be at stake than mere instrumentalization, even if fair measure of such labor is long overdue. The crucial shift lies in faculty seeing its capacity to run institutions as part of its expertise, as perhaps a more continuously expansive knowledge than shifting academic interests.

One irony of managerial competence is that within the university it is acquired but not taught, and in the professional field of management studies, it is continually taught but never finally acquired. Of course, educational management overlaps these realms, but for faculty at least, the process by which one sees oneself as able to assume greater organizational responsibility is voiced in terms of talent, personality, or will—individual attributes all—and not in the socializing processes of the learning environment. As already observed, management as an academic and practical field derives its productivity from its implication in lifelong learning. Best practices—the model derived from business innovation—expire after a year and must be reinvented. Innovators don't survive their innovations. Shareholder value runs the boss out of town to reenact the show in a different setting. Yet professional management knowledge is the ultimate version of preaching to the choir, while faculty self-governance would appear thoroughly unmoved by the interest in its own techniques. Certainly, there is the cadre of faculty members who are extremely adept and willing to step into governance roles. They are at times portrayed as promulgating a kind of "free rider problem" said to bedevil grassroots social movements more broadly.[6] Some pay with their voluntary service to the cause while others receive the benefits without making any contribution of their own.

Such explanations suffer the tautology of their own methodological individualism. The rationality of self-interest effaces the sociality that orients people to a cause in the first place. This is a deep fable of economic thought, the claim that pursuit of self-interest delivers social benefit, which Duncan Foley has cunningly labeled "Adam's Fallacy" (after Adam Smith). "The moral fallacy of Smith's position is that it urges us to accept direct and concrete evil in order that indirect and abstract good may come of it. The logical fallacy is that neither Smith nor any of his successors has been able to demonstrate rigorously and robustly how private selfishness turns into public altruism. The psychological failing of Smith's rationalization is that it requires a strategy of wholesale denial of the real consequences of capitalist development, particularly the systematic imposition of costs on those least able to bear them, and the implacable reproduction of inequities that divide people from one another in society."[7]

But if the limits to self-interest come fast and furious, the more vexing puzzle is the reverse—namely, how social benefits are recalibrated as self-interest. Beginning with the pervasive labors of administration is one step toward understanding how organization is accomplished and not simply who receives credit for its imputed gains. While formal innovation, identification with new programs, goals met on capital campaigns, expanded profiles, rankings, or other accouterment of reputation are the metric of designated leadership, organizational vitality is clocked to a different metronome, one with a more abiding temporality. For faculty, thinking the sociality of their own administrative capacity entails a different sidewise glance at staff work, at those outside the institution, as well as a different vertical gaze at how they make the place run. This is not to assume singular credit, as in the nostrum that faculty is the engine of the university but more to consider how we might have the run of the place if we can see how we move laterally to make explicit and available the linkages we devise in the expanded field of educational flows.

Gerald Raunig has advanced the term "transversality" to move beyond the twin traps of fixed hierarchy and the horizontal compulsory communication of networks. "Unlike centralist forms of organization *and* polycentric networks, transversal lines develop constellations that are *a-centric*, which do not move on the basis of predetermined strands and channels from one point to another, but right through points in new directions. In other words, transversals are not at all intended to be connections between multiple centers or points, but rather lines that do not necessarily even cross, lines of flight, ruptures, which continuously elude the systems of points and their coordinates."[8] That Raunig's figure of the transversal allows a more expansive sense of the spaces opened up within an organizational field need not compromise the tactical sense of how to work the traps of horizontal and vertical architectures. The trick would lie in how one shuttles between the parameters of decision and the critical faculties for making them. This might allow a revaluing of work within the institutional setting. Imagining the sociality of leadership entails a broader conception of how organization gets accomplished in the name of some ideal and also how that corporate figure might be embodied differently.

In organizational terms, we might consider a distinction between the virtual or imagined and the actual. Every action that places us somewhere, inscribes local knowledge, and accrues experience to a concrete particular also circulates elsewhere, has an impact, joins an interest, and ripples through some medium. This is frequently described as knowledge's immateriality, but it could just as easily refer to its mode of embodiment, how knowing something is activated by its travel somewhere else. Teaching is based upon this confidence. So is writing. So might our organizational efforts be conceived as such. Jürgen Habermas modeled his communication ethos on the exchange of rationally grounded viewpoints that might be encountered in a faculty meeting, where he saw polite turn taking providing a formal grounds for dialogue.[9] We might just as effectively inquire into the remainders of disagreement, the spillage of ideas unleashed but deferred, the consequential application of listening—all of which are constitutive of administrative labor. This work of judgment is not simply given by station or rank but is exercised through active facilitation. Turns may be taken among discrete voices, but they do not necessarily produce their own finding without a particular way to work the room, to parse what is productive, to amalgamate insights and activate interest.

The preparation of materials, the assemblage of decisions taken prior, the follow-through of connection to other offices or sites, are all examples of the work that goes into the conduct of the meeting undertaken in the name of administration. The voice that speaks for this work does incorporate all that other activity that has taken place and must silence its own opinion, perspective, or singularity if the ensemble is to be given space to roam. Holding forth would in this sense be the opposite of holding a meeting. Applied listening, what might be considered activated management, trolls for moments in conversation where something can be made of what is said, where intervention is suggested, where possibility might be identified. This is as much an identification of insight as of method, for example—a discussion of teaching in a faculty meeting that provides a form of evaluation in the middle of the term that is different from the one at the end, allowing students to see the change in course. Or the discussion of the hermeneutics of a personal statement in the promotion docket that articulates how diverse interests in professional work bear upon what one was hired to do. Collecting these mundane means is also an administrative task, one that shares authorship and renews itself in the kind of work that is subsequently given institutional value.

The learning that underwrites academic work at once occupies the position in the institution from which knowledge accrues. This learning also radiates through a larger arena that inscribes a kind of work in conversation across various sites. This doubling between site specificity and the arena in which an organizational logic moves is what I mean here by a register. An organizational register invokes circuits of affiliation, scope of activity, and impact, rather than a specific form or grouping. It references the potential through which organizational energies move and the dilemmas through which activists' efforts can become stymied. Rather than being prescriptive, mutually exclusive, or mandatory, organizational registers allow notice of the immanent logic of administrative labor, of the paths such work travels through, and of the implications for what it can connect, build, and render durable. If applied listening imagines the disposition of the administrator who is critically alive to the differences that might be made, the organizational register pertains to the circuits within which that work moves and through which it accrues value. Immanence must be acted upon; organization needs to be registered.

While much writing is now done that would consider this labor-in-motion as a network, here I want to reserve (and hopefully revive) a more conventional and grounded organizational vocabulary. My aim is to specify some of the political implications of the differences in the virtual worlds we weave through administrative endeavors. The active force of creativity, the openness of categories, and the indeterminacy of outcome that are part of the political itinerary of current network approaches developed in counterpoint to institutional fixities can fruitfully be applied back to the organizational architecture we presently inhabit. The imagery of networks has been deployed to maintain an expansiveness against the closure associated with bureaucratic organization and to redirect knowledge production from proprietary to communal considerations.[10]

The typifying personality of administrative leadership, what James Duderstadt (in the discussion in Chapter 5) called the capacity to engage in deciding upon and allocating resources for an "essential singularity," looks like an overbearing attention to the exceptional case as a substitute for the comprehensive view by which institutional interests might be ascertained. This focus on singularity is the inverse of the appellate function, in which presidential review culminates in a sequential decision process from the grassroots. In contrast, singularity grounds the personification of the leader in the other. It lends the sense of supreme decision in the moment to a position that cannot always reconcile the *longue durée* of institutional direction with the appreciative engagement that would inspire ongoing expenditure of effort. While the effect may be the charisma of which Max Weber spoke, this phenomenology of decision descales the massive setting into an availability to affirm agency at the top in the form of special projects or initiatives.[11]

Such moments disclose the value in the hierarchy to the inhabitation of a decision conventionally resolved at a lower level to the core of work by which executive deliberation takes place. The leader reaches into the loam of mundane activity, connects to the base, and shows how work gets done. This display can be public, but it can also be confined to the inner circles, where leaders generate and maintain their self-concept. Appropriation of work takes place by a kind of role switching, in which a sensory touch is achieved from what otherwise seems an inaccessible place. Broken down thus, the quotidian aspects of administration are fed into their cognate positions of higher authority. Such exercise of decision does not leave a residue of policy, of formalization as rule, but rather it points to the self-production of a subjectivity where protocol would seem to render it lost.

While it is common to catalog these interventions as whimsies of office, egocentricity, or ungainly distractions, they also speak to the inner life of decision, the intimacy with difference making that momentarily suspends scale and organizational position. This insight can also be applied to the daily administration machinations undertaken by faculty and staff, after all, this is the scene where the singularity is given its ongoing expression. What is a state of exception for the leader is the unexceptional capacity for those manufacturing the work of institutional matter. While this phenomenological inversion allows us to see how administration operates throughout, it is not undifferentiated. My interest here is to name the organizational registers historically in terms of what is structurally immanent. Thus, the process of social transformation comes to reflect and make legible some of the inert formations and resources that we can continue to draw upon.

Having identified the immanence of labor's managerialism, I want to move now to trace the simultaneity of this work through three primary organizational registers that have given shape to academic and other forms of labor in the past century—the professional association, the industrial union, and the political party. Each can be read as supposing a certain kind of occupational formation or subject, an interdisciplinary formation, a social formation, and an organizational formation. This series of terms is meant to provide a basis of differentiating the stakes of various practical commitments faculty members engage as well as offering a way to recognize the overlain and multivalent consequences of our administrative labors. Faculty has built up a range of administrative competencies that travel through these diverse organizational registers. The undervaluation of this work is matched by its powers of association to carry us through and beyond the university.

PROFESSIONAL ASSOCIATION

As a kind of guild, the professional association or learned society predates the formation of modern academic disciplines. The Scholarly Societies Project (www.scholarly-societies.org), based at the University of Waterloo in Ontario, Canada, is a digital archive that tracks more than four thousand learned bodies worldwide. The oldest it lists (dating to 1323) is the Compagnie du Gai Savoir originally founded by a group of Toulouse patrons of poetry. While not exhaustive, the list serves to indicate the range of endeavors that have undergone professional self-organization. The 614 listed associations for the United States cover a range of occupations and vocations, like the Air Conditioning Contractors of America (1914) and the American Antiquarian Society (1812), not all of which center themselves inside the university, and some of which reflect regional Republican affinity, such as the Virginia Historical Society (1831). But the Modern Language Association (1883), American Mathematical Society (1888), American Psychological Association (1892), American Anthropological Association (1902), American Political Science Association (1903), and College Art Association (1911) correspond to disciplinary foundation. The continued establishment of such entities for the subsequent hundred years is one indicator of the development in the professional division of labor whereby specialties gain credentialing autonomy (e.g., Urgent Care Association of America, 2004) or protocols congeal around emergent forms of professional practice (e.g., U.S. Distance Learning Association, 1987). And the work of these associations has itself become professionalized. The American Society of Association Executives (1920) supports its 22,000 member executives with advice on management and strategic planning for expansion of individual groups.[12]

Maintenance of this private self-interest would seem to impose a highly conservative charge on professional associations to maintain the perquisites of their station that would make them unlikely sites of effective change. Lennard Davis searingly referred to the species as a kind of "compulsory bureaucracy" and Stephen Watt underscores the continuities with the medieval "gentleman's club" and the sorting and exclusionary functions of extant societies.[13]

And yet, driven by the practical loss of autonomy broadly experienced by the professions and spearheaded by critiques of precisely this sort, new openings are now detectable among professional associations that place pressure on these conventional functions. Among professional fields themselves, the rubric of social responsibility has been both a rearguard action to protect credibility and a platform from which more comprehensive critique and renewal becomes possible. The professional society promises to police its field by applying expertise to the higher calling of public good. But socially responsible proposals often are more explicit regarding the particular technical interest they are beholden to than what they articulate about the kind of sociality they would want to enhance.

The most notorious case here is the field of accounting, which lost much of itself to its intimacy with its business client. Tony Tinker documents the conversion of the technical aspects of financial regulation that accountancy is to perform for a business-services model along the lines of professional education. As a run-up to the collapse of Arthur Andersen as the company moved (literally) inside the corrupt energy conglomerate Enron, Tinker notes "the elite firms begin hiring at the prestige graduate schools of accountancy and MBA programs, where three course credits of accounting are not uncommon. This flash exposure to auditing and accounting made sense to those who had no intention of auditing for the long-term, but who were destined for bigger killings in consulting." He concludes, "Far from providing a sanctuary, professional schools of accountancy have, in recent years, become the vehicles for furthering the accumulation pursuits of accounting firms and their corporate clients. This, arguably, has helped trigger a rolling depression that now threatens the livelihood of millions who are bound together in a global economy. Intensifying the commodification of business education with the professional school model will only create more instabilities."[14] Several years later, when unaccountable mathematical models did indeed help foment a much greater instability, calls for more comprehensive revisioning of the training curriculum could again be heard.[15]

While it is easy to dwell on the normative reproduction functions among these associations (what might be termed their will to replication), it is also possible to troll for the evidence of their openings to these more critical dispositions. The most basic shift that academic professions face is the limits to their ability to inculcate career goals that replicate professorial roles, which for many, have lost their allure. One large study of graduate students takes note of the shifting career expectations that take place in the course of their training. At the start of their PhD programs, 45 percent of men and 39 percent of women report a desire to become a professor with a research emphasis. Ultimately, those figures decline to 36 percent and 27 percent, respectively, with careers outside of academia garnering the greatest gains in interest (42 percent for men and 41 percent for women). The gender divide is significant as increasing numbers of women in graduate programs view an academic fast track as inhospitable to other life priorities. But the gap remains between what professionals expect of their charges and what emergent professionals learn of their horizons of expectation.[16] Socialization in this regard is as much a sorting machine as one of professional replication. In either case, the future glance bounces back as a reflection of where one will work, a departure from the promise that the life of the mind is its own reward for which material conditions need not be considered.

If the professional turn in the university is a move toward the instrumentalities of labor, what kinds of self-organization are springing from the existing quarters? The student radicals who made these critiques of professional false promises are themselves transferring their organizational savvy to these sites. While it would be naive to think that the internal conservatism upon which professionalization was grounded will suddenly disappear, the critique of privilege sounded most vociferously on the right speaks to a secular change in the strategies of socialization that a new crop of academic organic intellectuals and activists are coming to terms with. With the loss of autonomy has come the flood of the state and the market, of expectations of accountability voiced as both political and economic. The professional turn logically passes through its own means of association, pushes labor to the forefront of the very heart of its disavowal as a place of voluntary, if exclusionary, privilege. The laboring and epistemological critiques are nestled together in the professional association as the cognate to the fluorescence of managerialism within the university.

This is one more indicator that while skepticism toward experts marks public discourse, professionalization continues apace. Yet the formative divide between quality control or veracity in practice and advancement of self-interest has clearly transformed the work of professional associations, especially in the university. One can make a distinction between learned societies that have undertaken certification and post-professional training programs (common in the highly specialized medical societies) and academic associations that can no longer treat claims of control over epistemological domains as sufficient to maintain professional standing. We are now seeing a complication of the rift between professional public and private interest, which in Habermas's well-known account delineated the common values of advancing knowledge to serve a community (the life world) and the technical norms by which professions value their own advancement. The legitimation crisis that the disciplines face issues from the inability to maintain and apply technical reason as a sufficient insulation from instrumentalities of the life world.[17] Contrary to Habermas's understanding that the professional's own technical instrumentality would control community, the reverse is in evidence. Now, demands for value-added knowledge; accountability; relevance; jargon-free, transparent language; and the like appear as public demands that compromise professional sovereignty.

If loss of sovereignty is a condition of professional expansion, we still walk the grounds of those earlier landscapes even as the significance of doing so has changed. For the wave of professional associations established in the late nineteenth and early twentieth centuries, occupational specialization was supported institutionally by departmentalization. The self-governing departments rendered the internal geography of the university into the equivalent of well-bound nation-states, but the legitimation for autonomous rule (over curriculum and career advancement) came from a scale of measure outside the individual institution. This was provided by the professional association, which was not simply national in scope but permitted the measure of the nation to be taken up by faculty members whose allegiance was derived by their standing in the field first and secondarily to the institution. The result was a sequestering of knowledge politics from labor economics, of the power to judge work that was disconnected from the capacity to give that same work value, something that only employment could provide.

If the conceit of tenure was that a worthy professor was able to move freely in the national space (switch from institution to institution to confer status on a department), only the local site (the existence of a tenured appointment) could provide the means to do so. While tenure is now derided as an immobility of labor that is effectively unmanageable, its initial marking was the opposite—that of a small coterie who could teach anywhere and by so doing exemplify the national reach of what were newly invented disciplinary domains. The naturalization of the academic hierarchy mimicked that of the nation itself. Both would propose fair access to equal merit as grounds for advancement. The privileges conferred through a particular legislation of rights appeared as a matter of locational entitlement or institutional address. Professional citizenship, like its national cognate, masked its own internal hierarchies.

Recall from the discussion in Chapter 4 that the AAUP (the American Association of University Professors) itself incorporated this double movement into its own foundation. Sociology, anthropology, and political science broke off from economics in a self-interested disciplinary specialization that forged the first of these various departments at the likes of Johns Hopkins, Columbia, and Chicago. Simultaneously, the AAUP brokered a reamalgamation of these same constituencies that could subsequently make a claim for national representation of university faculty across all fields. The AAUP's proximate occasion was the dismissal of economics professors, but its own creation was the reintegration of the domains that had once belonged to this field. Economics would instantiate this split between polity and economy, between subjective and ideological values. The conviction that the truest expressions of the individual lie with markets and not society would come to provide cover for policy decisions and inspire claims toward a scientific account of the operations of a discrete object—namely, the economy. Negotiating these tensions relied upon invocation of nations themselves that would look like academic departments, amenable to the rule of reason, governable by technical logics, professionally interested and oriented toward quantifiable measures of rank (in the case of national progress, the measure would be GDP growth). Comparative advantage, development, and globalization would permit the nation to be thought of as a politically autonomous universal, despite the impossibility during any of those moments of global reign that nations would in actuality encounter each other on equal terms.

At the same time, as the financial meltdowns of the past twenty years have revealed, the interdependence and shared volatility of national markets speak to the undoing of even the most privileged nation's abilities to master its domains. As with the often-confounded discussion of national states in the light of globalization, the erosion of boundaries does not make the administrative operations of regulation disappear, and we have certainly not seen the elimination of departments and disciplines as managerial units. But it is the alignment of population with a certain logic of production that has been most dramatically displaced. Nations have clearly not gone away, but national interest as a means of rallying populations to the likes of war and sacrifice, or of claiming that free trade policies are of general benefit, or even of assuming that tax reductions provide comprehensive economic stimulus become tough sells even if they were initially promulgated as the common sense of the times. Professional associations of all stripes have had to confront the job crisis that they were designed to defer by substitution with meritocractic parceling of their own knowledge economies. The protocols for deciding what is best—the work of peer review has certainly not gone away even if it now no longer delivers the career track it once promised. The work of peerage that the professional association corroborates proceeds undiminished even as the practical capacity for controlling the demographics of the professoriate continues to decline. But as this work proliferates, it also opens up to other prospects of rule, other registers of organizational capacity where the fates of professional and other kinds of labor are indeed being decided.

The growth of administrative professional work is meeting with a more expansive sense of the scope and activities of professional associations. The MLA (Modern Language Association) was dramatically shaken by the organization of graduate students in its midst during the nineties. Not only did this impact the approach to professional socialization; it also began to reorient the discipline's own grammar in a way that staged a fundamental interdisciplinary opening of the sort discussed in Chapter 6. As a distinct field, writing instruction or composition has entwined pedagogical professionalization with a model of contingent labor subject to active managerial oversight. The activist response has called for collective action and a refusal to conflate the critical functions of teaching with bureaucratic operations, a move that Donna Strickland describes as a managerial unconscious:

Composition professionals committed to equity and social justice must find ways to infuse administrative work with political meaning and action. Rather than simply taking administrative work as a pragmatic given, which often leads to taking business practices as models, composition specialists are in a unique position to expose the political and economic interests of such models as they reach the academy and to look to models outside of business. Situated at the border between traditional faculty and managerial professionals, composition specialists can use their intellectual function as faculty to critique practices and their managerial function to enact new ones.[18]

The implications of Strickland's insights are to make explicit the intersections between professional specialization and administrative labor in organizing strategies that expand beyond traditional affiliations.

The AAUP itself has undergone a significant modulation under increasingly ambitious leadership to think across the various organizational registers considered here. Given the historic role of the Association, these changes deserve a closer look, as they suggest ways in which organizational hybridity is becoming a feature of existing professional bodies. The leadership changes are also significant for the way they position the organization at the intersection of academic labor and knowledge capital. Cary Nelson, elected AAUP president in 2006, is a faculty veteran of the graduate student struggles within the MLA and, in addition to his extensive work as author and editor on *Anthology of Modern American Poetry* and senior appointment as Jubilee Professor of Liberal Arts and Science at the University of Illinois, Champaign-Urbana, has one of the most prominent and sustained scholarly records theorizing academic activism (in books such as *No University Is an Island*, 2010; *Manifesto of a Tenured Radical*, 1997; *Academic Keywords: A Devil's Dictionary for Higher Education*, 1999; and *Office Hours: Activism and Change in the Academy*, 2004, the last two coauthored with Stephen Watt).[19]

Gary Rhoades, named general secretary in 2008, was himself former president of the Association for the Study of Higher Education. He trained as a sociologist and has written on faculty unionization and on the turn to the market in higher education *(Managed Professionals: Unionized Faculty and Restructuring Academic Labor*, and with Sheila Slaughter, *Academic Capitalism and the New Economy)*. Nelson and Rhoades are, in effect, organic intellectuals who came out of the recent turn in faculty activism, one that is stalwart regarding the traditional issues of shared governance, academic freedom, and tenure but that is expansive in its critical regard of professional socialization and university privatization. Their willingness to shift from highly prominent and productive research positions to leadership roles undercuts the notion of administrative types who are outside the academic experience or of bureaucratic work being undertheorized by those who undertake it.

The AAUP now leverages its legitimating issues of governance, tenure, and academic freedom to a more expansive research and policy agenda that performs certain operations in the register of industrial union and party. It is a key producer of knowledge in the academic profession, tracking trends in faculty appointments, salaries, campus policies, gender and minority diversity, research, grading and teaching evaluation, international solidarity, legislative agendas, and public concerns and controversies, as well as providing through publications, such as its journal *Academe*, ongoing critical analysis of these various issues. It continues to draw upon its claims to expert knowledge of the university through sanction-producing investigations that exercise influence over how campus matters are conceived and controversies resolved. This was the case for its 1915 statement on tenure and its 1940 brief linking academic freedom to tenure, which arose in the context of departmentalization and the academic entrepreneurialism that would fuel the government-university knowledge compact during which time AAUP membership itself peaked. Without the control over credentialing or positions that characterize the strongest guilds, like the American Medical Association, the AAUP has exercised various kinds of moral and intellectual suasion to shape specific institutional behavior. Illustrative here is its list of censured institutions, the very existence of which has assisted in local conflict resolution in the highly reputation-sensitive environment of higher education administration.[20]

The AAUP not only provides knowledge of professional organizations but also serves as an agent in collective bargaining on some seventy campuses—something it began to undertake in 1972 after much internal discussion and changes in labor law during the sixties and seventies led to rapid unionization across many campuses, especially in the Northeast. As a collective bargaining agent, the AAUP is smaller than many other faculty unions, such as the National Education Association (which represents more than 200,000 employees in higher education—not just faculty, but support staff and other professionals), the United Automobile Workers (which has organized among adjuncts as well as graduate and postgraduate employees at public and private universities, with 16,000 teaching assistants among its bargaining units), and the American Federation of Teachers (which represents some 160,000 employees in higher education).[21] Yet the AAUP engages its various roles to effect a hybridization of theory and practice that is significant in the way it expands the organizational reach of the professional association. The environment for self-organization is ultimately shaped by the cultural conceptions of faculty as framed in the public sphere, the legislative mechanisms at various levels of government, and various funding and entitlement programs.

The AAUP seeks to intervene on all these fronts. It developed a response to David Horowitz's Academic Bill of Rights, exposing it as an effort to use a language of internal imbalance on campus to shift the assignment of positions to state legislatures that could then employ their own ideological criteria for program support. It also crafted approaches and organized lobbying on behalf of specific laws, in an effort to counter state conceptions of faculty and higher education as undeserving of public support. It maintains four principles that cut across specific initiatives, access (financial aid), quality (faculty-centered evaluation), diversity (of students, faculty and institutions), and openness (internationally in terms of students and languages of instruction). In conventional terms, the AAUP operates as an interest group among others in the syntax of pluralistic pressuring among divergent constituencies. But given its own modest presence among all of the various devices of control over higher education, the professional association is compelled to make the most of its own state effects, whether these pertain to educational policy or more general claims about the nature of education in the national imaginary.

The turnover in leadership corresponds to a larger change in the conditions of professional self-organization that must increasingly look to affiliations with other laborers on campus and off. The industrialization of knowledge confronts the old clubs and networks with a different strategic ambit. Professors are not being left alone in their ivory towers. Teaching is not merely at the discretion of experts. Knowledge on the market is a private good subject to increasing public scrutiny. That attention is focused on an often ungovernable mix between consumerist demands for deliverable quality and affirmation of values claimed as expressions of civic virtue. This is an abiding antinomy of privatization. Ultimately, commerce is about capturing revenue by making private proprietary claims on publicly and socially constituted values. Doubtless this has occurred in higher education as elsewhere, especially in the knowledge sector. The organizational implications for the once self-governing professions are only now becoming legible.

INDUSTRIAL ORGANIZATION

In conventional terms, unions are the formal expressions of labor in industrial organization. Until 2007, when the ranks of the newly unionized reversed course and outstripped membership losses, unionization rates have been in decline over the prior twenty years, from slightly more than one in five workers to one in eight.[22] Collective bargaining is now highly concentrated in the public sector where nearly 40 percent of employees are represented by unions as opposed to just slightly more than 8 percent for private industry. Interestingly, professional and related occupations have a higher rate of union membership at 18.2 percent than do workers in mining (9.3 percent), construction (13.9 percent), or manufacturing (11.3 percent). The professions' unionization is anchored by education (37.2 percent), followed by community and social services occupations (14.9 percent) and healthcare (13.5 percent). Arts, design, entertainment, sports and media are lower (7.8 percent), as are legal occupations (5.5 percent). Within the information sector, telecommunications union rates are highest, with nearly one in five members.[23] While these numbers help decouple unions from narrow conceptions of industrial manufacturing, and insinuate them in the largest occupational category, they do not speak to the national historical changes to industrial organization itself.

The shift from craft to industrial unions, from single occupation to sectoral control reflected the advent of large industrial conglomerates. The historic compromise between big business and national unions that was brokered by the government formed the foundation of the post–World War II social compact that extended the material entailments of the American Dream well beyond unionized shops.[24] The promise of professionalization was yet more ambitious; namely, knowledge gained through merit-based advancement would lead self and society toward meaningful, self-fulfilling labor and leisure. The use of knowledge to decide one's fate would also be underwritten by a social compact, this one taking the form of financial policies that placed more consumer credit, risk management, and portfolio assessment in the hands of the half of the population that would benefit from these initiatives, the investors. An investor is the consummate information processor, the one whose claims to expertise over the economy helped organize a constituency for the industrialization of financial services (which, at 8.8 million for finance, insurance and real estate is larger than the 3.5 million employed in educational services).[25] The point is that professionalization is not simply an occupational shift but has far-reaching impact on culture, policy, and economy—and it influences the *ways* in which these processes are organized in society. Finance and education, culture, management, and information are the touchstones of the knowledge economy. The industrialization of these fields from their craft origins has organizational implications that must now be dissected.

Historically, autonomy has been both the resource and the limit of professional associations. Self-regulation typically leaves alone the contractual obligations that can compel employers to act. But what has been described here as the professional turn reflects the industrialization of these academic occupations. The move away from liberal arts toward professional degrees among students over the past forty years corresponds to the shift from tenured to contingent part-time and then full-time positions, and the incorporation of higher education into the broader field of the knowledge industries. The growth in the number of students and the expansion of continuing education fits the rising tide of professional workers. The free trade frameworks that go by the name of globalization expand forms of commerce to intellectual and cultural property, biotechnological emulations of life, networked information technologies, and internationally produced and distributed films, music, and games. The millions employed in these various productive activities form the heart of what needs to be considered today's industrial economy.

As with prior industrializations, of agrarian small-holding into textiles, cottage manufacture into industrial combines, and scaled networks of transit, energy, and materials into national monopolies, laboring populations are forged out of both a loss or enclosure of prior access to their productive base and a newly forced interdependence or socialization.[26] The migrant tutors and scholars from Plato to Erasmus may see their precarity echoed in today's adjunct but the enclosure of that knowledge commons is associated by profession and disciplinary order not available to earlier itinerant minds. This is not to discount the flight from enclosure, the ongoing production of inventive marginality and the vast surplus populations that have been an ongoing feature of what modernization leaves behind.[27] Yet, even this mass of dissidence and alternative is interconnected informationally and institutionally in ways previously unimaginable. Further, the traffic in knowledge is not simply an excursion in learning, but moves what can now be said to constitute industrialization as such.

Contrary to the promises of postindustrial society to move beyond mass aggregates of expropriated labor the flexibility associated with knowledge-work aims to extend factory discipline wherever informational products are sold. But industrial orders yield more than greater discipline and docility, the compression of labor makes for its own excess, scales of creativity, technical competencies that are only partially absorbed and admired in work. The lived experience of interdependence advances its own palette of cultural expressions—minstrelsy and cinema, baseball and dance hall—as well as a menu of organizational responses. These last often come deferred or emerge as industrializing furnaces choke on their own violence. Such responses are evident in the craft-based Knights of Labor and the anarchist-inspired International Workers of the World, or Wobblies, at the turn of the nineteenth century, as well as in the Congress of Industrial Organizations and the mass movements of the United Front of the thirties. How do we begin to detect the equivalent organizational responses in the proletarianization of professional labor and the industrialization of knowledge in which higher education finds itself today?

Just as the efficacy and form of the professional association continues to morph in our midst, that of the industrial union (whose heyday is rooted in the decades that clustered around the hegemonic ascent of the United States through the second world war), remains an uncompleted history. In terms of an historical formation, the most sensible point of reference to grasp this intersection between organization and the industrialization of knowledge making is in what Michael Denning called the cultural front, which is "the result of the encounter between a powerful democratic social movement—the Popular Front—and the modern cultural apparatuses of mass entertainment and education."[28] If the industrialization of culture forged a lineament of labor into a kind of spatial density or front, that formation seized the moment and crafted cultural expressions that articulated the experience of the day. These Denning treats as "two notions of the politics of art: 'cultural politics,' the politics of allegiances and affiliations, and 'aesthetic ideologies,' the politics of form. The first, cultural politics is at one level simply the politics of letterheads and petitions, the stances taken by artists and intellectuals, the pledges of allegiance and declamations of dissent. But it is also the politics of the cultural field itself, the history of the institutions and apparatuses in which artists and intellectuals work. For the kinds of political stances artists and intellectuals take depend upon their understanding of the ground on which they work."[29]

The creation of mass art, the varieties of political response, and the formation of an industrial proletariat from the cultural work of intellectuals and the new middle class, is understood in its day most perspicaciously by Marxists Antonio Gramsci and Lewis Corey. Denning juxtaposes their conceptions succinctly in the following passage: "One can say," he concludes, "that not only does the philosophy of praxis not exclude ethico-political history but that, indeed, in its most recent stage of development, it consists precisely in asserting the moment of hegemony as essential to its conception of the state and to the 'accrediting' of the cultural fact, of cultural activity, of a cultural front as necessary alongside the merely economic and political ones." Gramsci's sense of the importance of the cultural front in understanding social struggles has a remarkable echo in Corey's major work of 1934, *The Decline of American Capitalism*. "Every revolutionary class must wage war on the cultural front," Corey maintains. "The university, science, technology, and learning were in general manifestations of bourgeois development, under bourgeois control, waging the bourgeois cultural struggle against the feudal order. But now all these forces, in their dominant institutional forms, are opposed to the proletariat; its revolutionary culture, while it includes many concrete achievements, is necessarily and mainly potential, a culture of revolutionary criticism and ideological struggle, interpreting, clarifying, projecting, capable of becoming dominant only after the revolution."[30]

In this reckoning, the cultural front amalgamates a particular array of creative energies through which intellectuals undertake a critical formation, with a principal of lateral political affiliation as well as a kind industrial transformation. The Congress of Industrial Organizations is animated by the creative sensibilities of popular front modernism and by an expansive sense of participation in social movements. Denning wants to unseat the spatial and temporal singularity of the cultural front. He departs from the view that core ideas radiate from Communist Party leadership to members to fellow travelers—a fragile chain of influence whose reach and significance crested at one moment in the mid-thirties. In a way, he plays this big bang conception of radicalism in reverse and unpacks the antecedent and consequent reverberations that could account for the organizational strength even if the vehicle of these divergent waves could not sustain them for more than a few years.

Viewed strictly from within the trajectory of the professoriate, it is tempting to look at the history of proletarianization as one of lost organizational opportunity, assimilation of autonomy, and co-optation of radical critique. Hence, Clyde Barrow argues, "The corporate ideal as applied to the university was actually a class-political program designed to conquer ideological power. The program was directly and precisely linked to the emergence of modern corporations through the property connection established in the material means of mental production. In this respect, the emergence of American universities is best understood as a cultural component of the Industrial Revolution, related transformations of class structure, and the culmination of these upheavals in the social rationalization movements of the progressive era."[31] At issue is how to make legible what eludes conquest, and what continues to drive organizational prospects despite corporate consolidation and rationalization of more radical impulses through policy channels. This tragic narrative of organization forecloses imagination of what alternate routes, unabsorbable excesses, and radical critiques are generated through the internal contests over means and aims.

While Denning is writing about the CIO in the thirties and Barrow is focusing on the progressive era in the decades before, both have an eye toward the organizational consolidation and dispersion in the present. Within the knowledge sector, the mergers of firms (such as AOL Time-Warner, Disney, Bertelsmann, Viacom, News Corporation, and Vivendi Universal) and the integration of analog and digital (from film to music, publishing to telecommunications) has seen a cognate response among labor unions through what is termed convergence.[32] Vincent Mosco has studied this phenomenon among unions in North America, where, for example, the International Typographical Workers Union, the Newspaper Guild, and the National Association of Broadcast Employees and Technicians have consolidated with the Communications Workers of America (CWA). Mosco recognizes that such moves are taken by unions to be defensive in the face of declines in those kindred fields. "But significantly, they also see labour convergence as an attempt to take advantage of synergies brought about by growing convergence in the nature of their work. Since these unions represent workers who are increasingly involved in producing for a converging electronic information services arena, they see improved opportunities for organizing, for bargaining, and for advancing a political program including a communication policy that expands the public service principle. In essence, converging technologies and converging companies have led workers to come together across the knowledge industry."[33]

Convergence is organizational but also operates on the conception of what is to be organized. The Newspaper Guild within the CWA has begun to organize other word workers, such as court reporters and interpreters. It also reached out to the AAUP to organize a conference "dealing with intellectual workers, academic freedom, and freedom of the press. They noted that a 'profit-at-all-costs atmosphere . . . pervades campuses and newsrooms alike,' and must be resisted to protect the 'dignity, freedom and independence of our professions.'"[34] While a medium of labor or principle of its exercise may be a basis for affiliation, corporate consolidation can also have geographical effects. Ursula Huws has tracked the formation of what she terms the "cybertariat"—digital service workers who are part of the raced and gendered international division of knowledge labor. These largely contingent laborers populate workplaces such as call centers, which support any number of customer service departments. Huws notes an agreement jointly signed with Air Canada by the Canadian Auto Workers and sister unions in the United Kingdom and United States. The agreement covers these workers as well as a 1999 strike by call center employees at British Telecom and unionization drives in the Caribbean and Brazil. Together these actions brought attention to this dispersed yet focused segment of the industry.[35] There is, of course, no guarantee that the circumstances that lead unionists to explore convergence, mergers, or other forms of alliance will result in successful or sustainable organizations, as in the fracture in spring 2009 that followed efforts to affiliate hotel and food service workers and garment workers under the umbrella of Unite Here.[36] Organizational amalgamation from whatever source comes with its share of disruption to patterns of leadership, labor culture, workplace knowledge, communications strategies, and the like. When organization is labor's own, expectations of unity further complicate the challenges that are bound to ensue.

In higher education, the swell in faculty unionization during the seventies can be understood in the context of convergence. The growth of the multicampus conglomerate expanded the market but also led to a series of labor displacements, of PhD production that exceeded tenured appointments, labor reservoirs of part-time then full-time faculty. A new cohort of faculty that had experienced its own cultural front of campus activism in the sixties confronted the managerialism and corporatization of the university, and the conflicted culture on campus fueled unionization and led to the expectation among some observers that more is to come.[37] Another explanation for organizing stems from a kind of prestige gap stemming from a perceived weakness, a phenomenon that can be found in another expression of convergence—a collaborative effort between the AAUP and MLA that surveys various aspects of collective bargaining. "That is why academics who are confident that they can protect academic and professional standards through their individual bargaining power or who are confident in the effectiveness of shared governance in their particular institution are less likely to pursue collective bargaining than faculty members in troubled institutions. This pattern is consistent with the legislative history and purpose of the NLRA [National Labor Relations Act], which established legal protections for concerted action only by those employees who lacked the bargaining power sufficient to balance that of their employers."[38]

The logic of convergence, which relies on all manner of lateral affiliations among service and clerical workers, graduate student workers, part-time faculty, and undergraduates concerned with the campus as a nexus of social justice issues, such as No Sweat. At Yale, for example, the mobilization of graduate students was tied to the treatment of service workers during the nineties and led to coordinated actions over the following decade. Individual faculty commonly work in conjunction with knowledge sector unions, and the links between faculty and museum workers was a feature of UAW organizing. In light of these interconnections, some of these hierarchies of privilege are themselves beginning to shake under the weight of the larger displacement of privilege in higher education. Stanley Aronowitz, stalwart activist in the labor insurgency of his own union, the PSC/CUNY (Professional Staff Congress at the City University of New York), has been a force in new social movements and a close student of the myriad transformations of society. Aronowitz proposes that unions must deliver gains to their membership, but they also must be the site for posing greater ambitions and alternatives for their own profession and beyond:

> For academic unions there can be no question of reversing the tendency toward the de facto end of mass public higher education through collective bargaining. Having successfully shown that the professoriat in some academic precincts can act like traditional trade unionists without seriously damaging their academic integrity or standing, the unions are now faced with the awesome task of becoming institutions of alternative as well as resistance. In short, they are challenged to accept responsibility for the academic system rather than remaining representatives of specific interests of faculty and staff within its technocratically defined boundaries. The challenge is to become agents of a new educational imagination—that is, to join with others in counterplanning that aims *both* to retain mass higher education as a *right* and to suggest what education is in the new, postregulation, postwork era.[39]

The two posts in question refer respectively to the erosion of higher education as a self-contained realm within the knowledge sector and the demise of the academic career as an autonomous occupational sphere. The challenge here is to reimagine what education is for, if it can no longer be for itself, and what is to be done with knowledge labor if it is no longer contained and sustained as a self-regulating career. Clearly, formal organization draws upon the principles of association and interdependence generated in the course of class formation and decomposition. The integrated mass of the industrial proletariat yields to the derivative intersections of the professional-managerial class. Convergence needs to be imagined, therefore, as a feature of both the professions and the knowledge industries. It needs to be considered alongside the current trajectories of expanded higher education—continuing education, lifelong learning, and management itself. More than a redistribution from primary intake of fees to advanced research or other niche, rank, and prestige-generating functions, strategic planning might begin to imagine how knowledge making circulates as a value, what to do with this enormous social capacity, and how its means might be reconciled with particular productive ends.

Clearly, this was the alignment of industrial policy and consumer credit promised by Fordism and purchased by mass exclusion, along racial and gendered lines, from the professional ranks. The claim that everyone is an entrepreneur in an ownership society is of a piece with the industrialization of the professions, for the enclosure of the professional's own domain in exchange for its universalization suggests the condition whereby labor has nothing to sell but its capacity to peddle ideas—but lacks meaningful means for disseminating them without the university/intellectual property/telecommunications complex. These are the conditions of casualization, contingency, and precarity that mark the sector. Such circumstances provide an ironic twist on craft conceptions of intellectual or artistic freedom, and also reference a thicket of outsourced, networked, commuting, and mediated project-based researchers, freelancers, artists, teachers, designers, organizers, service providers, and the like. Surely, this experience generates its own cultural front, a hive of gamers and video posters, activity-based associations and start-up NGOs, commons squatters, and neo–myth makers. The capacity to work is generally unmoored from the conditions of labor.

Where is the intersection of and for faculty in all this? Certainly, there are consultancies, moonlighting, volunteering, community work, and organizing that weave particular expertise with the industrial expression of the same. There is also teaching nontraditional students (increasingly traditional), credentialing, distance learning, and myriad other ways in which instruction opens beyond the normal channels. And there is the work between professional associations, with unions, and through neighborhood associations in which administrative faculty labor is articulated in various industrial circuits. These are existing features of faculty experience, the ones that augur other affiliations and organizational directions, the basis of the weft by which what is lost of professional self-interest poses a gain of what can be made of and with knowledge committed to the expansion of these social circuits, the pleasures of ongoing learning and the politics of divining what problems should receive creative attention, dissection, and application.

These matters of affiliation and intercalation present different vistas and logics of interdisciplinarity and various questions of how these diverse sources and ethics of knowledge can share a stage. Cocreation between varieties of expertise inside and outside the university is already evident in collaborative research models, community-based arts, and progressive regional development. The decomposition of the professional-managerial class trades autonomy for these various kinds of association, the terms of which have yet to be theorized but whose practices make evident an increasing palette of options for faculty and kindred knowledge makers. Consulting with unions outside the university would conventionally be considered service work. The organization of labor lies at the heart of what administration does. It is vital to recognize this kind of work as a capacity of faculty as well. How this work is valued, how this landscape of association is mapped, and how these entangled interests might find organizational expression are only beginning to become apparent, but their foundations are already extensively laid in the groundwork that has been prepared.

POLITICAL PARTY

Knowledge that addresses issues of what a national interest might be, of who gets served and what is serviced, of what kind of public is being made good—these are matters of state. The desire to monopolize legitimate means of knowledge becomes fragile and exposed in its particularity when scholars of the Middle East, or of science and technology, or of heteronormativity are attacked, as if what they know places at risk the silencing monologics of the state. These dissident voices index the activist intellectual's resonance with the state and invocation of that organizational register that encompasses the exercise of state power in its myriad forms—namely, the political party. At times, the violation of this code of silence is explicit, as when it touches upon the capacity to wage war against errant populations either directly or by proxy. Unsurprisingly, area knowledge borne of foreign-policy instrumentality has been treated as a pariah in this context. In other moments, the relation between critique and the state is refracted to epistemological and disciplinary turf, as seen in the cordon around big science, which goes to the heart of what should properly be funded as research on behalf of the public.[40] However we think of ourselves, state responses suggest that the party form is seen in us, that some knowledge is already attached to this kind of power. For many in academia, this connection between critique and the party form is most elusive. Certainly, a corrective would begin with the recognition of how critical endeavors already insinuate organizational reach.

Yet, of all the organizational registers through which administrative labor flows, that of the political party presents the greatest challenge. The party form seems to have been usurped by new social movements and then networks. What was for hundreds of years a vehicle for the radicalism of both capital and labor is now just as likely to be the object of radical suspicion that large-scale organization and state bureaucracies can do much more than squelch the impetus for profound social change. The discipline of working within a party platform, the occurrence of internecine battles, and the compromise of principle to the exigencies of broad appeal often seem at odds with the iconoclasm, individualism, or self-critical cast nurtured by faculty. Whatever the internal limits may be, the external constraints visited upon those who would seek to meld appeals for comprehensive change with the organizational form of a party disclose a deeper intolerance to political difference that has circumscribed what democratic convention allows.

The repression is as much in evidence with respect to mass parties like the Communist Party USA as with the cadre-based organizations, both kinds of groups having been targeted by the FBI's Counter Intelligence Program (Cointelpro, 1956–1971).[41] The witch hunts, purges, and firings of professors with Communist Party affiliation leave a residue of repression that has silenced even consideration of what such engagement might entail. Insofar as communism is linked with sedition (the condition that tenure, in its own historic formulation, cannot protect), affiliation (or even ideational sympathy) with any organizational expression becomes the limit case for academic freedom and therefore faculty appointment. The potency of anti-communism, particularly on the Left, has had the effect, in Michael E. Brown's terms, of making the Left's own history inaccessible to itself. Accordingly, the Left could persist not through a constant reckoning with its own contradictions but via an idealization of formal, organized political engagement that impels a disengagement from what it has done in the past as a litany of compromise, mistaken idols, and bad faith:

> In summary, it is understandable that post–Cold War discussions among progressives about the future of the Left began to separate it from its past. However, this had the effect of making the present Left seem altogether indeterminate, as if waiting in a kind of hopeful innocence for an integrative idea with less controversial pedigrees than "socialism" and "Marxism," possibly a new party or program aimed at promoting "radical democracy." At the same time, there remains a growing literature aimed at confirming anti-communism and, by inferences often explicitly made, denigrating the Left in general. The desire to separate the Left from its past poses a dilemma for those who are currently advocating a yet newer Left than the new Lefts of before. The Left can have a future only if it has a present that is somehow related to a memorable past. If it has such a past, it must repudiate or ignore it for the sake of its own progress. Otherwise, something different from a Left needs to be constructed and the idea of social progress redefined accordingly. But, then, there is no imagining a future for what we might have thought was under discussion, and what was under discussion was not just a particular Left but the indispensable critical notion of social progress. To undo the Left is, in that sense, to empty the expression "social progress" of all political meaning, which, I take it, was the aim of official anti-communism from the outset.[42]

The specter of communism is deeply tied to the organizational register of the party itself. As state leadership that can transform institutional methods and practices, a party also stands for the means to actualize an imagined horizon of progress as something other than more of the present. Imbuing social progress with political meaning entails a shift from the dull logic of expansion to an interrogation of what there needs to be more of and what needs to be removed—of what difference the passage of time, duration of engagement, or sustenance of struggle might make to an imaginable future. Even the campaigns to evict communists from campuses during the Cold War, which Ellen Schrecker has meticulously documented, proved incredibly effective in their own terms without explaining why party affinity in the United States was so thoroughly banished in concept when it survived in other far less hospitable environments elsewhere in the world.[43]

Outside of policy circles—in which the Kennedy School, Hoover Institute, and the myriad think tanks of Republican or Democratic orientation that might warehouse party intellectuals who operate within the state apparatus—many campus radicals would be loath to think of their own political aspirations in party terms. Even where the critique of state actions is comprehensive enough to require a response that undertakes activities of governance, management, and administration, the logical link to a party is averted. Given the narrowness of ideological range in policy discourse, such hesitation is certainly understandable, but the absence of a suitable vehicle tends to negate the kinds of faculty work that corresponds to the political operations and reach of the party form, even as faculty members suffer consequences as if they were part of an illegitimate oppositional political party.

The register of the party is surfaced when faculty deploy critical knowledge that challenges state authority. The governmental claim that its policies align a national interest with a popular will, has, particularly in the realm of foreign policy, operated as a matter of faith. Major military incursions in Vietnam, or more recently Afghanistan and Iraq, failed on their own terms to deliver containment of communism or an end to the spread of terrorism. Area knowledge designed to apologize for imperial expansion has lost much of its capacity for legitimation and has largely been jettisoned in favor of culture-less protocols for risk management, privatization, and micro-credit stimulus. The major triumph of marginalist economics used to reorient policy away from government support of public goods has been incapable of explaining its own market failures in terms other than the moralism and psychology it had claimed to be free of. In the case of the recent financial meltdown, fingers have been pointed at the excessive greed of a handful of financiers, at the herd mentality engendered by irrational exuberance, and at the overreliance on flawed mathematical models.[44] The larger issues of what such technical knowledge is subservient to is thereby conventionally avoided.

The underlying link between knowledge failure and crisis is not restricted to finance. The failures of Cold War area knowledge and the failure to produce or apply appropriate area knowledge in the wars on terror have also had catastrophic results. In these instances, the insinuation with the state is difficult to deny. Yet, when academics with specific knowledge of the internal dynamics of a region criticize foreign policy, they are also addressing themselves directly to state authority by challenging its monopoly as well as its means of legitimation of governing knowledge. So too do political economists insinuate themselves with the state when they disclose the limits of conventional economic doctrine to explain the behavior of labor or capital, price-making markets or economic growth. Through whatever channels such knowledge is disseminated, whether a seemingly obscure academic journal, a specialized conference, a teach-in, or rally, it appears and is treated by its critics as a kind of state address—alien, unpatriotic, anti-democratic. Surely, that is a reason that the scholarship of Middle Eastern studies, ethnic studies, Native American studies, political economy, community studies, collaborative research, and all the other interdisciplinary formations that disrupt the implied consensus around policy legitimation can be received with such consternation and anxiety by state authorities and off-campus bodies acting as their proxy.

As with the work in interdisciplinarity, the critical voice that operates in the register of the political party is derivative of the state. It provides a counter-knowledge that while comparatively minuscule in scale can generate ideological volatility that the state will not abide. As with political correctness on campus, a seemingly minor dissidence disrupts the confidence in a monologic truth. Critical worldly knowledge suggests that the premise for deployments of state violence are erroneous and therefore undeserving of monopoly, but that the world itself might be imagined along different lines. When deployments of military might or massive social surplus (as in the $787 billion financial bailout at the conclusion of the Bush administration or the even more costly $12 trillion tax cuts that it opened with) appear to be discretionary instead of natural, inevitable, or urgently necessary (or even evidence of an emergency), the specter of rule by deliberation rather than decree is raised. It is not enough for critical knowledge to rely on the protocols of rationality to advance its case. Such confidence would keep specialized academic research within its professional cocoon. Recognition of the organizational register of the party implies a knowledge of how critical ideation circulates in the world, how it gains an impact, how it intersects with various mobilizations, and how it begins to imagine a comprehensive approach to the direction of discretionary wealth, power, and critical understanding.

It is certainly the case that the figure of the state overconsolidated the relation between knowledge and power and organization and interest in a manner that curtailed radical imagination of how to value emergent political energies.

The theories of new social movements, micrological or rhizomatic struggles, multitudes, and networks and commons have contributed to an active language of political mobilization that takes us beyond the conventional conception of the state as an institution of inert political will. This far more dynamic understanding of the political was typically achieved at the expense of any attention or consideration of formal organization, as if an application of what was learned about this new physics of power would disappear into a vortex of state centricity. A very perceptive critique of this lacuna in new political theorizations has been advanced by Ned Rossiter, whose concept of organized networks seeks to return a conception of organizational immanence to what might be considered exhausted institutional forms:

> The network models of sociality made possible by information and communication technologies have resulted in new forms of social-technical systems, or what I am calling emergent institutional forms of organized networks. While these networks can be called institutional forms in so far as they have a capacity to organize social relations, they are radically dissimilar to the moribund technics of modern institutional forms—or "networked organizations"—such as governments, unions and firms whose logic of organization is predicated on vertical integration and representative tenets of liberal democracy. Such dynamics are profoundly unsuited to the collaborative and distributive culture of networks peculiar to digital communications media and their attendant socialities.[45]

Unlike many observers of digital cultures that might take antihierarchical and decentralizing claims of information technologies at face value, and open source collaboration as sufficient alternative to property-based regimes, Rossiter is attuned to the issues of scale and organization and contradictions of administration that such networks continue to face. "However, it is a mistake to think the horizontal, decentralizing and distributive capacities of digital networks as immune from a tendency to fall back into hierarchical and centralizing modes of organization and patterns of behaviour. Indeed, there are times when such a move is necessary. Decisions have to be made . . . the so-called 'open' systems of communication are frequently not only not open, they also elide hierarchical operations that enable networks to become organized. Let us not forget that flexibility is also the operative mode of post-Fordist labour and its attendant double-edged sword of economic precarity and ontological precariousness."[46]

Rossiter is quite careful in mining the immanent organizational alterities in the otherwise ignored institutional sites of firms and unions but is reluctant to consider what this might entail in the case of government. Declaring that "The time of parties is over!" and that "It is now time for modest, pragmatic engagements with localized networked politics," he still wants knowledge workers to attend "to the question of how we think the relationship between communications media and the new institutional possibilities they enable."[47] And yet, if this relationship between labor, networks, and institutional possibilities is already mediated by the state (as it itself seems persistently wont to point out), then the exclusion of the party form from consideration or recognition seems to open a return of an ungoverned omission of some very consequential hierarchical considerations. Surely, there is the question of how creative labor relates to labor designated otherwise, with how those situated in a relation of marginality to institutional conventions coalesce with those who are not, or how those subject to state mandates, coercions, or interventions within the national frame join those subject to similar attention outside a given nation-state.

The sense that the party form is exhausted as a medium for posing or advancing radical or comprehensive trajectories for society reflects a tangible and vital expansion of the realm of politics beyond formal state mandates. As with post-Fordism, what has been termed neoliberalism has also been a governmental initiative for labor, citizens, and investors to assume responsibility for security, regulation, and welfare—operations once confined to state institutions. Whether this shift amounts to a retreat or expansion of the state is a matter of important debate, especially in Michel Foucault's recently translated account of neoliberalism, which provides a revision from the laissez-faire conception of a passive state to an activist, interventionist relation to both economy and civil society.[48] But by no account can it be said that the state has gone away. It is surely too soon to pronounce the political efficacy of the organized networks of young activists—said to number in the tens of thousands with an ability to reach many millions—that were occasioned by the drive of Barack Obama to gain the nomination of a political party and subsequently the presidency. It soon became clear that the organizational residues of this mobilization could not be readily subsumed to Obama's policy agenda despite the efforts at formal subsumption.[49]

If the state and the party form remain, so to speak, historically moving targets, the inability to evade the state because it continues to morph and not go away must be joined by a question of what political movements and aspirations would want of it. The dismissal through irrelevance is understandable in the context of so much of the theorizing of the party form—whether by Marx, Lenin, or Gramsci—taking place in what appears an altogether different context where the mass party was historically emergent.[50] At this time, its relation to its base was still indeterminate, and its patterns of operation were still being decided. In these instances, the party is a nomenclature for a class and the process of representation helps constitute how the class sees itself and how it gives shape to or reconfigures the state. This dynamics of struggle as making the actual terrain of the state was taken farthest in the work of Nicos

Poulantzas.[51] But in the United States, at least since the alignment of corporate labor and business from the New Deal to the Great Society came to unravel, the party has become as much the nomenclature of a kind of market ideal as of a class interest. The bipartisan attention to polling and communications strategies seems an acknowledgment of this, as does the niching of constituencies through wedge issues and targeted mobilizations of contestable constituencies. Rather than sitting on the mass and securing its interest, this national politics of party organizing acknowledges the volatility of the electorate, and it treats every segment of the population as a potential swing vote that may tip the balance in one direction or the other. This politics of volatility was certainly in evidence in the Tea Party's use of networked means to leverage highly instrumental organizational ends, especially in the 2010 midterm elections when Republicans assumed a majority in Congress.

Here too we observe the derivative logic of the post-partisan politician, the one who displaces the center in order to capture it as a space liberated from the professional's grasp. The post-professional politician—claiming the space of the outside, treating state power as a market to be managed, and crafting policy positions through arbitrage—all align with what is here called the professional turn. What becomes evident is the way in which this turn from the outside to some putative inside imagines a party register, not simply the capture of the state but the invocation of a comprehensive view of societal transformation ("change"—or "hope" in the lexicon of the 2008 Obama campaign, shorting or wagering that government will fail in the tactics of Tea Party–inspired Republicans). This invocation of change or failure, like the financial hedges that market prices will rise or fall, is nominally without content. These approaches to leveraging the future in the present are not a rejection of the party; they are directions for its use. They provide the knowledge for how this derivative logic—this small difference that will make all the difference, this wager of change that is to become change—permits what Stefano Harney called "state work." "Perhaps a phenomenology of government work might soon show that there is something about laboring in the state that becomes laboring on the state and in turn becomes activity for others without bounds, a place of fantasy. Moreover, it may be an activity not only for others but with others, where administered publics are sparked to recognize something of the labor in themselves, a labor that is not a displacement of society but a practice of it, a practice of society on society."[52]

This slippage from the inside to the outside, from the laboring subject to the knowing object makes the bureaucrat appear both empty and full, vacant and occupied. The generalization of this condition that Harney marks as a move of public administration shows how this lateral movement across registers serves to become part of the administrative labor of the professor as well as the politician, the post-professional moment in the professional turn. The marketing of knowledge, as with that of the political itself, transforms how we understand the administrative labor in the register of the political party. For what was once the sinecure of class, its stable representation is now reconstituted as a matter of the market, less as a realization of want, need, or desire than of a professionalized technics of creating use value through consumption, of making momentarily manifest the affirmation of an otherwise volatile and circulating worldly knowledge and will. The burgeoning administrative labor within the university makes for its own manifestations of state work. While there is little concern that all organizing effort will be subsumed to the party form, the question of how to manage the whole of society continues to be asserted by higher education's own condition. The need for something like a party to tackle these problems is posed not only by the limits to what institutions can do to solve their immediate obstacles of student debt, faculty precarity, budget problems, and the like but also by what critical knowledge conveys to the world about what is realizable beyond mere affirmation of existing states rights.

8

(Out) from Under New Management?

That new management would spell trouble for faculty comes as little surprise. That it would press us into something other than service, something perhaps unwanted but entirely more serviceable, is rather more unexpected. Making these latter prospects legible might require some narrative sleight of hand. Let us return to the Dickensian figure of best and worst times for higher education with which this book opens. The trick in retelling the tale is in seeing whether we can get to a different ending. On first glance, those who see education as experiencing its best years would most likely be its principal beneficiaries: students who get into the most selective institutions and come out debt-free; faculty with unprecedented perquisites and globally expansive mobility; administrators who raise their campuses' profiles, bequeathing a legacy of signature initiatives, advancing comparative advantage, and thereby increasing the stock of singular leadership; and patrons whose investments change the face of the institution, reap dividends on new intellectual properties, and ennoble their good names so as to define the substance of excellence. Among each of these constituencies could also be counted a growing casualty list: students discouraged to apply, drowned by a lifetime's debt, and numbed by mounting hours of work; faculty dispirited by diminished opportunity for secure positions with meaningful influence on their institution's governance and by their poor prospects for advancement; administrators churning in permanent turnover, squeezed between ceaseless fund-raising and external need, and exhausted by the incessant demands of the few troublemakers and the passive body of unappreciative faculty; and policy makers who see in higher education undeserved want but diminishing returns.

The double view from on high and from the trenches reflects higher education's dual operations to provide faith in knowledge-driven meritocractic mobility on the one hand, and on the other, to deliver an occupational and organizational hierarchy to society. Accordingly, if the methods of the former were seen as fair and objective based upon talent and drive, the outcomes of the great sorting machine nod in the direction of options foreclosed, choices denied, and the coercive aspects of market-based selection, that, while not just, are treated as justifiable. And yet, there is now considerable doubt about the solidity and reasonableness of both the temporality of mobility and the spatiality of hierarchy. The luster of the professional-managerial class is clouded by the decomposition of its cherished autonomy while its ranks continue to expand. The popular skepticism toward expertise as more and more of it is sought, acts to compromise merit and mobility's entrepreneurial spirit, which lies at the heart of the knowledge society's social compact. If to the victors goes autonomy, educational expansion may prove Pyrrhic from both sides now.

ORGANIZATION: TOO MUCH OR TOO LITTLE?

And so, if autonomy as a measure of value has lost its cachet, then perhaps association, or more pointedly, organization, may be the far more promising figure to rise from the ashes. Here too, it may turn out, we can see the best and worst of our times. Surely, there are faculty who will see the proliferation of organizational proposals on offer here as being way too much, and others for whom they are far too little. For faculty members born and raised under new management, the excess of organizational potential, which derives from the preponderance of administrative labor, is already upon them. This new management is them and us—not in the sense of some felicitous unity of purpose imagined by a leadership training session—but in the sense of engendering the practical knowledge for running institutions that can be applied to contest what our knowledge circuits, workplaces, and society are being run for. When administrative labor only looks like work to be refused or minimized, the prospect of seizing the means of institutional operation for different purposes will be lost.

To the extent that autonomy is indeed being traded for administratively forged connections of mutual association, the greatest challenge to activating colleagues may be to convince them of the value and prospect of the administrative work they are presently doing, so as to redirect it rather than to implore them to undertake more of it or simply to be overtaken by it. As has been the case for every other kind of productive endeavor, the enclosure of the knowledge commons undeniably inflicts losses on the qualities of intellectual life as it has been known. Yet, for increasing numbers, enclosure also awakens a more profoundly interdependent professional labor and the possibility of revaluing the work we are forced to do together. The unpaid and undervalued activities conventionally marginalized as service gain credence for compensation, but they also reference that vast surplus of knowledge that feeds life's organizational necessities. A century ago, Frederick Winslow Taylor was quick to recognize the need to enlist the participation of the manual industrial worker in the project of increasing productivity.[1] Today, new management, with its expectations of financial literacy and emotional and spiritual participation, demands a good deal more. Behaviorally savvy and affectively sensitive, "debiased" management expects from employees nothing less than a greater investment in the revitalization of the means and end of the organization—and therefore makes available a tacit knowledge of how to produce organization as such.[2]

While this revaluation of faculty labor will prove vertiginous for some, it must also be appreciated that for others it will seem insufficiently transformative—paradoxically for those who have put the most energy toward rendering their environments otherwise. For many activists—especially those whose formative experiences have been involvement in such phenomena as the 1999 protests in Seattle against the World Trade Organization, the World Social Forum convened in 2001 at Porto Alegre, Brazil, and Internet-centered actions, such as that orchestrated by the Independent Media Center (http://www.indymedia.org)—the current condition of organizations can be part of the problem. As if a displacement from the traditional mantle of the professionals, autonomy is a key category in these political initiatives, and self-organizing is crucial to their creation of alternate sites, mobilizations, and institutions in a manner that yields tacit knowledge similar to what is here called administrative labor. Self-management is part of the longer history of anarchism and council communism of the late nineteenth century, which serve as one inspiration for these European and North American activisms of the past few decades.[3] While the welfare state was expanding, it broke free from its paternalistic grasp, which was different in significance than present state policies aimed at freeing the welfare state from the social demands of marginalized (or at risk) populations. Many of these protests look to be chasing the state (or its proxies) down as the state takes flight from prior commitments and demanding that resources (like free education) be redeployed toward social purposes. When successful, as ACT UP (AIDS Coalition to Unleash Power) was in securing health care for those with HIV, governments are loath to acknowledge the impact of protests on policy. The official nonrecognition of this efficacy obscures the dialectic of institutionalization, which for gay activists has expanded to decouple what bodies may be entitled to beyond those covered by conventional marriage vows.

Certainly, there are radicals whose activism has led them to engage in graduate student organizing, the critiquing of professional societies, or the joining of electoral-based parties. These radicals have found that each group can pose impasses to more comprehensive change that consequently can be profoundly deradicalizing.[4] And is it not uncommon to see members of cadre-based parties and other activists find common cause around a particular issue. But impatience or frustration can reign when joining an organization is presented as a condition for further organizing or a challenge in coming to agreement on what tactical moves might best further a more revolutionary agenda. Without doubt, the history of organizing is full of this tension between the radical ambition that can energize organizing and the pragmatics of compromise that seem to divert those drives. This narrative of revolution and reform—wherein radical impulses when not suppressed are co-opted or assimilated by legislation and institutionalization, of longstanding pedigree—tends toward a tragic account of political engagement by which oppositional politics are found forever insufficient to alter the status quo.[5] Yet this reckoning makes it difficult to account for the ongoing generation of new activism, the expansion of political contestation into new domains or dimensions of human experience. The episodic dynamic of political intervention (whether protest or revolution) does not map smoothly onto the *longue durée* of social transformation. At the moment, activism is typically met with forceful efforts at dispersal and disavowal of the very effects that form part of its subsequent efficacy. Granted, from within any political position or engagement, it is often difficult to recognize how it is dependent on other positions or affects further prospects, contexts, or the repertory of practices.

If the evaluative criteria shift from individual careers (what can sustain a life of activism) to organizational density (what accounts for the expansion of the political field), the appraisal of what politics yields can reorient perspective from one of scarcity to surplus. The concern for the sustainability of the activist is that insufficient political gain leads to burnout. The perspective of organizational density recognizes not only that more of life is subject to organizational rationality (with its attendant Weberian disenchantment) but also that organizations generate an excess they cannot reabsorb. The flip side of the winnowing process that leads to concrete institutional outcomes is that alternate routes are opened, proposals vetted that may get introduced in another context, and experiences gleaned that get reapplied under different circumstances. That excess includes aspirations, critique, coalition, and collaboration. These are the loam of administrative engagement from which further radicalism springs.

One consequence of the organizational immanence explored here is that the lateral pathways to other commitments, interventions, and affiliations are already present in particular activist moments. While there are certainly those who will cease operations, many more are likely to compile an intricate inventory of activist experiences that continue to build organizational possibility in disparate settings. The efforts to retain traditional perquisites, especially those that flow from academic freedom, tenure, and professional autonomy, and those mobilizations aimed at altering what institutions are for (or replacing them altogether) present a sturdy version of the inside-outside problem posed persistently for agents of social change. Yet one argument advanced in this book has been that the once stable separation between what is inside and outside the university is now being effaced. Whether, when, and how such entanglements lead to direct coalitions between designated insiders and outsiders, and when the effects of the efforts of each result in strange new polyrhythms that neither had been playing at the time, cannot be readily forecast. Hopefully, a critical framework can be capacious enough to show how political pursuits—that may seem incompatible in their immediate program or disposition—are joined in the larger field of possibilities that they together open up. The simultaneity of protests that entwine campus and extracurricular issues, and of organizational trajectories that entangle professional, unionist, and party considerations, evident among various activisms today, are tangible signs of this expanded field. This recognition of how difference constitutes a field could itself be seen as part of an administrative temperament that facilitates what it cannot alone give voice to, listens for what it does not say, and co-relates what it encounters from distinct settings. Consequently, value is derived not from what it makes but from what it does with the variation it meets. The recent financial crisis has disclosed the ways in which what seem the most tenuous connections and minor variations are interconnected in ways that are hugely consequential. The socializing effects of capital on labor convey an intricate web of mutual associations that can link practices through the most delicate filigree, but the result can be a sudden disruption or abiding critique. The best use of a critical analysis is not to get everyone doing the same thing at the same time but to allow all to notice what their particular interventions contribute toward, what they push existing arrangements to be, and what emergent practices they valorize and make legible.

Nothing in the preceding analysis suggests that such outcomes are guaranteed. If anything, the university under new management presents a series of dilemmas that further unsettle existing circumstances and open up a range of possible outcomes. The hope here has been that mapping these various antinomies can enhance the evaluation of activities that faculty is currently engaged in. Each chapter of this book indeed offers a cluster of dilemmas that, taken together, could begin to describe the general circumstances of higher education in the United States today. In the first chapter, expansion of higher education proceeds in tandem with the industrialization of knowledge, such that the proletarianization of faculty becomes part of the larger decomposition of the professional-managerial class. The regulatory framework for higher education pairs defunding with privatization. Credentials pass from public to private goods in need of ongoing reinvestment. The generalized skepticism toward professional expertise, synecdochically expressed on campus as the culture wars—which in turn cover for comprehensive accountability measures, such as benchmarking—comes with a more pervasive drive from government-sponsored security to self-management of life's risks, whether through information glut or incessant expectations of measurable gain. With more and more of the population under the sway of new management, and even traditional disciplines subject to the professional turn, technical reason swells and yet it is insufficient to govern conditions of judgment. For better and for worse, values are rendered more contingent, and ripe are the conditions for opening to consideration what education might be for when it is neither evidently a thing merely for itself nor a reliable means for launching and sustaining a career. What is expansive in education, professionalization, and managerialism is not simply access and reach but an opening toward other criteria by which this participation in judgment might be mobilized, together with the requisite organizational and administrative wherewithal.

That such fissures do not begin with college but are of a piece with the longer preparation for it gets emphasis in Chapter 2. While saving for college from birth might be preparation for a lifetime of debt, managerialist primary education can't wait to get started with protocols of accountability. Laboring to learn establishes a dual authority between what is valued in the classroom and what one must be accountable to from without. The reductive scoring of high-stakes testing in reading and math leads a double life with collaboration and interdisciplinary projects sustained through the arts. Parental free labor forms a coalition with managerialist protocols of child rearing, while even the alternative elementary school studied here delivers its escape routes under the cover of conventional accomplishment. While this experience is not generalizable, it does indicate where planning meets its limit, where time-management opens to decolonization, and where a kind of holism or contextualism emerges in the student work that bubbles up through the carefully constructed cracks in the edifice that teachers, administrators, and parents make available.

For college students who embark upon higher learning under the regime of the professional turn, education is never simply for itself. Yet, as Chapter 3 demonstrates, instrumentalization leaves its own outcomes uncertain. The push for relevance reinscribes the question of what education is for as more people access it without benefit of assured occupational placement. Curricular initiatives that help niche-campus offerings are also a site for reimagining connections across fields, communities, work, and worlds, through which students will enroll in the task of learning to generalize beyond themselves and from their own experience, and in so doing, question the passively asserted universalism of general education. The breakdown in disciplinary replication assures that graduate student experience will be supplemented by lessons in the general conditions of academic labor, denials that their work is such to the contrary. The activisms that issue from campuses, while far from universal, perform a generalizing move from the specific circumstances of students to their broader context, linkages abetted by the meshing of what lies on campus and off when the dual market failure of disciplinary replication and risk-driven professional advancement occasions its own forms of politicization. The tactical continuity of interventions, like building occupations, joins an imaginary of institutional appropriation and reassembly while allowing a strategically diffuse coalition of campus constituencies and interests.

Loss of faculty autonomy has been entwined with erosions of security. The persistence of tenure through conditions of its general decline highlights the limited purchase that disciplinary peerage has on university governance. As the Al-Arian and Churchill cases in Chapter 4 make plain, critique of the state poses tenure's limit, but these cases also point to a broader need to advance the conditions of critique beyond what occupational perquisites can protect. The absent term of "administrative labor," masked by the present unpaid and undervalued category of service, indicates where the current means of account places faculty in the circumstance of a population at risk. Service work disproportionately performed by women and people of color meets an indifference when merit pay is apportioned, which stands in marked contrast to the elevated worth of senior administrators.

The emphasis on leadership is another arena where higher education adopts, albeit in its own key, certain mandates of the corporate world at the same time that lifelong learning animates the knowledge economy and well-practiced management. Heightened learning as an indissociable capacity of all labor is deemed incommunicable to external stakeholders for whom education must be translated into immediate if ephemeral measures of gains in output. The focus on public and private university presidents in Chapter 5 speaks not only to the erosion of the difference between these sectors more broadly but also to the logic of singularity by which an exceptional investment yields the productivity norms by which all will be measured. While the research universities on which these two cases are based turn out not to be generalizable (a conceit of the drive to excellence itself), the resulting justification of risk and the race to positional advantage that affects most institutions is exemplified in these models even as higher education itself becomes differentiated institutionally in ways that strain conceiving of it as a single sector. So too, the focus on leadership engenders a vulnerability and a volatility that spring from leveraging the institution's fate to key strategic initiatives while the employees of the university partake of their own accursed share of mounting managerial tasks.

The last two chapters of the book, on interdisciplinarity and organizational registers, can be read together to compose a response to the managerialism expressed in the first five chapters. The substance of academic labor lies in the braiding together of what knowledge is, how it is made, and what it is for. The promise that expert knowledge could rationally command society, what drove the formation of the professional-managerial class, was undone as expertise passed into a generalized condition of management—mastering risk, which consequently meant losing the security and pervasive judgment that rendered accountability unaccountable. The slicing and dicing of our production and circulation of knowledge—of affiliation to what learning does with association to what it joins—points to an underlying development of the past thirty years, the rise of a derivative logic. The dominance of finance in the current conjuncture has been underscored by its spectacular failures of late, of models that could no longer yield truth effects and of broken capital circuits that could not explain themselves. Finance-driven wealth demanded technical information subsumed to a disinterested mastery. But for all the destructive impact of the fall as well as the rise of finance, its socializing effects have been to spread the mandates of risk management to myriad facets of social life, including that of the professions themselves.

This is not to say that the move from security to risk—from the certainties of technical expertise to effervescent appeals of professional arbitrage—are readily reducible to the growth of financial services or attendant instruments of risk management, such as derivatives. Rather, the specific expansion of finance and the transformation of professional labor are joined by a social impetus, which amplifies the leverage of small interventions and shared attributes of otherwise disparate entities in the constitution of a whole field, precisely what is meant by derivative logic. Intriguingly, the emphasis on leverage aligns with the central trope of *mochlos* in Jacques Derrida's account from the eighties of what would become the professional turn, whereby he sees academics acting upon the Kantian divide between the liberal and professional faculties to create a surplus responsibility, in a manner consistent with the ripple effects of interdisciplinarity noted here.[6] The bundling together of difference and the transit of analytic methods across dissimilar sites would seem to reference deconstruction and financialization alike, not in some facile analogy of fragmentation and loss of reference but in a more nuanced circulation of associated attributes, of manifest difference placed in mutual debt. The point is not that this logic explains or exhausts all of any given social domain but rather that it allows us to think about aspects of life that otherwise appear disparate. With this conjuncture of finance in mind, it is now possible to construct a framework that allows us to join the labor of learning with that of making the settings within which that work comes to have value. Setting to work on the what and where of knowledge production allows consideration of both interdisciplinarity and administrative labor as kinds of arbitrage that follow a derivative logic.

THE FATEFUL MULTIPLE

It should now be apparent that the discussion of faculty work around the rubric of waves of interdisciplinarity Chapter 6 presents and the organizational registers Chapter 7 considers can be seen as intersecting one another. Recall that the figure of the wave is, in contrast with that of periodization, meant to suggest that formations can be historically rooted and introduced without their coming to an end, that organizational registers can persist in a different context without being anachronistic, that even futurity is a feature of the present conjuncture. While the waves of interdisciplinarity roughly and respectively crest at the turn of the last century, during the two decades following World War II, and according to the risk society has promoted since the early eighties, each swell continues to ripple in the present. While the terms and conditions of departments and nations can change, they remain consequential features of our social geography. If the disparate forces of interdisciplinarity are all still available to us, both as they continue to differentiate academic training and interconnect circumstances of labor, we can say the same of organization itself. Professional associations, unions, and parties are inscribed in institutional histories, but they also carry logics of affiliation that continue to bear upon us, as their founding conditions (autonomy, development, mass) have passed or been transformed into other principles of connection.

Loss of autonomy has not diminished the demands for higher education or the professionalization of occupations. The mapping of individual career to societal advancement generates its own anxieties now that it is unmoored from the assurances of smooth, linear, and developmental progress. The dispersion of mass movements and parties has accompanied an expansion of the political domain, as movement organizations proliferate and major parties expend more effort and consume more material resources in assembling governing pluralities. "Register" here is being used as both verb and noun to indicate the act of compiling, recording, and inscribing knowledge as well as the domain or site within which these flows take place. Registers mark our own accretions of knowledge on a persistent, daily basis—dutiful responses that add up beyond immediate measure. The kinds of knowledge work we engage in invoke an organizational logic and horizon and they move and circulate through thickening associations, whether or not we name ourselves or settings in such organizational terms. We do not choose between registers, but our administrative labor carries us through these intersecting logics, scales, and imaginaries.

The polychronic pressure of waves can be articulated with the polyvocal organizational registers. The present is composed of many segments of time and we speak in many voices. Novelty and innovation do not erase earlier formations but instead recontextualize organizational forms and rearrange principles of mutual association. As such, each emergent wave is already a mixture, already hybridized and intersectional, and already interdisciplinary and organizationally heterodox. Certainly, our dependencies upon one another have deepened, even as the ways in which we rely upon one another have changed, linking more of us more diffusely along myriad but commonly recognizable attributes. The dialectic of class formation and decomposition generates a sense of lost ground in which nascent integuments nestle. Faculty over the past hundred years bears at once an occupational, disciplinary, and organizational formation. If a complex of occupation, discipline, and organization institute academic work at a particular conjuncture, each of these historical waves is in turn pulled by nation, class, and market.

These social formations, often what justifies and legitimates the emerging conjuncture, frame the professoriate in different ways. They delimit a zone of sovereignty (in the case of nation, whose territorial architecture the departmentalized university mimics), a productive capacity (within what was taken to be a hitherto "nonproductive" professional-managerial class), and a link between judgment or assessment and value in what is taken as a newly universalized market. Occupationally, each formation promotes a particular subject position that encompasses both continuity and change of academic protagonists over the past century: the professional specialist, who authorizes academic departments, makes a dazzling entrance with the rise of academic professionalization; the academic entrepreneur, whose interdisciplinary programs from area studies to laboratories serve to advance knowledge industrialization, emerges with the postwar government-university social compact; the arbitrager—who makes much with small differences in value through project-based work, consultancy, and proprietary endeavors that drive the post-professional links between the university's inside and outside—manifests the derivative logic as finance marks its ascent.

Such exemplary figures of action in turn imply specific organizational registers within which they move and emerge, and to which they craft particular expressions. The professional associations founded their grammar of governance in academic freedom and tenure that would allow those so anointed limited national mobility and influence. The unionization of faculty was the organizational inflection of the great expansion of higher education and knowledge making. The anxiety of influence over expertise, derided as a politicization of the university, speaks to the address of knowledge to the state when its interests and value must be demonstrated and not treated as axiomatic, a voicing of judgment that aligns critical intervention with the comprehensive claims of the political party. The disavowal of government's monopoly over legitimate knowledge, its self-proclaimed end, which was one conceit of neoliberalism, also spelled the proliferation of the political in that very space said to be free of it—namely, the value-making market. These conditions of production yield not only particular kinds of knowledge but also the capacities to place this knowledge in circulation, to make organizations run, to shift between various institutional masters and settings, to distribute attributes of affiliation among otherwise disparate participants. The managerialism that courses through every social capillary challenges particular expertise, but it also raises the expectation that performance could be adequate to collective expectation, that society itself might be adequate to its ideals. The array of these relations can be presented as shown in Table 8.1.

TABLE 8.1   KNOWLEDGE WORK AND ADMINISTRATIVE LABOR

	Occupational Formation	Disciplinary Formation	Organizational Formation	Social Formation
First wave	Professional specialization	Departmentalization	Professional association	National
Second wave	PMC-entrepreneur	Interdisciplinary programs	Industrial union	Class
Third wave	Professional-turn-arbitrager	Post-professional alliances	Political party	Market

In stressing that these spatial and temporal relations are already immanent to faculty work, both in how knowledge is made and how it is put into circulation, what is being proposed here is a revaluation of where we find ourselves and not an exhortation to do more, better, or entirely different work. As with the discussion of identification that rested upon notions of multiple subject positions, organization too is intersectional and hybridized, simultaneous and dispersed.[7] All these might be considered consistent with what Henry Giroux calls "a strategy to retake the university," which entails "multiple interventions, extending from taking control of academic departments to organizing larger faculty structures and organization."[8] It may certainly become necessary to start a new professional association, form or converge collective bargaining along newly legible industrial rather than occupational lines, or organize under the mantle of a political party.

The leadership skills, patience and perseverance, mastery of strategy and tactics, and analytic acumen all must be developed and drawn upon. But such work must itself first be imagined as already with us, as bubbling up from the ways we have been pressed together, from experiences that nestle among us and not as inspiration for those who cannot recognize their own. Shannon Jackson, reflecting on what she terms the "enmeshment" of mental and manual labor displayed in the interdisciplinary formation of performance studies, makes a sympathetic translation to the feeling that administrative labor is impossibly outside the orbit of creative intellectual work. She appreciates the bind to do it all that invites professionally active faculty to turn away from what seems like the manual work of the university. But she adds, "I am also sympathetic, not only to the idea that someone has to keep the place running, but that that running is also part of 'my own work.'"[9]

This array of relations is one approximation of the multiplicity and complexity that we manage every day. Surely, these forces move in different and indeterminate directions. Growth in the number of professionals has accompanied loss of autonomy borne by the professional turn; continued specialization shuttles between the star entrepreneur and the arbitrager. Interdisciplinary programs can be administrative rationalizations and provide new critical horizons; departments are increasingly permeable to post-professional alliances. We swim in these currents not able to readily isolate tidal pulls and cresting swells. The challenge lies not simply in staying afloat but in recognizing what is being formed and what may be durable amid these myriad forces.

If elementary school children are being prepared for higher education in the ways of a proletarianized professional-managerial class by learning to recognize the limits to accountability regimes, even as they gain fluency in them, college students today show signs that campus activism is awash in these various organizational registers that flow through the university. While senior professors confront the limits to disciplinary socialization and graduate students encounter themselves in the setting of industrial labor, undergraduates are being taught to recognize how their local experience extends to questions of state. When the allocation of hundreds of billions of dollars to bail out financial institutions is coupled with a bailing out on students, whether through rising costs or perfidies of debt, the global is installed in particular locations that cross boundaries of public and private institutions, national and international students, research and teaching campuses. The installation of grief, of dispossession and enclosure, meets another kind of authorizing presence, one reminiscent of interventionist art that takes the existing social fabric as its canvas and possibility rather than longevity as its terms of accomplishment. In the rush of occupations that interlaced with the financial crisis, the latter's socializing effects—its invigorating urge to interconnection—are forcefully on display. In one example, on February 18, 2009, a group of students at New York University occupied a campus building. Their demands were extensive:

Amnesty for all parties involved.

Full compensation for all employees whose jobs were disrupted during the course of the occupation.

Public release of NYU's annual budget and endowment.

Allow student workers (including T.A.'s) to collectively bargain.

A fair labor contract for all NYU employees at home and abroad.

A Socially Responsible Finance Committee that will immediately investigate war profiteers and the lifting of the Coke ban.

Annual scholarships be provided for thirteen Palestinian students.

That the university donates all excess supplies and materials in an effort to rebuild the University of Gaza.

Tuition stabilization for all students, beginning with the class of 2012. Tuition rates for each successive year will not exceed the rate of inflation. The university shall meet 100% of government-calculated student financial need.

That student groups have priority when reserving space in the buildings owned or leased by New York University, including, and especially, the Kimmel Center.

That the general public have access to Bobst Library.[10]

After two days, the university evicted the demonstrators and suspended the students. The provost explained that the students "were not suspended because they protested or opposed University policies—rights to which they were entitled and which make the University a stronger institution—but because they refused to leave the building and were involved in destruction of University property, harmful behavior, and other violations of the University's rules—conduct at odds with our creed of reasoned exchange of ideas."[11] The building they occupied stood on ground that had once been a student center that was torn down to erect a more hybrid facility that houses a food court, commuter lounge, suite of offices for student organizations, theater, and conference facility (the latter on a fee-for-service basis). The property violation in question referred to breaking a lock on a door that led to a balcony overlooking Washington Square Park, where hundreds of students had gathered. Those inside the building had set up a live video stream to link with others and garner solidarity for their action.

The conflict between communicational entitlements and property entailments leads back to questions of organizational immanence. Some faculty expressed concern about the lack of organizational preparation of the students, the scattershot nature of the demands, and the overinvestment in tactics. Graduate students who had themselves taught many of the activists issued a public statement responding to such criticisms. The undergraduates had been organizing for two years, had a coalition of some twenty-two student groups, and the range of demands incorporated this diverse constituency and linked this protest to those occurring at other campuses in the United States and Europe. Slogans, tactics, demands, and strategy sharing mingled among these various actions. A building occupation at the New School two months prior, involving some of the same students, called for the removal of their then-president, Bob Kerry. Tens of thousands of students in Italy occupied campus buildings in what they called the "anomalous wave," while many more students marched through downtown Athens, Greece, demanding that students not bear the burden of the financial crisis. Several months after the NYU event, the deportation of immigrant cleaning-service workers in the midst of an organizing campaign led to a student and faculty occupation at the School of Oriental and African Studies, while protests flared in Berlin and Belgrade over a new European higher education framework called the Bologna Process.[12]

In 2010, students mobilized across the University of California system, where promised fee hikes were being used by university managers to secure favorable loan terms on capital projects, while at California State campuses, students demanded fuller access to facilities, such as at Fullerton, where students demanded that the library, not the bowling alley, be kept open around the clock. This season of interventions was derived from a political sensibility and critique that invoked global organizational circuits without membership.

The phalanx of demands have yet to coalesce organizationally while the mobilizations show little sign of abating. The linkage between governance and political economy, locally and internationally, must include registers of interdisciplinary study and labor but also flows through the state. The emergence of this comprehensiveness takes on the appearance (or is accused) of being fragmentary, scattershot, transient, and spontaneous. And yet perhaps this is what the immanence of organization produces, a feeling of disruption at the moment that unwanted connections, attention to how things are run, and periods of unauthorized decision are being joined. Indeed, in June 2010, students at the University of Puerto Rico, Río Piedras, ended a two-month campus shutdown with a successful negotiation with the governor's office (only to resume it months later when the governor issued more austerity measures).

The university architecture that internally mimicked the boundaries of the nation and that sought to affirm a national culture still stands and makes waves, as does the institutional mandate of higher education to manage the expansion of the professional-managerial class and education as a private good that renders the university a competitor in a larger knowledge market. Antoinette Burton has formulated the interdisciplinary sensibility that accompanies the gambit for administrative labor described here. As one good turn deserves another, she coins "the imperial turn" as the accelerated attention paid, within the North American university, to anticolonial, feminist, and racial, social, and political movements that has yielded a glacial and incomplete democratization but also a reaction formation within the university. She observes, "The ways in which disciplines have been constructed as nations, revealing the territorial investments of scholars and departmental curricula, as well as the imperial fantasies of 'self' and 'other'" lead not to a disappearance, but a "reprise of the nation."[13]

This complicated imbrication of expansion and enclosure, socialization and segmentation, and interdependence and isolation suggest that no simple inversion of management and labor is available or achievable. Rather, a more delicate parsing of the realms of possibility lies in what can be derived from the combinations that currently obtain and the resonance that echoes elsewhere in critical and creative activity. The protests, occupations, and organizing being unleashed across campuses challenge the self-assured hegemony of the educational model of U.S.-based research universities. These students may see in their counterparts around the world very different options for how the future can be brought into the present than the one offered by the professional turn. They may refuse their own marginalization in higher education to noninstructional revenue streams and thereby reassert their place in the knowledge economy that was to be given over to the property-enhancing applications of research.

The simultaneous participation of knowledge making and administrative work, which assumes the organizational logic of professional organizations, unions, and parties, has transformed each of these entities into more hybridized forms that intersect with one another. This makes it all the more likely that administrative labor will continue to travel across these registers, responding to new managerialisms with ever more comprehensive critiques whose linkages may be tenuous but nonetheless mutually affecting. What looked like an impassable divide between administrators and faculty is transgressed in the way managerialism is disbursed throughout the work of knowledge making, braiding interests, competencies, desires, and strategies for what can be made of what we know. Making the most of these inchoate opportunities will require a different calculus—a well-placed leverage—on that fateful multiple, a recombinant form of worthiness that our labors lead to. This book is offered in the service of that longer term investment, the one for which we can already begin to see returns.

Pursuing these challenges will allow us to move beyond the tragic tales that echo through the cognitive corridors of autonomy lost, mission misunderstood, authority fragmented, public spheres debased, and culture wars surrendered. Defenses along these lines quickly become the casualties from the attacks on exceptionalism, even as the assaults barely conceal their own protection of privilege. The rise of new managerialism has altered the script that reads an increase in professionalization produces a fragmentation and loss of unifying belief by which rightist ideology is said to triumph. Yet it also points to the high road of knowledge democratization after the professional turn that is the most salient promise of still-expansive higher education. For academic labor, broadly realizing this potential would mean trading mastery for affiliation, embracing interconnection at the limit to specifiable knowledge, and finding other ways of valuing small differences that circulate together in a wider field. The derivative logics of interdisciplinarity and organizational immanence, the association of attributes and multiplication of profiles—their combination and commensurability across sites of knowledge production— invite a focus that concentrates more on the techniques of practical accomplishment of this work than on its unitary and orienting belief. Appropriating the terms and trajectories of these techniques—realizing the value of administrative labor—affords a comprehensive, if dizzying recognition, of a dispersed and appreciating means for making the world.

Notes

CHAPTER 1

1. While the term "knowledge society" has entered common parlance, its provenance is typically traced from an argument concerning the shift from manual to mental labor, variously referred to as a knowledge or information economy, or postindustrial, postmodern, or network society. See Fritz Machlup, *The Production and Distribution of Knowledge in the United States* (Princeton, NJ: Princeton University Press, 1962); Peter Drucker, *The Age of Discontinuity* (London: Heinemann, 1969); Daniel Bell, *The Coming of Post-industrial Society: A Venture in Social Forecasting* (New York: Basic Books, 1973); Manuel Castells, *The Rise of the Network Society. The Information Age: Economy, Society, and Culture*, vol. 1 (Malden, MA: Blackwell, 1996).

2. Christopher Jencks and David Riesman, *The Academic Revolution* (Garden City, NY: Doubleday, 1968), 480.

3. Alain Touraine, *The Academic System in America* (New Brunswick, NJ: Transaction Books, 1997 [1974]), xxii, 6.

4. Harold Perkin, *The Third Revolution: Professional Elites in the Modern World* (Routledge: London, 1996), 1.

5. Donald Clark Hodges, *Class Politics in the Information Age* (Chicago: University of Illinois Press, 2000), 3. See also James Burnham, *The Managerial Revolution: What Is Happening in the World* (New York: John Day, 1941); Alfred D. Chandler Jr., *The Visible Hand: The Managerial Revolution in American Business* (Cambridge, MA: Harvard University Press, 1977); Milovan Djilas, *The New Class: An Analysis of the Communist System* (New York: Praeger, 1957).

6. Andrew Abbott, *The System of Professions: An Essay on the Division of Expert Labor* (Chicago: University of Chicago Press, 1988), 16.

7. Ibid., 61.

8. Elliot Friedson, *Professionalism: The Third Logic* (Chicago: University of Chicago Press, 2001), 14.

9. Ibid., 209.

10. Charles Derber, *Professionals as Workers: Mental Labor in Advanced Capitalism* (Boston: C. K. Hall, 1982), 14. Andre Gorz, *Farewell to the Working Class* (London: Pluto, 1982); Serge Mallet, *Essays on the New Working Class* (St. Louis, MO: Telos Press, 1975); Milovan Djilas, *The New Class: An Analysis of the Communist System* (New York: Praeger, 1957).

11. Charles Derber, William A. Schwartz, and Yale Magrass, *Power in the Highest Degree: Professionals and the Rise of a New Mandarin Order* (New York: Oxford University Press, 1990), 4. See also Jethro K. Lieberman, *The Tyranny of the Experts: How Professionals Are Closing the Open Society* (New York: Walker, 1970).

12. Barbara and John Ehrenreich, "The Professional Managerial Class," *Radical America* 11: 2, 29; part 1, 11 (March–April 1977): 7–31; part 2, 11 (May–June 1977): 7–22.

13. Derber, *Professionals as Workers*, 226.

14. Students for a Democratic Society, inaugurated with the Port Huron Statement in 1962, was a broad student movement with a million members. Disbanded in the seventies, it was relaunched in 2006. The history of the first wave is told in Kirkpatrick Sale, *SDS: The Rise and Development of Students for a Democratic Society* (New York: Vintage Books, 1973) and a graphic novel, Harvey Pekar, Gary Dumm, and Paul Buhle, *Students for a Democratic Society: A Graphic History* (New York: Hill and Wang, 2008).

15. John Beverly, "Higher Education and Capitalist Crisis" in *Professionals as Workers*, by Derber, 101.

16. Mike Dent and Stephen Whitehead, "Configuring the 'New' Professional," in *Managing Professional Identities: Knowledge, Performativity, and the "New" Professional*, eds. Mike Dent and Stephen Whitehead (London: Routledge, 2001), 1.

17. Rosabeth Moss Kanter, *On the Frontiers of Management* (Cambridge, MA: Harvard Business Review, 1997), xii.

18. Peter F. Drucker, *Management Challenges for the 21st Century* (New York: HarperCollins, 1999), 159.

19. Henry Mintzberg, *Managers Not MBAs: A Hard Look at the Soft Practice of Managing and Management Development* (San Francisco: Berrett-Koehler Publishers, 2004), 1.

20. Ibid., 24.

21. Ibid., 377.

22. See Rakesh Khurana, *From Higher Aims to Hired Hands: The Social Transformation of American Business Schools and the Unfulfilled Promise of Management as a Profession* (Princeton, NJ: Princeton University Press, 2007), 368.

23. Jeff Schmidt, *Disciplined Minds: A Critical Look at Salaried Professionals and the Soul-Battering System that Shapes Their Lives* (Lanham, MD: Rowman and Littlefield, 2000), 14.

24. Ibid., 16.

25. The more restrictive conception is common in sociological taxonomies of class. See for pertinent examples, Dennis Gilbert, *The American Class Structure* (New York: Wadsworth Publishing 1998); Paul Fussel, *Class, A Guide through the American Status System* (New York, NY: Touchstone, 1983); Rhonda Levine, *Social Class and Stratification* (Lanham, MD: Rowman and Littlefield, 1998). As of 2001, the number of persons holding professional and doctoral level degrees in the United States was 5,860,000. See U.S. Department of Education, *Digest of Education Statistics* (Washington, DC: National Center for Education Statistics, 2009), table 9 ("Number of Persons Age 18 and Over, by Highest Level of Education Attained, Age, Sex, and Race/Ethnicity: 2009"), available at http://nces.ed.gov/programs/digest/d09/tables/dt09_009.asp (accessed November 19, 2010).

26. U.S. Bureau of Labor Statistics, table A-13 ("Employed and Unemployed Persons by Occupation, Not Seasonally Adjusted"), March 2010, available at http://www.bls.gov/news.release/empsit.t13.htm (accessed May 25, 2010). Professional

and related occupations were one of the few job categories to show growth in a year of recession between March 2009 and March 2010, with more than 300,000 positions created (although unemployment rates also rose from 3.9 to 4.3 during this period, much less, however than the general rate of unemployment, which went from 9.0 to 10.2 during the same time).

27. The more expansive measure comes from U.S. Bureau of Labor Statistics, *Statistical Abstracts of the United States,* table 627 ("Full-Time Wage and Salary Workers"), available at http://www.census.gov/compendia/statab/2010/tables/10s0633.pdf (accessed December 21, 2010). Between 2000 and 2008, employment in these categories had grown nearly 20 percent to more than forty million of a workforce made up of 106 million people. Many other occupations in the service economy, notably in sales and office occupations and other service occupations, which together comprise another forty million workers, include a number of jobs considered to be professional by various measures. In its National Occupational Employment and Wage Estimates, the BLS has managerial jobs listed across its forty-two job categories, including those in farming, mining, and manufacturing. See Occupational Employment Statistics, BLS 2008, http://www.census.gov/compendia/statab/tables/08s0627.pdf.

28. See Ian D. Wyatt and Daniel E. Hecker, "Occupational Changes during the 20th Century," *Monthly Labor Review,* March 2006, 35–57 ("Groupings of Occupations," 36; college completion in 1910, 42).

29. For historical data, see U.S. DOE, *Digest of Education Statistics* (2009), table 188 ("Historical Summary of Faculty, Students, Degrees, and Finances in Degree-Granting Institutions: Selected Years, 1869–70 through 2007–08"), available at http://nces.ed.gov/programs/digest/d09/tables/dt09_188.asp (accessed November 19, 2010).

30. Ibid., table 200 ("Recent High School Completers and Their Enrollment in College, by Sex: 1960 through 2008"), available at http://nces.ed.gov/programs/digest/d09/tables/dt09_200.asp (accessed November 19, 2010).

31. Ibid., table 9 ("Number of Persons Age 18 and Over, by Highest Level of Education Attained, Age, Sex, and Race/Ethnicity: 2009"), available at http://nces.ed.gov/programs/digest/d09/tables/dt09_009.asp (accessed November 19, 2010).

32. *Projections of Education Statistics to 2018,* "Section 4: Degrees Conferred," National Center for Education Statistics, September 2009, available at http://nces.ed.gov/pubs2009/2009062.pdf (accessed November 19, 2010).

33. Aviva Aron-Dine and Arloc Sherman, "New CBO Data Show Income Inequality Continues to Widen: After-Tax-Income for Top 1 Percent Rose by $146,000 in 2004," Center on Budget and Policy Priorities, January 23, 2007, available at http://www.cbpp.org/cms/?fa=view&id=957 (accessed November 19, 2010). The top quintile of households saw after-tax income gains of 69 percent between 1979 and 2004, whereas the top 1 percent increased their income by 176 percent during the same period. For the bottom fifth of the income distribution, income went up 6 percent in this thirty-five-year spell during which taxes were cut and stock markets soared.

34. Randall Collins, *The Credential Society: A Historical Sociology of Education and Stratification* (New York: Academic Press, 1979), 192.

35. Ibid., 194.

36. Jean-François Lyotard, *The Postmodern Condition: A Report on Knowledge* (Minneapolis: University of Minnesota Press, 1984), 50.

37. Ibid., 53.

38. Ibid., 63–64.

39. Ibid., 81.

40. Jürgen Habermas, "Modernity: An Incomplete Project," in *The Anti-aesthetic: Essays on Postmodern Culture*, ed. Hal Foster (Port Townsend, WA: Bay Press, 1983), 3–15.

41. Harry Collins and Robert Evans, *Rethinking Expertise* (Chicago: University of Chicago Press, 2007), 2. The authors provide a strikingly modest corrective that relies on the tacit knowledge of the transitive and interactional mediators of specialization (like themselves in the sociology of science), "in spite of the fallibility of those who know what they are talking about, their advice is likely to be no worse, and may be better, than those who do not know what they are talking about."

42. See Micki McGee, *Self-Help, Inc.* (New York: Oxford, 2006).

43. On the home and the financial labors of maintaining it as a new revenue stream or liquidity, see Dick Bryan and Mike Rafferty, "Financialization and the Subsumption of Labour before and after the Subprime Crisis," *Historical Materialism* (forthcoming). For a look at this new phenomenology of home ownership, see Fiona Allon, *Renovation Nation: Our Obsession with Home* (Sydney: University of New South Wales Press, 2008), and for an account of the mortgage debacle, see Paul Mason, *Meltdown: The End of the Age of Greed* (London: Verso, 2009).

44. See Randy Martin, "Subprime—A Different Cut," *Mute Magazine*, June 2008.

45. Jonathan D. Glater, "Student Loans Start to Bypass 2-year Colleges," *New York Times*, June 2, 2008, A1, A13.

46. Steven Brint, *In an Age of Experts: The Changing Role of Professionals in Politics and Public Life* (Princeton, NJ: Princeton University Press, 1994), 5.

47. Andrew Ross, *No Respect: Intellectuals and Popular Culture* (New York: Routledge, 1989), 229.

48. Thorstein Veblen, *The Higher Learning in America* (1916; repr., New Brunswick, NJ: Transaction, 1993).

49. Alex Williams, "The Falling Down Professions: For Lawyers and Doctors, Gold-Embossed Diplomas Are No Longer So Golden." Style, *New York Times Sunday*, January 6, 2008, 1, 8–9.

50. John Craig, "Production Values: Building Shared Autonomy," in *Production Values: Futures for Professionalism*, ed. John Craig (London: Demos, 2006), 14. Craig calls for a realignment of producer and consumer needs and interests to yield what he terms "shared autonomy" (13–25).

51. Lynn Curry et al., *Educating Professionals: Responding to New Expectations for Competence and Accountability* (San Francisco: Jossey-Bass Publishers, 1993), xi.

52. Michael F. Middaugh, *Understanding Faculty Productivity: Standards and Benchmarks for Colleges and Universities* (San Francisco: Jossey-Bass Publishers, 2001), xvi.

53. Barbara Bender and John H. Schuh, eds., *Using Benchmarking to Inform Practice in Higher Education* (San Francisco: Jossey-Bass, 2002), 1.

54. Gary Becker, *Human Capital: A Theoretical and Empirical Analysis with Special Reference to Education*, 2nd ed. (New York: Columbia University Press, 1977), 37.

55. For a synopsis of Bourdieu's conception, see his "The Forms of Capital," in *Handbook of Theory and Research for the Sociology of Education*, ed. John G. Richardson (New York: Greenwood Press, 1986), 241–258. Bourdieu's writings on

education are extensive and can be found in *Homo Academicus* (Stanford: Stanford University Press, 1988), and in *Reproduction in Education, Society, and Culture* (Thousand Oaks, CA: Sage, 1977), which he coauthored with Jean-Claude Passeron. Bourdieu is careful to distinguish his position from the naturalized differentiation of human capital theories, such as those of Gary Becker, but the historical specificity for the conditions of autonomous fields of distinction—the contingencies of boundary maintenance—are not always considered in discussions of his work.

56. For a nuanced recent treatment of this transformation see Matteo Pasquinelli, *Animal Spirits: A Bestiary of the Commons* (Rotterdam, Netherlands: NAi Publishers/Institute of Network Cultures, 2008).

57. See Alan Liu, *The Laws of Cool: Knowledge Work and the Culture of Information* (Chicago: University of Chicago Press, 2004), 299. Liu posits a deep antinomy within the inner experience of knowledge-making, that for all the team-building corporate ethos that has migrated through the knowledge economy and into the university, there is "the 'gesture' of ambivalent recusant oppositionality (not quite a 'statement,' 'expression,' or even 'representation' of defiance within knowledge work" (293). This coolness toward the enthusiasm of managerialist self-confidence is for Liu a sleeper cell of the new economy.

58. National Science Foundation, *Science and Engineering Indicators, 2008*, in "Chapter 6: Industry, Technology, and the Global Marketplace," January 2008, available at http://www.nsf.gov/statistics/seind08/c6/c6h.htm (accessed November 22, 2010).

59. Laura G. Knapp et al., *Enrollment in Postsecondary Institutions, Fall 2005* (National Center for Education Statistics, 2007), table A-8 ("Revenues and Expenses and the Percentages Input for Title IV Institutions"), A24–A25.

60. At $363.5 billion, this figure of expenditures is substantially less than the total revenues and earnings figure cited in table A-8, note 59. For historical data on expenditures, see U.S. DOE, *Digest of Education Statistics* (2006), (table 25, "Expenditures of Educational Institutions Related to the Gross Domestic Product, by Level of Institution: Selected Years, 1929–30 through 2005–06"), available at http://nces.ed.gov/programs/digest/d06/tables/dt06_025.asp?referrer=report (accessed November 22, 2010).

61. U.S. Patent and Trademark Office (USPTO), Electronic Information Products Division, Patent Technology Monitoring Team (PTMT) Historic Data, Extended Year Set—All Technologies (Utility Patents) Report, Parts A1, A2, and B granted: January 1, 1963, to December 31, 2006, *A Patent Technology Monitoring Team Report*, available at http://www.uspto.gov/go/taf/h_at.htm#PartA1_1 (accessed November 22, 2010).

62. See National Science Foundation, *Science and Engineering Indicators, 2008*, "Chapter 5: "Academic Research and Development," January 2008, available at http://www.nsf.gov/statistics/seind08/c5/c5s3.htm (accessed November 22, 2010).

63. Ibid., appendix table 5-42, "Academic Licensing and Patenting Activities: 1991–2005," available at http://www.nsf.gov/statistics/seind08/append/c5/at05-42 .xls (accessed November 22, 2010).

64. "Academic Patenting: Patents Awarded to U.S. Universities," National Science Foundation, Science and Engineering Statistics, available at http://www.nsf .gov/statistics/seind96/ch5_acad.htm (accessed November 22, 2010).

65. For a discussion of the complexities of what changes in patent granting measure in terms of technological innovation, see Zvi Griliches, "Patent Statistics

as Economic Indicators: A Survey," *Journal of Economic Literature* 28 (December 1990): 1661–1707.

66. USPTO Electronic Information Products Division PTMT Historic Data (see note 61).

67. Knapp et al., *Enrollment in Postsecondary Institutions, Fall 2005*, 3.

68. See, for example, John Thelin, *A History of American Higher Education* (Baltimore: Johns Hopkins University Press, 2004); Christopher J. Lucas, *American Higher Education: A History* (New York: Palgrave Macmillan, 2006); Hugh Davis Graham and Nancy A. Diamond, *The Rise of American Research Universities: Elites and Challengers in the Postwar Era* (Baltimore: Johns Hopkins University Press, 1999).

69. William Clark, *Academic Charisma and the Origins of the Research University* (Chicago: University of Chicago Press, 2006), 3.

70. Steve Fuller, "University Leadership in the Twenty-first Century: The Case for Academic Caesarism," in *Geographies of Knowledge, Geometries of Power: Framing the Future of Higher Education*, ed. Debbie Epstein et al. (New York: Routledge, 2007), 50–66.

71. Sheila Slaughter and Gary Rhoades, *Academic Capitalism and the New Economy: Markets, State, and Higher Education* (Baltimore: Johns Hopkins University Press, 2004), 1. Sheila Slaughter and Larry Leslie's earlier formulation of the concept appeared as *Academic Capitalism: Policies, Politics, and the Entrepreneurial University* (Baltimore: Johns Hopkins University Press, 1997).

72. Slaughter and Rhoades, *Academic Capitalism and the New Economy*, 15.

73. Gregg Pascal Zachary, *Endless Frontier: Vannevar Bush, Engineer of the 20th Century* (Cambridge, MA: MIT Press, 1999), 4.

74. These articulations are discussed by Slaughter and Rhoades in *Academic Capitalism and the New Economy* (cf 28) but also by Paul Edwards, *The Closed World: Computers and the Politics of Discourse during the Cold War* (Cambridge, MA: MIT Press, 1996); Christopher Simpson, ed., *Universities and Empire: Money and Politics in the Social Sciences in Cold War America* (New York: New Press, 1998); Noam Chomsky et al., *The Cold War and the University: Toward an Intellectual History of the Postwar Years* (New York: New Press, 1997).

75. Christopher Newfield, *Ivy and Industry* (Durham, NC: Duke University Press, 2003).

76. Slaughter and Rhoades, *Academic Capitalism and the New Economy*, 52–53.

77. This discussion draws directly from Chapter 2, "The Policy Climate for Academic Capitalism," in *Academic Capitalism and the New Economy*. See also the work of Henry Etzkowitz—for example, Henry Etzkowitz and Loet Leydesdorff, eds., *Universities and the Global Knowledge Economy: A Triple Helix of University-Industry-Government Relations* (London: Pinter, 1997); Henry Etzkowitz, Andrew Webster, and Peter Healey, eds., *Capitalizing Knowledge: New Intersections of Industry and Academia* (Albany, NY: SUNY Press, 1998); Henry Etzkowitz, *MIT and the Rise of Entrepreneurial Science* (London: Routledge, 2002).

78. Slaughter and Rhoades, *Academic Capitalism and the New Economy*, 42.

79. T. B. Hoffer et al., *Doctorate Recipients from United States Universities: Summary Report 2004*, National Opinion Research Center, quoted in The Project on Student Debt, available at http://projectonstudentdebt.org/files/pub/Debt_Facts _and_Sources.pdf (accessed November 22, 2010).

80. "Quick Facts about Student Debt," The Project on Student Debt, http://www.projectonstudentdebt.org. Between 1993 and 2009, average debt levels

increased from $9,250 to $24,000, while unemployment climbed from 5.8 percent in 2008 to 8.7 percent in 2009. "Student Debt and the Class of 2009," http://projectonstudentdebt.org/files/pub/classof2009.pdf. Of the tenth with the greatest debt, those who attended public institutions left with at least $32,994, those from private colleges $40,000 or more, and those from proprietary schools $45,000 or more. In 2010, student debt at $829.785 billion surpassed credit card debt of $826.5 billion. Mary Pilon, "Student Debt Surpasses Credit Card Debt," *Wall Street Journal*, August 9, 2010, available at http://blogs.wsj.com/economics/2010/08/09/student-loan-debt-surpasses-credit-cards (accessed January 15, 2011).

81. See *Morgan Adamson, "The Financialization of Student Life: Five Propositions on Student Debt," Polygraph* 21 (Summer 2009).

82. Knapp et al., *Enrollment in Postsecondary Institutions, Fall 2005,* table 1 ("Enrollment at Title IV Institutions"), available at http://nces.ed.gov/pubs2007/2007154.pdf (accessed November 22, 2010).

83. Kwang Kim et al., "National Household Surveys of 2001: Participation in Adult Education and Lifelong Learning: 2000–2001" (Washington, DC: National Center for Education Statistics, 2004), xi, available at http://adulted.about.com/cs/studiesstats1/a/participation.htm.http://adulted.about.com/gi/dynamic/offsite.htm?zi=1/XJ&sdn=adulted&cdn=education&tm=57&gps=262_26_1020_53 8&f=00&su=p554.2.150.ip_&tt=2&bt=0&bts=0&zu=http%3A//nces.ed.gov/pubsearch/pubsinfo.asp%3Fpubid%3D2004050 (accessed November 22, 2010).

84. National Center for Education Statistics, E.D. TAB: "Adult Education Participation in 2004–05," May 2006, available at http://nces.ed.gov/pubs2006/adulted/06.asp (accessed November 22, 2010). This report does not tabulate actual revenue as it is based on a survey of nearly nine thousand and extrapolations are made on the basis of the findings.

85. See Mary Lindenstein Walshok, *Knowledge without Boundaries: What America's Research Universities Can Do for the Economy, the Workplace, and the Community* (San Francisco: Jossey-Bass Publishers, 1995). For a look at state-education relations in a broader frame, see Michael W. Apple, ed., *The State and the Politics of Knowledge* (New York: RoutledgeFalmer, 2003).

CHAPTER 2

1. Phillipe Aries's seminal *Centuries of Childhood* (New York: Knopf, 1962) treated it as a wholly modern discovery, a view that has been tempered by subsequent historians to emphasize shifts in the conception of life's early episodes. See, for example, Colin Heywood, *A History of Childhood: Children and Childhood in the West from Medieval to Modern Times* (Malden, MA: Polity, 2002). The politics of this backward-looking gaze is critically interrogated by Stephanie Coontz, *The Way We Never Were: American Families and the Nostalgia Trap* (New York: Basic Books, 1992).

2. See Diane Ravitch, *Left Back: A Century of Failed School Reform* (New York: Simon and Schuster, 2000), 362. Ravitch, an assistant secretary of education in the George H. W. Bush administration, treats departures from academic tradition as undermining the democratic promise of education by denying the highest quality instruction to those deemed incapable of comprehending it (460). She is equally suspicious of tendencies that understand themselves to have a politics: "Anything in education that is labeled a 'movement' should be avoided like the plague. What American education most needs is not more nostrums and enthusiasms, but more

attention to fundamental, time-tested truths" (453). Ravitch's formulations, profoundly contentious as educational policy, were voiced as being outside politics in a manner consistent with those who would accuse dissenting positions with less institutional authority as agents of "political correctness."

3. For Gardner's account of this exchange with Reagan, see David Pierpont Gardner, *Earning My Degree: Memoirs of an American University President* (Berkeley: University of California Press, 2005), 115.

4. "A Nation at Risk: The Imperative for Educational Reform," U.S. Department of Education, National Commission on Excellence in Education (Washington, DC: The Commission: [Supt. of Docs., U.S. G.P.O. distributor], 1983), 5.

5. *No Child Left Behind Act of 2001*, Public Law 107-110, 107th Cong., 20, *U.S. Code* 6472, (January 8, 2002), section 1432, available at http://www.ed.gov/policy/elsec/leg/esea02/107-110.pdf (accessed December 4, 2010).

6. Barack Obama quoted February 24, 2009. See "The American Recovery and Reinvestment Act of 2009: Saving and Creating Jobs and Reforming Education," U.S. Department of Education, March 7, 2009, http://www2.ed.gov/policy/gen/leg/recovery/implementation.html.

7. This analysis is a highly synoptic account of arguments developed in my previous work. See Randy Martin, *Financialization of Daily Life* (Philadelphia: Temple University Press, 2002), and *An Empire of Indifference: American War and the Financial Logic of Risk Management* (Durham, NC: Duke University Press, 2007).

8. The extensive critiques of testing from among education experts have strained to influence policy directions. See, for example, Sharon Lynn Nichols and David Berliner, *Collateral Damage: How High-Stakes Testing Corrupts America's Schools* (Cambridge, MA: Harvard Educational Press, 2007).

9. Information on the mission and history of the school can be found on its Web site: "About: History," PS3, http://PS3nyc.org/blog/?page_id=1112. This account is compiled from conversations with numerous people in the school community.

10. The claim that New York's schools were a national model was made locally and by Education Secretary Arne Duncan, and inserted into the controversy over Klein's stewardship and the larger issue of mayoral control of schools. For an account, see Elissa Gootman, "Controlling Interests: Taking Sides on New York's School Chancellor," *New York Times*, March 5, 2009, available at http://www.nytimes.com/2009/03/06/nyregion/06klein.html (accessed December 4, 2010).

11. This figure is taken from a report prepared for New York Assemblyman James F. Brennan based on 2007 statistics by Brena Cascini, "Student Achievement: New York City and the Big Four," New York City Department of Education, New York State Assembly, March 2009, available at http://assembly.state.ny.us/member_files/044/20090319/report.pdf (accessed December 4, 2010).

12. Figures taken from Diane Ravitch, *The Death and Life of the Great American School System: How Testing and Choice Are Undermining Education* (New York: Basic Books, 2010), 45. Ravitch profiles the changes both demographic and educational in District 2 (see her chap. 3, "The Transformation of District 2"). The book provides a reversal of her earlier positions (see note 2) in favor of testing and choice regimes of which she observes, "The more I saw, the more I lost faith" (4).

13. Charly Greene, interview by Randy Martin, July 12, 2007.

14. Ibid.

15. For some context and case studies of mayoral control as a political issue in the United States, see Joseph P. Viteritti, ed. *When Mayors Take Charge: School Governance in the City* (New York: Brookings Institution Press, 2009).

16. "About Us: Children First History," New York City Department of Education, July 2008, http://schools.nyc.gov/AboutUs/ChildrenFirstHistory/default.htm.

17. "Who We Are," NYC Leadership Academy, http://www.nycleadership academy.org/who-we-are.

18. Elissa Gootman and Robert Gebeloff, "Controlling Interests: Principals Younger and Freer, but Raise Doubts in the Schools," New York Times, May 25, 2009, available at http://www.nytimes.com/2009/05/26/nyregion/26principals .html?scp=5&sq=Elissa%20Gootman&st=cse (accessed December 4, 2010).

19. "Times Topics: People: Cathleen P. Black," New York Times, November 30, 2010, available at http://topics.nytimes.com/top/reference/timestopics/people/b/ cathleen_p_black/index.html (accessed December 22, 2010).

20. Information available at http://www.community-lso.org (accessed July 2008).

21. "About Us," New York City Department of Education, July 2008, http:// schools.nyc.gov/AboutUs/default.htm.

22. Ibid.

23. Ibid.

24. The DOE's 2005 manual "Creating a Quality IEP" defines it as the documentation process required for provision of special services. It also uses the language of "at-risk" populations; in this case, those who may not proceed to the next grade. "Creating a Quality IEP," New York City Department of Education, July 2008, http://schools.nyc.gov/NR/rdonlyres/69D78629-9B1B-4247-A23B-C09B581A FAB1/2962/THENEWIEPMANUALJANUARY2005.pdf.

25. Elissa Gootman, "In Elite N.Y. Schools, a Dip in Blacks and Hispanics," New York Times, August 18, 2006, available at http://www.nytimes.com/2006/08/18/ education/18schools.html (accessed December 5, 2010). "Still, during 2005–6, blacks made up 4.8 percent of the Bronx Science student body, according to city figures, down from 11.8 percent in 1994–95, when the institute was created. At Brooklyn Technical High School, the proportion of black students has declined to 14.9 percent from 37.3 percent 11 years ago, and at Stuyvesant, blacks now make up 2.2 percent of the student body, down from 4.4 percent."

26. Sam Roberts, "In Surge in Manhattan Toddlers, Rich White Families Lead Way," New York Times, March 23, 2007, available at http://www.nytimes .com/2007/03/23/nyregion/23kid.html (accessed December 5, 2010). "The analysis shows that Manhattan's 35,000 or so white non-Hispanic toddlers are being raised by parents whose median income was $284,208 a year in 2005, which means they are growing up in wealthier households than similar youngsters in any other large county in the country. . . . Their ranks expanded by more than 40 percent from 2000 to 2005. For the first time since at least the 1960s, white children now outnumber either black or Hispanic youngsters in that age group in Manhattan. . . . In comparison, the median income of other Manhattan households with toddlers was $66,213 for Asians, $31,171 for blacks and $25,467 for Hispanic families." One parent interviewed for the article, reflecting on public education said, "We have every intention of sending our kids to P.S. 6. New York is a wonderful place to raise children, especially if there are more of them and more resources devoted to them."

27. Elissa Gootman, "Gifted Kindergarten Programs Expand," New York Times, May 4, 2009, available at http://cityroom.blogs.nytimes.com/2009/05/04/ gifted-kindergarten-programs-expand.html (accessed May 4, 2009).

28. Jennifer Medina, "Standards Raised, More Students Fail Tests," New York Times, July 28, 2010, available at http://www.nytimes.com/2010/07/29/

education/29scores.html?scp=1&sq=drop%20in%20NYC%20school%20test%20 scores&st=cse (accessed December 22, 2010).

29. Michael W. Apple, *Educating the "Right Way": Markets, Standards, God, and Inequality*, 2nd ed. (New York: Routlege, 2006), 186. Within five years, an increase of nearly 30 percent was reported.

30. See, for example, the fact sheet produced by Brian Ray of the National Home Education Research Institute, which claims 20 percent to 60 percent improvement in standardized test scores compared to children in public schools. Brian Ray, "Facts on Homeschooling," National Home Education Research Institute, available at http://www.nheri.org/content/view/174/51 (accessed December 5, 2010).

31. Linda M. McNeill, *Contradictions of School Reform* (New York: Routledge, 2000), xxvii.

CHAPTER 3

1. Profiles are constructed annually by the Comparative Institutional Research Program of the Higher Education Research Institute at UCLA. See *The American Freshman: National Norms 2009*, January 2010, http://www.heri.ucla.edu/PDFs/pubs/briefs/brief-pr012110-09FreshmanNorms.pdf. On political attitudes, self-designated liberals have outnumbered conservatives every year save 1981, with Reagan's election (19.2 percent to 21.5 percent, respectively), and the liberals spiked in 2008, with the election of Obama, to 31 percent, versus 20.7 percent conservative, and those reporting volunteering as a form of civic engagement hit a record high of more than 30 percent. While concerned about future finances and undertaking greater debt, freshmen polled by CIRP are shifting away from business-related fields.

2. See, for example, Herbert Marcuse, *One Dimensional Man: Studies in the Ideology of Advanced Industrial Society* (Boston: Beacon, 1964); Erich Fromm, *Escape from Freedom* (New York: Avon Books, 1965); Paul Goodman, *Growing Up Absurd: Problems of Youth in the Organized Society* (New York: Vintage Books, 1960).

3. Irving Louis Horowitz and William H. Friedland. *The Knowledge Factory: Student Power and Academic Politics in America* (Chicago: Aldine Publishing, 1970), 118.

4. Ibid., 120.

5. Ibid., 125.

6. Greg Ip, "The Declining Value of Your College Degree," *Wall Street Journal*, July 17, 2008, available at http://online.wsj.com/article/SB121623686919059307.html (accessed December 7, 2010).

7. Steven C. Riggert et al., "Student Employment and Higher Education: Empiricism and Contradiction," *Review of Educational Research* 76, no. 1 (Spring 2006): 63–92 (esp. 64).

8. U.S. Department of Labor, Bureau of Labor Statistics, "College Enrollment and Work Activity of 2006 High School Graduates," April 2007, available at http://www.bls.gov/news.release/hsgec.nr0.htm (accessed December 7, 2010).

9. U.S. Department of Education, *Digest of Education Statistics* (Washington, DC: National Center for Education Statistics, 2006), table 177 ("Total Fall Enrollment in Degree-Granting Institutions, by Attendance Status, Age, and Sex: Selected Years, 1970 through 2015"), available at http://nces.ed.gov/programs/digest/d06/tables/dt06_177.asp (accessed December 7, 2010).

10. With respect to the privileged citizen-subject entitled to participation, the universalist aspirations of the liberal arts help to naturalize a particular national

identity. See, for example, Raymond Williams, *Culture and Society* (New York: Harper and Row, 1966); David Lloyd and Paul Thomas, *Culture and the State* (New York: Routledge, 1998); Bill Readings, *The University in Ruins* (Cambridge, MA: Harvard University Press, 1996).

11. The relevant figures here are John Henry Cardinal Newman, whose *The Idea of the University* was originally published in 1852 (New Haven, CT: Yale University Press, 1996); Abraham Flexner, whose formulation of research in *Medical Education in the United States and Canada* (Boston: Updyke, Merrymount Press, 1910) was based on professional education; Clark Kerr, whose *The Uses of the University*, 4th ed. (Cambridge, MA: Harvard University Press, 1995), was first published in 1963; and Larry Leslie and Sheila Slaughter (*Academic Capitalism* [Baltimore: Johns Hopkins University Press, 1999]).

12. Data on Degree-Granting Postsecondary Enrollment are from U.S. DOE, *Digest of Education Statistics* (2002), 205 (table 171, "Historical Summary of Faculty, Students, Degrees, and Finances in Degree-Granting Institutions: 1869–70 to 1999–2000") and from *Digest of Education Statistics* (2006), table 260 ("Degrees Conferred by Degree-Granting Institutions, by Control of Institution, Level of Degree, and Discipline Division: 2004–05), available at http://nces.ed.gov/programs/digest/d06/tables/dt06_260.asp (accessed December 7, 2010). For 2007–2008 data, see *The Condition of Education 2010: Contexts of Postsecondary Education*, sec. 5, U.S. Department of Education (Washington, DC: National Center for Education Statistics, 2010), available at http://nces.ed.gov/pubs2010/2010028_6.pdf (accessed December 7, 2010).

13. The numbers for professional and liberal arts degrees are based on my own aggregation of categories in table 252 ("Bachelor's Degrees Conferred by Degree-Granting Institutions, by Discipline Division: 1970–71 to 2001–25"), available at http://nces.ed.gov/programs/digest/d03/tables/dt252.asp (accessed December 7, 2010).

14. U.S. DOE, *Digest of Education Statistics* (2002), 306 (table 254, "Doctor's Degrees Conferred by Degree-Granting Institutions, by Discipline Division: 1970–71 to 2000–2001"), available at http://nces.ed.gov/programs/digest/d03/tables/dt254.asp (accessed December 7, 2010).

15. Stanley Aronowitz, *The Knowledge Factory: Dismantling the Corporate University and Creating True Higher Learning* (Boston: Beacon Press, 2000), 137–138.

16. For a history, see Timothy P. Cross, *An Oasis of Order: The Core Curriculum at Columbia College* (New York: Columbia College, Office of the Dean, 1995), chap. 1 ("The Insistent Problems of the Present"), available at http://www.college.columbia.edu/core/oasis/history1.php (accessed December 7, 2010).

17. "The Core Curriculum," Columbia College, http://www.college.columbia.edu/bulletin/core.

18. Boyer's survey (as Cross observes in *An Oasis of Order*) lists the five most important places with core curricula, and although the survey doesn't mention Columbia's program, it precedes all of them: (1) Harvard University, (2) University of Chicago, (3) Alverno College (Wisconsin), (4) Saint Joseph's College (Indiana), and (5) Brooklyn College of the City University of New York. See Ernest L. Boyer, *College: The Undergraduate Experience in America* (New York: Harper and Row, 1987), 99–100. In the twenty years since, the claim to importance itself would become far more difficult to sustain.

19. This, at least, was the assessment of skeptic, Harry R. Lewis, in his *Excellence without a Soul: How A Great University Forgot Education* (New York: Public Affairs, 2006).

20. "Report of the Task Force on General Education," Harvard University, 2007, 1, available at http://www.fas.harvard.edu/~secfas/General_Education_Final _Report.pdf (accessed July 2008).

21. "Curriculum: The Ideal of a Liberal Education," University of Chicago Admissions: Academics, https://collegeadmissions.uchicago.edu/level2.asp?id=7.

22. College Catalog 2007–2008, Shoreline Community College, http://www .shoreline.edu/catgenedcore.html.

23. Derek Bok, *Our Underachieving Colleges: A Candid Look at How Much Students Learn and Why They Should Be Learning More* (Princeton, NJ: Princeton University Press, 2006).

24. Among the titles that Bok references, intending to be ideologically ecumenical but clearly inflected toward the rightist assault on higher education, are the books by former heads of the National Endowment for the Humanities: William J. Bennett, *To Reclaim a Legacy: A Report on the Humanities in Higher Education*, and Lynne Cheney, *Tyrannical Machines: A Report on Educational Practices Gone Wrong and Our Best Hopes of Setting Them Right*; books that got considerable public attention, such as Allan Bloom, *The Closing of the American Mind: How Higher Education Has Failed Democracy and Impoverished the Souls of Today's Students*; Dinesh D'Souza *Illiberal Education: The Politics of Race and Sex on Campus*; Charles Sykes, *Profscam*; Roger Kimball, *Tenured Radicals: How Politics Has Corrupted Higher Education*; as well as the radical critique of Bok's own liberal humanist nationalism, Bill Readings, *The University in Ruins*.

25. For this longer historical view, see Frederick Rudolph, *Curriculum: A History of the American Course of Study since 1636*; and Lawrence Veysey, *The Emergence of the American University*.

26. Bok, *Our Underachieving Colleges*, 331.

27. Ibid., 315

28. Derek Bok, *Universities in the Marketplace: The Commercialization of Higher Education* (Princeton, NJ: Princeton University Press, 2003).

29. Donald M. Stewart, "Standardized Testing in a National Context," in *Higher Learning in America: 1980–2000*, ed. Arthur Levine (Baltimore: Johns Hopkins University Press, 1993), 344–359 (esp. 354).

30. See William V. Spanos, *The End of Education: Toward Posthumanism* (Minneapolis: University of Minnesota Press, 1993), esp. 118–161 (chap. 4, "The Violence of Disinterestedness: A Genealogy of the Educational 'Reform' Initiative in the 1980s").

31. James W. Hall, ed., *In Opposition to the Core Curriculum: Alternative Models for Higher Education* (Westport, CT: Greenwood, 1982), xvi.

32. Paul Willis, *Learning to Labour: How Working Class Kids Get Working Class Jobs* (New York: Columbia University Press, 1981).

33. Randy Martin, "Introduction," in *Artistic Citizenship: A Public Voice for the Arts*, eds. Mary Schmidt Campbell and Randy Martin (New York: Routledge, 2006), 16–17.

34. A selection of student essays from around New York University is published annually in a piece called "Unchained Cannibals" in the NYU journal *Mercer Street*, eds. Pat C. Hoy II et al. (2007): 157.

35. Ibid., 162.

36. Ryan Chassee, "Battling for Bethesda: Public Space in Play," *Mercer Street* (2005): 126.

37. Ibid., 131.

38. An open call to faculty for course proposals was made along the following lines:

> (1) *Content:* Proposed courses should address questions of public policy broadly construed as the means for the support, making, and dissemination of the arts. Issues to be considered could include day-to-day decisions of artists; creation of institutions such as theaters or production companies and their internal dynamics, diversity, and approaches to programming; means for creating public spaces and engaging audiences; interfaces with governments and private funding agencies, regulations, and legislation; comparisons between localities, regions, nations, and/or the spaces in between. By establishing the affiliations and commitments of artists through a whole range of institutional sites, public policy poses key questions of ethical and esthetic connections for the arts. (2) *Interdisciplinary:* Interdisciplinarity has a variety of meanings all of which will be considered. Proposed courses can draw from a range of critical approaches—be they historical, ethnographic, textual, phenomenological. Courses can incorporate diverse creative media and expressions that mix various professional fields in the arts. Courses can undertake a reflection on different approaches to or aspects of a field (such as comparative approaches to performance or relations between writing, directing, and production). These courses present an opportunity for Tisch students to draw the links between their creative endeavors and to reflect on the context for all of their professional interests. (3) *Collaboration:* Courses in the Department of Art and Public Policy provide opportunities for collaboration among faculty in different TSOA Departments, or between TSOA and other faculty. When a course is to be co-taught, the proposal should indicate how the collaboration is to take place (e.g., will faculty teach different course modules, codirect a production, participate in a community project together?).

Randy Martin (associate dean of faculty), memo: Department of Art and Public Policy—Call for Proposals, September 27, 2002.

39. Pat C. Hoy II, e-mail message to the office of the NYU president, December 5, 2007. The e-mail was written in response to a student complaint, voiced in a public forum, about the course.

40. Howard Singerman, *Art Subjects: Making Artists in the American University* (Berkeley: University of California Press, 1999), 3–8.

41. See Monika Krause et al., eds., *The University against Itself: The NYU Strike and the Future of the Academic Workplace* (Philadelphia: Temple University Press, 2008). A chronology of pertinent events compiled by the editors appears on pages 115–122.

42. Philip G. Altbach, "Students: Interests, Culture, and Activism," in *Higher Learning in America: 1980–2000*, ed. Arthur Levine (Baltimore: Johns Hopkins University Press, 1993), 203–221 (esp. 214).

43. "Students for a Democratic Society (SDS)," CampusActivism.org, April 14, 2007, http://www.campusactivism.org/displaygroups-701.htm.

CHAPTER 4

1. Immanuel Kant, *The Conflict of the Faculties*, trans. Mary J. Gregor (Lincoln: University of Nebraska Press, 1992), 23.

2. Even the self-managerial inclinations of the faculty, identified by Luc Boltanski and Eve Chiapello as the appropriated legacy of the May '68 movement—which they term the artistic critique for greater workplace freedom and self-criticism—modeled a new flexibility for labor evident in the casualization of the faculty. Luc Boltanski and Eve Chiapello, *The New Spirit of Capitalism*, trans. Gregory Elliott (London: Verso, 2005).

3. For an updated brief on the links between governance, academic freedom, and faculty organization from the perspective of the current AAUP president, see Cary Nelson, *No University Is an Island: Saving Academic Freedom* (New York: New York University Press, 2010).

4. B. Robert Kreiser, ed., *AAUP: Policy Documents and Reports,* 9th ed., (Washington, DC: American Association of University Professors, 2001), 292.

5. Ibid., 293.

6. Ibid., 295.

7. Ibid., 294.

8. See Paul Baran and Paul Sweezy, *Monopoly Capital: An Essay on the American Economic and Social Order* (New York: Monthly Review Press, 1966).

9. Robert O'Neil, *Academic Freedom in the Wired World: Political Extremism, Corporate Power, and the University* (Cambridge, MA: Harvard University Press, 2008), 99.

10. Ibid., 107.

11. Ibid., 102.

12. See Louis Menand, ed., *The Future of Academic Freedom* (Chicago: University of Chicago, 1996) and Stanley Fish, *Save the World on Your Own Time* (Oxford: Oxford University Press, 2008).

13. Ibid., 2–3.

14. Ibid., 89.

15. "Transcript: O'Reilly Interviews Al-Arian in September 2001," *The O'Reilly Factor*, Fox News, September 26, 2001, available at http://www.foxnews .com/printer_friendly_story/0,3566,61096,00.html (accessed December 10, 2010).

16. For a summary of the case, see Stephen Lendman, "Sami Al-Arian's Long Ordeal," March 24, 2008, *Counterpunch*, available at http://www.counterpunch .org/lendman03242008.html (accessed December 10, 2010).

17. Ward Churchill, "Some People Push Back: On the Justice of Roosting Chickens," *Pockets of Resistance* (September 2001), 20–22.

18. See Chalmers Johnson, *Blowback: The Costs and Consequences of American Empire* (New York: Metropolitan Books, 2000).

19. Kirk Johnson and Katharine Q. Seelye, "Jury Says Professor Was Wrongly Fired," *New York Times*, April 3, 2009, available at http://www.nytimes .com/2009/04/03/us/03churchill.html?_r=1&scp=3&sq=Ward%20Churchill%20 %20court&st=cse (accessed December 10, 2010).

20. O'Neil, *Academic Freedom in the Wired World*, 84.

21. "Colorado University Investigation of Ward Churchill," University of Colorado at Boulder, May 16, 2006, available at http://www.colorado.edu/news/ reports/churchill/churchillreport051606.html (accessed January 17, 2011).

22. This point was made by Cornell Professor Eric Cheyfitz. See John Gravois, "University of Colorado Board of Regents Fire Ward Churchill, Who Vows to Sue,"

The Chronicle of Higher Education, July 25, 2007, available at https://chronicle
.com/article/University-of-Colorado-Board/123484 (accessed January 17, 2011).

23. Robert Post, "The Structure of Academic Freedom," in *Academic Freedom after September 11*, ed. Beshara Doumani (New York: Zone Books, 2006), 64.

24. Ibid., 69.

25. Judith Butler, "Academic Norms, Contemporary Challenge: A Reply to Robert Post on Academic Freedom," in *Academic Freedom after September 11*, 115–116.

26. Ibid., 128.

27. Ibid., 132.

28. Ibid., 137.

29. See Christopher Simpson, *Universities and Empire: Money and Politics in the Social Sciences during the Cold War* (New York: New Press, 1998).

30. See Immanuel Wallerstein, *The End of the World as We Know It: Social Science for the 21st Century* (Minneapolis: University of Minnesota Press, 1999).

31. The reference comes from Dwight D. Eisenhower's televised exit speech given January 17, 1961. Dwight D. Eisenhower, "Military-Industrial Complex Speech," Matrix, January 17, 1961, available at http://coursesa.matrix.msu .edu/~hst306/documents/indust.html (accessed December 10, 2010).

32. Peter Burke observes: "One of the most important intellectual trends in early modern Europe was the rise of skepticism of various kinds concerning claims to knowledge." See his *A Social History of Knowledge: From Gutenberg to Diderot* (Cambridge, UK: Polity Press, 2000), 197.

33. For an early critique of the trend, see Emily Abel, *Terminal Degrees: The Job Crisis in Higher Education* (New York: Praeger, 1984), and for a pointed gender critique, see Eileen E. Schell, *Gypsy Academics and Mother-Teachers: Gender, Contingent Labor, and Writing Instruction* (Portsmouth, NH: Boynton/Cook Publishers, 1998). That the model of casualization is now globalized is registered in Rudolphus Teeuwen and Steffen Hantke, eds., *Gypsy Scholars, Migrant Teachers, and the Global Academic Proletariat: Adjunct Labour in Higher Education* (Amsterdam: Rodopi, 2007).

34. U.S. Department of Education, *Digest of Education Statistics* (Washington, DC: National Center for Education Statistics, 2007), 359 (table 238, "Number of Instructional Faculty in degree-granting institutions"), available at http://nces .ed.gov/programs/digest/2009menu_tables.asp (accessed January 17, 2011).

35. U.S. DOE, *Digest of Education Statistics* (2007) (table P62, "Percentage of Teaching Faculty in 4-Year and 2-Year Institutions Working Full-Time and Part-Time"), available at http://nces.edu.gov/surveys/ctes/tables/P62.asp (accessed July 2008).

36. U.S. DOE, *Digest of Education Statistics* (2009) (chap. 3: Postsecondary Education, Digest), available at http://nces.ed.gov/programs/digest/d09/ch_3.asp (accessed January 1, 2011).

37. U.S. DOE, *Digest of Education Statistics* (2007), 373 (table 246, "Average Base Salary of Full-Time Instructional Faculty and Staff in Degree-Granting Institutions, by Type and Control of Institution and Field of Instruction: Selected Years, 1987–88 through 2003–04").

38. Ibid., 262 (chap. 3, Postsecondary Education, Summary).

39. Ernest Boyer, *Scholarship Reconsidered* (New York: Carnegie Foundation for the Advancement of Teaching, 1990), 37.

40. Marc Bousquet, *How the University Works: Higher Education and the Low-Wage Nation* (New York: New York University Press, 2008), 21.

41. Ibid., 27.

42. For explanation of how the rankings are constructed, see "America's Best Colleges: Undergraduate Ranking Criteria and Weights," *U.S. News and World Report*, August 17, 2007, available at http://colleges.usnews.rankingsandreviews .com/usnews/edu/college/rankings/about/weight_brief.php (accessed June 19, 2008).

43. The internal process of peer review and the tacit consensus established through the acts of deliberation is detailed in Michele Lamont's *How Professor's Think: Inside the Curious World of Academic Judgment* (Cambridge, MA: Harvard University Press, 2009). Lamont's study is based upon interdisciplinary panels deliberating on prestigious fellowships, and it points to the substantive limits to understanding work that generates a kind of customary deferral.

44. Scott Jaschik, "Battle Lines on *U.S. News*," *Inside Higher Education*, May 7, 2007, available at http://www.insidehighered.com/news/2007/05/07/usnews (accessed December 10, 2010).

45. See the report produced by the collective initiative of representatives of research universities and Campus Compact to renew the civic mission of higher education. Timothy Stanton, "New Times Demand New Scholarship II: A Conference Report 2007," Campus Compact, available at http://www.compact.org/initiatives/ research_universities/Civic_Engagement.pdf (accessed December 10, 2010).

46. Ibid., 26.

47. Julie Ellison and Timothy K. Eatman, *Scholarship in Public: Knowledge Creation and Tenure Policy in the Engaged University* (Syracuse, NY: Imagining America, 2008).

48. Ibid., xiii.

49. See Stefano Harney and Fred Moten, "The University and the Undercommons: Seven Theses," *Social Text* 22.2 (2004): 101–115.

50. See Brian Pusser, *Burning Down the House: Politics, Governance, and Affirmative Action at the University of California* (Albany: SUNY Press, 2004).

51. For an inside account, see then-chair of history at University of Minnesota Kinley Brauer, "The Tenure Crisis at Minnesota," Organization of American Historians, November 1996, http://www.oah.org/pubs/nl/96nov/brauer1196.html. Another participant, biochemistry professor Vic Bloomfield, observed that the episode was perhaps "destructive of faculty governance, but in terms of what we care about, it's ended up positive," because a strong tenure and academic freedom code prevailed along with community support that had not existed previously. See Stanford Lehmberg and Ann M. Pflaum, *The University of Minnesota: 1945–2000* (Minneapolis: University of Minnesota Press, 2001), 252.

52. See President of the Council of UC Faculty Associations Bob Meister, "They Pledged Your Tuition (An Open Letter to UC Students)," Keep California's Promise, October 2009, http://keepcaliforniaspromise.org/wp-content/uploads/2009/10/ They_Pledged_Your_Tuition.pdf.

53. This position has been articulated well in a recent book by Frank Donoghue, *The Last Professors: The Corporate University and the Fate of the Humanities* (New York: Fordham, 2008). He sees denial of the humanist predicament and familiar defenses of academic freedom rendering the faculty powerless in the face of new developments. "Minimizing the economic realities of higher education represents a desperate attempt by professors to retain some power over its future direction" (137). His call for the study of institutional histories is fruitfully augmented by a rethinking of administrative labor.

CHAPTER 5

1. Representative of this literature is Jim Collins, *Good to Great: Why Some Companies Make the Leap and Others Don't* (New York: Harper Collins, 2001).

2. Despite their dramatic declines following the 2008 stock market crash, top university endowments have been offered as general investment models. See, for example, Matthew Tuttle, *How Harvard and Yale Beat the Market: What Individual Investors Can Learn from the Investment Strategies of the Most Successful University Endowments* (New York: Wiley, 2009).

3. For a recent literature review that makes this point, see Allan L. Scherr and Michael C. Jensen, "A New Model of Leadership," Negotiations, Organizations, and Markets: Research Papers, Harvard NOM Research Paper No. 06-10, Barbados Group Working Paper No. 06-02, August 2007.

4. Quotes from James J. Duderstadt, *The View from the Helm: Leading the American University during a Time of Change* (Ann Arbor: University of Michigan Press, 2007), 101.

5. Ibid., 58.

6. Ibid., 314. One distinctive feature that remains for public universities is the amount of budget information they disclose. University of Michigan's is available at http://sitemaker.umich.edu/obpinfo/files/greybk_aasum_fy08.pdf (accessed July 2008). For 2007–2008, athletics took in some $72 million with nearly $10 million in net revenue, as compared with the $2.2 billion that health care collected while netting more than $50 million.

7. Duderstadt, *View from the Helm*, 132.

8. Ibid., 106.

9. Ibid., 110.

10. Ibid., 112.

11. Ibid., 329.

12. Ibid., 331.

13. Ibid., 282.

14. Ibid., 275.

15. Ibid., 178.

16. Merriam-Webster, http://www.merriam-webster.com.

17. Duderstadt, *View from the Helm*, 272.

18. Gary Hamel and C. K. Prahalad, *Competing for the Future* (Boston: Harvard Business School Press, 1994). See also Henry Mintzberg, *The Rise and Fall of Strategic Planning: Reconceiving Roles for Planning, Plans, Planners* (New York: Free Press 1994).

19. Edward Whalen, *Responsibility Center Budgeting: An Approach to Decentralized Management for Institutions of Higher Education* (Bloomington: Indiana University Press, 1991).

20. Duderstadt, *View from the Helm*, 275.

21. Ibid., 335.

22. Ibid., 338.

23. Gary Rhoades, "Who's Doing It Right? Strategic Activity in Public Research Universities," *Review of Higher Education* 24, no. 1 (Fall 2000): 41–66.

24. Morris Llewellyn Cooke, *Academic and Industrial Efficiency* (New York: Carnegie Foundation, 1910).

25. Robert Birnbaum, *Management Fads in Higher Education: Where They Come From, What They Do, Why They Fail* (San Francisco: Jossey-Bass, 2000).

26. Allan Schofield, *Benchmarking in Higher Education*, UNESDOC Database, United Nations Educational, Scientific, and Cultural Organization, 1998, 14, http://unesdoc.unesco.org/images/0011/001128/112812eo.pdf.

27. Daniel James Rowley and Herbert Sherman, *From Strategy to Change: Implementing the Plan in Higher Education* (San Francisco: Jossey-Bass, 2001), 178.

28. As one recent collection of "stories" of strategic change puts it, "With increased competitiveness . . . more senior staff are engaging with the thorny issue of how best to bring about transformational, embedded and lasting change." Stephanie Marshall, ed., *Strategic Management of Change in Higher Education: What's New* (London: Routledge, 2007), 2.

29. Eric Hoyle and Mike Wallace, *Educational Leadership: Ambiguity, Professionals, and Managerialism* (London: Sage, 2005), viii and ix.

30. Birnbaum, *Management Fads in Higher Education*, 207.

31. Ibid., 216.

32. See the NYU public affairs office's account: Joan Marans Dim and Nancy Murphy Cricco, *The Miracle on Washington Square* (Lanham, MD: Lexington Books, 2000).

33. NYU Tuition Reform Campaign, available at http://www.makenyuaffordable.org/reform.html (accessed July 2008).

34. It ranks thirty-sixth among research institutions in the more rigorous Florida State ranking, thirty-fourth in *U.S. News and World Report*'s national universities, thirtieth among Shanghai Tiao Tong University's top 500, and forty-ninth in the *Times* Higher Education top 100.

35. John Lombardi, Elizabeth D. Capaldi, and Craig W. Abbey, *The Top American Research Universities, 2007 Annual Report*, 5, The Center for Measuring University Performance, Arizona State University, http://mup.asu.edu/research2007.pdf.

36. "Installation address of John Sexton," September 26, 2002, http://www.nyu.edu/about/leadership-university-administration/office-of-the-president/redirect/speeches-statements/installation-address.html.

37. Brian Leiter, *The Philosophical Gourmet Report: Brian Leiter's Report of Graduate Programs in Philosophy in the English-Speaking World*, 2009, http://www.philosophicalgourmet.com/overall.asp.

38. "Rankings: Economics," *U.S. News and World Report*, 2009, available at http://grad-schools.usnews.rankingsandreviews.com/best-graduate-schools/top-economics-schools/rankings (accessed June 7, 2010).

39. John Sexton, "Fire and Ice: The Knowledge Century and the Urban University," New York University, August 10, 2007, http://www.nyu.edu/about/leadership-university-administration/office-of-the-president/redirect/speeches-statements/fire-and-ice-the-knowledge-century-and-the-urban-university.html.

40. John Sexton, "The Common Enterprise University and the Teaching Mission," New York University, http://www.nyu.edu/about/sexton-teachingmission04.html. (The document accessed online July 28, 2008, is without pagination.)

41. Ibid.

42. Ibid.

43. Ibid.

44. Ibid.

45. Ibid.

46. Ibid.

47. John Sexton, "The University as Sanctuary," New York University, http://www.nyu.edu/about/leadership-university-administration/office-of-the-president/redirect/speeches-statements/the-university-as-sanctuary.html.

48. Ibid.

49. Ibid.

50. Ibid.

51. John Sexton, "Dogmatism and Complexity: Civil Discourse and the Research University," New York University, http://www.nyu.edu/about/leadership-university-administration/office-of-the-president/redirect/speeches-statements/dogmatism-and-complexity-civil-discourse-and-the-research-university.html.

52. See, for example, Daniel Bell, *The Cultural Contradictions of Capitalism* (New York: Basic Books, 1976).

53. John Sexton on *The Colbert Report*, Comedy Central, December 6, 2006, http://www.comedycentral.com/colbertreport/videos.jhtml?videoId=79177.

54. Gary Rhoades, "The Higher Education We Choose: A Question of Balance," *Review of Higher Education* 29, no. 3 (Spring 2006): 381–404.

55. Joan Wallace Scott, "The Critical State of Shared Governance," *Academe* 88, no. 4 (July/August 2002): 41–48.

56. Edwin E. Vineyard, *The Pragmatic Presidency: Effective Leadership in the Two-Year College* (Bolton, MA: Anker Publishing, 1993), 3.

57. Rakesh Khurana, *From Higher Aims to Hired Hands: The Social Transformation of American Business Schools and the Unfulfilled Promise of Management as a Profession* (Princeton, NJ: Princeton University Press, 2007), 257.

CHAPTER 6

1. Joe Moran, *Interdisciplinarity* (London: Routledge, 2002), 15.

2. Mieke Bal, *Traveling Concepts in the Humanities: A Rough Guide* (Toronto: University of Toronto Press, 2002), 34.

3. Theodor Adorno, "Culture and Administration," in *The Culture Industry* (London: Routledge, 2001), 107.

4. Ibid., 128–129.

5. See John Rajchman and Cornel West, *Post-analytic Philosophy* (New York: Columbia University Press, 1985).

6. W. Hofkirchner et al., "ICTs and Society: The Salzburg Approach: Towards a Theory for, about, and by Means of the Information Society," in *ICT&S Center Research Paper Series*, no. 3 (2007), 12, available at http://icts.sbg.ac.at/media/pdf/pdf1490.pdf (accessed December 10, 2010). I thank Marcus Breen for providing this link.

7. Ibid., 22.

8. Ibid., 23–25.

9. Michael Burawoy, tracks these discussions on his Web page, Public Sociologies, at the University of California, Berkeley, Web site: http://burawoy.berkeley.edu/PS.Webpage/ps.mainpage.htm. He provides the following bibliography: Vincent Jeffries, ed., *The Handbook of Public Sociology* (Lanham, MD: Rowman and Littlefield, 2009); Michael Hviid Jacobsen, ed., *Public Sociology: Proceedings of the Anniversary Conference Celebrating Ten years of Sociology in Aalborg* (Aalborg, Denmark: Aalborg University Press, 2008); Dan Clawson et al., eds., *Public Sociology: Fifteen Eminent Sociologists Debate Politics and the Profession in the Twenty-First Century* (Berkeley: University of California Press, 2007); Andrew Barlow, ed., *Collaborations for Social Justice: Professionals, Publics, and Policy Change* (Lanham, MD: Rowman and Littlefield, 2007); Ben Agger, *Public Sociology: From Social Facts to Literary Acts* (Lanham, MD: Rowman and Littlefield, 2007); Lawrence Nichols, ed., *Public Sociology: The Contemporary Debate* (Piscataway, NJ: Transaction Publishers, 2007); Judith Blau

and Keri E. Iyall Smith, eds., *Public Sociologies Reader* (Lanham, MD: Rowman and Littlefield, 2006).

10. For a critique of this disciplinary and epistemological Trinitarianism, see Immanuel Wallerstein, *Unthinking Social Science: The Limits of 19th Century Paradigms* (Cambridge, UK: Polity Press, 1991).

11. Michael Burawoy, "For Public Sociology," in Clawson et al., *Public Sociology*, 32–33.

12. Talcott Parsons, *The Structure of Social Action* (New York: McGraw-Hill, 1937).

13. Burawoy, "For Public Sociology," 59.

14. Ibid., 241.

15. Patricia Ticineto Clough, *The Ends of Ethnography: From Realism to Social Criticism* (New York: Peter Lang, 1998).

16. Evelyn Nakano Glenn, "Whose Public Sociology?" in Clawson et al., *Public Sociology*, 217.

17. Ibid., 228.

18. Michael E. Brown, *The Production of Society: A Marxian Foundation for Social Theory* (Totowa, NJ: Rowman and Littlefield, 1986), 145.

19. Philip Mirowski, *The Effortless Economy of Science?* (Durham, NC: Duke University Press, 2004), 16.

20. Ibid., 18.

21. Mario Biagioli, "Postdisciplinary Liaisons: Science Studies and the Humanities," *Critical Inquiry* 35 (Summer 2009): 816–833.

22. Patricia Ticineto Clough, "Future Matters: Technoscience, Global Politics, and Cultural Criticism," *Social Text* 80 (Fall 2004): 1–24. See also Roddey Reid and Sharon Traweek, eds., *Doing Science + Culture* (New York: Routledge, 2000); Sandra Harding, *Is Science Multicultural?: Postcolonialisms, Feminisms, and Epistemologies* (Bloomington: Indiana University Press, 1998); Steve Fuller, *New Frontiers in Science and Technology Studies* (Cambridge, UK: Polity Press, 2007).

23. Mirowski, *The Effortless Economy of Science?*, 191.

24. One recent reflection on interdisciplinarity finds that its success in contributing to a more just society "remains an open question." Joseph D. Parker, Ranu Samantrai, and Mary Romero, *Interdisciplinarity and Social Justice: Revisioning Academic Accountability* (Albany: SUNY Press, 2010), 2.

25. Roland Barthes, "From Work to Text," in *Image, Music, Text*, trans. Stephen Heath (New York: Hill and Wang, 1977), 155–164.

26. Julie Thompson Klein, *Humanities, Culture, and Interdisciplinarity: The Changing American Academy* (Albany: SUNY Press, 2005), 78.

27. Ellen Messer-Davidow, David R. Shumway, and David J. Sylvan, eds., *Knowledges: Historical and Critical Studies in Disciplinarity* (Charlottesville: University of Virginia Press, 1993), 2.

28. Keith Hoskins and Richard Macve, "Accounting as Discipline: The Overlooked Supplement," in Messer-Davidow, Shumway, and Sylvan, *Knowledges*, 32.

29. Evelyn Fox Keller, "Fractured Images of Science, Language, and Power: A Postmodern Optic or Just Bad Eyesight?" in Messer-Davidow, Shumway, and Sylvan, *Knowledges*, 56.

30. Andrew Pickering, "Anti-discipline or Narratives of Illusion," in Messer-Davidow, Shumway, and Sylvan, *Knowledges*, 115.

31. Timothy Lenoir, "The Discipline of Nature and the Nature of Discipline," in Messer-Davidow, Shumway, and Sylvan, *Knowledges*, 79.

32. Mary Louise Pratt, *Imperial Eyes: Travel Writing and Transculturation* (New York: Routledge, 1992).

33. The critique of this epistemological edifice under the notion of a "post-occidentalism" has been made by Walter Mignolo, *Local Histories/Global Designs: Coloniality, Subaltern Knowledges and Border Thinking* (Princeton, NJ: Princeton University Press, 2000).

34. For an interesting document of the issues surrounding interdisciplinarity of the seventies and a look at the relation between historically constituted disciplinary authority with special reference to the humanities, see Joseph J. Kocklemans, ed., *Interdisciplinarity and Higher Education* (University Park: Pennsylvania State University Press, 1979), 31.

35. Mary Poovey, "The Twenty-First-Century University and the Market: What Price Economic Viability?" *Differences: A Journal of Feminist Cultural Studies* 12.1 (2001): 1–16 (esp. 11).

36. Ibid., 12.

37. Ibid., 13.

38. Ibid., 13–14.

39. Gayatri Chakravorty Spivak, *Outside in the Teaching Machine* (New York: Routledge, 1993).

40. Mary Poovey, *A History of the Modern Fact: Problems of Knowledge in the Sciences of Wealth and Society* (Chicago: University of Chicago Press, 1998).

41. See Christopher Newfield, *The Unmaking of the Public University* (Cambridge, MA: Harvard University Press, 2008). In the case of the University of California, "half of the humanities instructional money and close to two-thirds of the social sciences money" are used to subsidize research in the sciences and engineering" (217). Rather than acknowledge or appreciate the handout, cultural fields are presented as dependent and deficient. "By equating commercially oriented research in technology with profitability, and culture with cost, culture warriors helped obscure budgetary reality that successful tech research depends on public subsidies—subsidies funneled in some significant part through teaching in cultural fields" (219).

42. Bill Readings, *The University in Ruins* (Cambridge, MA: Harvard University Press, 1996), 118.

43. Ibid., 89.

44. Ibid., 119.

45. Neil Smith, *American Empire: Roosevelt's Geographer and the Prelude to Globalization* (Berkeley: University of California Press, 2003).

46. Newfield, *Unmaking of the Public University*, 154.

47. Christopher Newfield, *Ivy and Industry: Business and the Making of the American University, 1880–1980* (Durham, NC: Duke University Press, 2003), 7–8.

48. Ibid., 219.

49. Ibid., 226.

50. Ibid., 221.

51. Ibid., 225.

52. This line of argument is elaborated in Randy Martin, *An Empire of Indifference: American War and the Financial Logic of Risk Management* (Durham, NC: Duke University Press, 2007).

53. On this contradiction between downsizing-driven leanness and the supervisory girth required to execute it, see Bennett Harrison, *Lean and Mean: The Changing Landscape of Corporate Power in an Era of Flexibility* (New York: Guilford, 1997);

David M. Gordon, *Fat and Mean: The Corporate Squeeze of Working Americans and the Myth of Managerial "Downsizing"* (New York: Free Press, 1996).

54. Derivatives are identified by the value or notional price of the commodities that they are tied to, rather than to the amount of money they yield, which is but a fraction of that price. So, if one is paying $1,000 for the option to purchase $1,000,000 worth of Euros at a certain date, the contract is entered as $1,000,000 not $1,000. Figures on the global derivatives markets can be found at the Bank of International Settlements Web site. See, for example, "OTC Derivatives Market Activity in the First Half of 2006," November 17, 2006, http://www.bis.org/press/p061117.htm. For a fuller explanation, see Dick Bryan and Michael Rafferty, *Capitalism with Derivatives: A Political Economy of Financial Derivatives, Capital and Class* (Houndmills, UK: Palgrave, 2006).

55. Michael Lewis, *Moneyball: The Art of Winning an Unfair Game* (New York: W. W. Norton, 2003). The emergence of these quantitative models in baseball, initially called sabermetrics in the early eighties by amateurs outside the scouting business, adaptation by managers like Beane a decade latter, and the flagging fortunes of the Oakland As several years after the book was published, correspond to the rise of risk management protocols and their loss of sheen with the financial crisis.

56. See the autoethnography of one such struggle by Jacqui Alexander in *Pedagogies of Crossing: Meditations of Feminism, Sexual Politics, Memory, and the Sacred* (Durham, NC: Duke University Press, 2005).

57. See Lisa Lattuca, *Creating Interdisciplinarity: Interdisciplinary Research and Teaching Among College and University Faculty* (Nashville: Vanderbilt University Press, 2001), 8.

58. Christopher J. Lucas, *American Higher Education: A History* (New York: St. Martin's Press, 1994), 179.

59. Laurence Veysey, *The Emergence of the American University* (Chicago: University of Chicago Press, 1965), 59.

60. Jurgen Herbst, "Diversification in American Higher Education," in *The Transformation of Higher Learning 1860–1930: Expansion, Diversification, Social Opening, and Professionalization in England, Germany, Russia, and the United States,* ed. Konrad H. Jarausch (Chicago: University of Chicago Press, 1983), 196–206 (esp. 206).

61. John S. Brubacher and Willis Rudy, *Higher Education in Transition: A History of American Colleges and Universities,* 2nd ed. (New Brunswick, NJ: Transaction Publishers, 1997),368

62. David R. Shumway, *Creating American Civilization: A Genealogy of American Literature as an Academic Discipline* (Minneapolis: University of Minnesota Press, 1993), 20.

63. See, for example, David Theo Goldberg, *Racist Culture: Philosophy and the Politics of Meaning* (Cambridge, MA: Blackwell, 1993).

64. Mark R. Nemec, *Ivory Towers and Nationalist Minds: Universities, Leadership, and the Development of the American State* (Ann Arbor: University of Michigan Press, 2006), 11.

65. Leslie Margolin, *Under the Cover of Kindness: The Invention of Social Work* (Charlottesville: University of Virginia Press, 1997), 2.

66. William C. Chase, *The American Law School and the Rise of Administrative Government* (Madison: University of Wisconsin Press, 1982).

67. William R. Johnson, *Schooled Lawyers: A Study in the Clash of Professional Cultures* (New York: New York University Press, 1978).

68. Quoted in The Sheffield Scientific School at Yale University 1847–1956, Yale School of Engineering and Applied Science, available at http://www.eng.yale.edu/content/historicSheffield.asp (accessed June 2008).

69. "History: Nation's First Engineering School," United States Military Academy at West Point, http://www.usma.edu/bicentennial/history/FirstESchool.htm.

70. Henry Sjoerd Van Klooster, "125 Years of Chemistry History at Rensselaer Polytechnic Institute," http://www.lib.rpi.edu/archives/chemistry/ess60.pdf, 3.

71. Bernadette Bensaude-Vincent and Isabelle Stengers, A History of Chemistry (Cambridge, MA: Harvard University Press, 1996), 4.

72. Ibid., 1.

73. Ibid., 10.

74. The concept comes from Antonio Gramsci, "Americanism and Fordism," in Selections from the Prison Notebooks, ed. Geoffrey Nowell Smith (New York: International Publishers, 1971), 277–318. But it gains wide attention when the phenomenon it names is said to come to a close, hence post-Fordism. For a discussion, see Ash Amin, ed., Post-Fordism: A Reader (Cambridge, MA: Blackwell, 1994).

75. Rustom Roy, "Interdisciplinary Science on Campus: The Elusive Dream," in Interdisciplinarity and Higher Education, ed. Joseph J. Kockelmans (University Park: Pennsylvania State University Press, 1979), 161–196 (quotation, 176–177). Roy considers 1960 to mark the birth of interdisciplinarity "on a major structural scale" (162), and also observes that materials science took off in the more entrepreneurial and less prestigious research universities that were not part of the initial government largess.

76. George Steinmetz, "Introduction: Positivism and Its Others in the Social Sciences," in The Politics of Method in the Human Sciences: Positivism and Its Epistemological Others, ed. George Steinmetz (Durham, NC: Duke University Press, 2005), 1–56 (quotation, 2).

77. Michael Dutton, "Area Studies/Asian Studies," in Steinmetz, The Politics of Method, 89–125 (quotation, 96).

78. Christopher Simpson, "An Introduction" in Universities and Empire: Money and Politics in the Social Sciences during the Cold War, ed. Christopher Simpson (New York: New Press, 1998), xi–xxxiv (quotation, xvii).

79. Bruce Cumings "Boundary Displacement: Area Studies and International Studies during and after the Cold War," in Simpson, Universities and Empire, 159–188 (quotation, 163).

80. Ellen Messer-Davidow, Disciplining Feminism: From Social Activism to Academic Discourse (Durham, NC: Duke University Press, 2002), 45.

81. Sucheng Chan, In Defense of Asian American Studies: The Politics of Teaching and Program Building (Urbana: University of Illinois Press, 2005), xiv.

82. Ibid., 197.

83. Kenneth P. Gonzalez and Raymond V. Padilla, Doing the Public Good: Latina/o Scholars Engage Civic Participation (Sterling, VA: Stylus, 2008), 8.

84. The reference to this other revolution entailing faculty autonomy (as discussed in Chapter 1) is Christopher Jencks and David Riesman, The Academic Revolution (Garden City, New York: Doubleday, 1968).

85. Malcolm Moos and Francis E. Rourke, The Campus and the State (Baltimore: Johns Hopkins University Press, 1959), 2.

86. Gary Rhoades, Managed Professionals: Unionized Faculty and Restructuring Academic Labor (Albany: SUNY Press, 1998), 10.

87. Frank T. Rhodes, *The Creation of the Future: The Role of the American University* (Ithaca, NY: Cornell University Press, 2001), xii.

88. Daniel Rowley, Herman Lujan, and Michael Dolence, *Strategic Choices for the Academy: How Demand for Lifelong Learning Will Re-create Higher Education* (San Francisco: Jossey-Bass, 1998), 254–255.

89. Ibid., 256.

90. Sharona Coutts, "At University of Phoenix, Allegations of Enrollment Abuses Persist," *Propublica*, November 3, 2009, http://www.propublica.org/feature/at-u-of-phoenix-allegations-of-enrollment-abuses-persist-1103.

91. See Straighterline at http://www.straighterline.com. Straighterline has won awards for its educational software, and it partners with accredited colleges to confer credits. Students of one such partner, Fort Hays State University, were none too happy with the arrangement and registered their protest on a Facebook page: "Larry Gould, as Provost, has taken steps that will inevitably cheapen the quality and value of a degree from Fort Hays State University by placing our university in bed with a private corporation that sells general education credits. What this means is that students will pay more per credit hour for poorly designed online courses than they would for quality courses taught on campus by actual FHSU faculty, yet they would appear the same on a transcript. Perhaps worse, the courses from Straighter Line can be viewed as competition for the classes FHSU offers through the Virtual College." "FHSU Students against Straighter Line," Facebook, http://www.facebook.com/group.phb?gid=58406687476.

92. See U.S. Department of Education, *Digest of Education Statistics* (Washington, DC: National Center for Education Statistics, 2005), "Number of Educational Institutions, by Level and Control of Institution: Selected Years, 1980–81 through 2003–04," available at http://nces.ed.gov/programs/digest/d05/tables/dt05_005.asp (accessed December 10, 2010). For-profits are not tabulated until 1996 and by then, at 2,573, are already more numerous than public (2,069) and private nonprofit (2,027). Recent enrollment data can be found at U.S. Department of Education, *Digest of Educational Statistics* (Washington, DC: National Center for Education Statistics, 2009), table 213 ("Total Fall Enrollment in Private Not-for-Profit Degree-Granting Institutions, by Attendance Status, Sex, and State or Jurisdiction: 2006 and 2007"), available at http://nces.ed.gov/programs/digest/d09/tables/dt09_213.asp (accessed December 10, 2010).

93. Between 1998 and 2008, there were more than 150 fewer public and nearly 200 fewer nonprofit private institutions, while the number of for-profits grew by 300 and added more than a million students to their ranks. *Digest of Educational Statistics* (2009), table 5 ("Number of Educational Institutions by Level, and Control of Institution: Selected Years, 1980–81 through 2007–08"), available at http://nces.ed.gov/programs/digest/d09/tables/dt09_005.asp (accessed December 10, 2010).

94. For example, for the year 2004 to 2005, 44 percent of adults report participating in some form of adult education. For a breakdown of the data, see *Digest of Education Statistics* (2005), "Adult Education Participation in 2004–2005," available at http://nces.ed.gov/pubs2006/adulted/01.asp (accessed December 10, 2010).

95. Karen Levesque et al., *Career and Technical Education in the United States: 1990 to 2005 Statistical Analysis Report* (Washington, DC: National Center for Education Statistics, 2008), 195 (table 4.1, "Number of Adults and Labor Force Members, and Percentage of Adults and Labor Force Members Who Participated in Work-Related Courses, by Selected Adult Characteristics: 2004–05"), available at http://nces.ed.gov/pubs2008/2008035.pdf (accessed December 10, 2010).

96. For a look at how these partnerships operate in the field of science, see Henry Etzkowitz, *The Triple Helix: Industry-University-Government Innovation in Action* (New York: Routledge, 2008).

97. Indicative of the proprietary nature of such programs, especially niched master's degrees, GetEducated.com lists 313 graduate certificate programs and more than 11,000 specialized master's degrees, while GradSchools.com claims a listing of more than 60,000 programs.

CHAPTER 7

1. Stanley Aronowitz, *The Last Good Job in America: Work and Education in the New Global Technoculture* (Lanham, MD: Rowman and Littlefield, 2001).

2. Linda Zimbler, "Figure B—Principal Activity of all Faculty and Instructional Staff, by Employment Status: Fall 1998," in *Background Characteristics, Work Activities, and Compensation of Faculty and Instructional Staff in Postsecondary Institutions: Fall 1998*, Office of Educational Research and Improvement, U.S. Department of Education (Washington, DC: National Center for Education Statistics, 2001), 10, http://nces.ed.gov/pubs2001/2001152.pdf.

3. The workweek averaged 52.5 hours for full-time faculty in 1992. Administrative and service hours are broken out only for the earlier period. For 2003, teaching and research accounted for 78.2 percent of time, the remainder was classed as "other." See U.S. Department of Education, *Digest of Education Statistics* (Washington, DC: National Center for Education Statistics, 2007), table 240 ("Percentage Distribution of Full-Time Instructional Faculty and Staff in Degree-Granting Institutions, by Type and Control of Institution, Selected Instruction Activities, and Number of Classes Taught for Credit: Fall 2003"), available at http://nces.ed.gov/programs/digest/d07/tables/dt07_240.asp?referrer=report (accessed December 10, 2010); and U.S. Department of Education, National Study of Postsecondary Faculty (NSOPF), *Digest of Education Statistics* (Washington, DC: National Center for Education Statistics, 1993), table 234 ("Full-Time Instructional Faculty and Staff in Institutions of Higher Education, by Instruction Activities and Type and Control of Institution: Fall 1992," prepared September 1996), available at http://nces.ed.gov/programs/digest/d00/dt234.asp (accessed December 10, 2010).

4. "What Do Faculty Do?" American Association of University Professors, http://www.aaup.org/AAUP/issues/facwork/facultydolist.htm.

5. Paolo Virno, "General Intellect," in *Lessico Postfordista*, trans. Arianna Bove (Feltrinelli: 2001), http://www.generation-online.org/p/fpvirno10.htm.

6. The classic formulation of this problem is in Mancur Olson, *The Logic of Collective Action* (Cambridge, MA: Harvard University Press, 1965).

7. Duncan Foley, *Adam's Fallacy: A Guide to Economic Theology* (Cambridge, MA: Harvard University Press, 2006), 3.

8. Gerald Raunig, *Art and Revolution: Transversal Activism in the Long Twentieth Century* (Los Angeles: Semiotexte, 2007), 205.

9. Jürgen Habermas, *The Theory of Communicative Action*, vols. 1 and 2 (Boston: Beacon [1984] 1987).

10. See Matteo Pasquinelli, *Animal Spirits: A Bestiary of the Commons* (Rotterdam, Netherlands: NAI Press, 2008).

11. See S. N. Eisenstadt, ed., *Max Weber on Charisma and Institution Building* (Chicago: University of Chicago Press, 1968). I should note that the term "singularity," which in the work of Hardt and Negri is borrowed from philosopher Baruch

Spinoza, has a parallel but unconnected meaning for administrators like Duderstadt, suggesting something of the immanent theoretical language evinced by this derivative logic. See Michael Hardt and Antonio Negri, *Multitude: War and Democracy in the Age of Empire* (New York: Penguin, 2004).

12. The Scholarly Societies Project, http://www.scholarly-societies.org.

13. Lennard Davis, "Dancing in the Dark: A Manifesto against Professional Organizations," *Minnesota Review* 45 and 46 (Fall 1996): 197–214; Stephen Watt, "What Is an Organization Like the MLA? From Gentleman's Club to Professional Organization," *Workplace* 1 (1998): 1, available at http://cust.educ.ubc.ca/work place/features1/watt.html (accessed January 17, 2011).

14. Tony Tinker, "The End of Business Schools? More than Meets the Eye," *Social Text*, no. 79 (Summer 2004): 67–80 (esp. 75 and 77).

15. See Stefano Harney, "Business Schools Must Spurn Rewards Structure that Shamed the City," *Times Higher Education*, November 28, 2008, available at http://www.timeshighereducation.co.uk/story.asp?storycode=404398 (accessed December 15, 2010).

16. Mary Ann Mason, Marc Goulden, and Karie Frasch, "Why Graduate Students Reject the Fast Track," *Academe* (January–February 2009): 11–16 (esp. 13).

17. Jürgen Habermas, *Legitimation Crisis* (Boston: Beacon, 1975).

18. Donna Strickland, "The Mangerial Unconscious," in *Tenured Bosses and Disposable Teachers: Writing Instruction in the Managed University*, eds. Marc Bousquet, Tony Scott, and Leo Parascondola (Carbondale: Southern Illinois University Press, 2004), 46–56 (quotation, 54).

19. Other poetry titles by Cary Nelson include *Our Last First Poets: Vision and History in Contemporary American Poetry* (Urbana: University of Illinois Press, 1981); *Repression and Recovery: Modern American Poetry and the Politics of Cultural Memory, 1910–1945* (Madison: University of Wisconsin Press, 1989); *Revolutionary Memory: Recovering the Poetry of the American Left* (New York and London: Routledge, 2001).

20. American Association of University Professors, "Censure List," http://www.aaup.org/AAUP/about/censuredadmins/default.htm.

21. These figures are taken from the following sources: NEA Higher Education Faculty and Staff, http://www.nea.org/home/1602.htm; United Automobile Workers, UAW Research Bulletin, Higher Education: Graduate Student Employees, January–February 2003, http://www.uaw.org/publications/jobs_pay/03/no1/jpe11.html; American Federation of Teachers "About AFT Higher Education," http://www.aft.org/higher_ed/about.htm.

22. "Government Workers Lead 428,000 Gain of Union Membership," *Minneapolis StarTribune*, January 28, 2009, available at http://www.startribune.com/business/38577097.html (accessed December 15, 2010). The gain of more than 300,000 members was followed by 428,000—the largest increase in unionized workers since 1983.

23. United States Department of Labor, Bureau of Labor Statistics, Economic News Release, table 3 ("Union Affiliation of Employed Wage and Salary Workers by Occupation and Industry"), available at http://www.bls.gov/news.release/union2.t03.htm (accessed December 15, 2010).

24. Kim Moody has provided a critical tracking of organized labor's travails over the years. See his *An Injury to All: The Decline of American Unionism* (London: Verso, 1988), and more recently, *U.S. Labor in Trouble and Transition: The Failure of Reform from Above, the Promise of Revival from Below* (London: Verso, 2007).

25. United States Department of Labor, Bureau of Labor Statistics, Economic News Release, table 3.

26. An early formulation of knowledge economy is Fritz Machlup, *The Production and Distribution of Knowledge in the United States* (Princeton, NJ: Princeton University Press, 1962). After the work of Alain Touraine and Daniel Bell, Manuel Castells provides a key account of the global dispersion of information technologies and their link to social movements in *The Rise of the Network Society. The Information Age: Economy, Society, and Culture*, vol. 1 (Malden, MA: Blackwell, 1996).

27. See Dimitris Papadopoulos, Niamh Stephenson, and Vassilis Tsianos, *Escape Routes: Control and Subversion in the 21st Century* (Ann Arbor, MI: Pluto Press, 2008).

28. Michael Denning, *The Cultural Front: The Laboring of American Culture in the Twentieth Century* (London: Verso, 1996), xviii.

29. Ibid., xix.

30. Ibid., 100–101.

31. Clyde Barrow, *Universities and the Capitalist State: Corporate Liberalism and the Reconstruction of American Higher Education, 1894–1928* (Madison: University of Wisconsin Press, 1990), 14.

32. These patterns of ownership are charted by MediaChannel.org; see http://www.freepress.net/ownership/chart/main.

33. Vincent Mosco, "The labouring of the Public Service Principle: Union Convergence and Worker Movements in the North American Communication Industries," *Info: The Journal of Policy, Regulation, and Strategy for Telecommunications, Information, and Media* 9, no. 2/3 (2007): 57–67 (quotation, 62).

34. Catherine McKercher, *Newsworkers Unite: Labor, Convergence, and North American Newspapers* (Lanham, MD: Rowman and Littlefield Publishers, 2002), 193.

35. Ursula Huws, *The Making of the Cybertariat: Virtual Work in a Real World* (New York: Monthly Review, 2003), 176.

36. For an account of the breakup between Unite Here and the Service Employees International Union, see Peter Dreier, "Divorce Union Style: Can the Labor Movement Overcome Unite Here's messy breakup?" *The Nation* 289, no. 6 (August 31, 2009/September 7, 2009), 11–18.

37. See Judith Wagner DeCew, *Unionization in the Academy: Visions and Realities* (Lanham, MD: Rowman and Littlefield Publishers, 2003), 23.

38. Ernst Benjamin, Introduction to *Academic Collective Bargaining*, eds. Ernst Benjamin and Michael Mauer (Washington, DC/New York: AAUP/MLA, 2006), 12–13.

39. Stanley Aronowitz, "Academic Unionism and the Future of Higher Education," in *Will Teach for Food: Academic Labor in Crisis*, ed. Cary Nelson (Minneapolis: University of Minnesota Press, 1997), 181–214 (quotation, 213–214).

40. No doubt, treating all scientific research as if it delivered a state interest is equally problematic. From the Science for the People project that emerged from the antiwar movement in 1970, which featured Stephen Jay Gould and Richard Lewontin, to contemporary science studies and professional insurgencies, like Physicians for a National Health Plan, the critical range of scientific means and ends opens an expanded field that challenges both epistemological and policy claims of the state. Science for the People itself was relaunched as an international body in 2002, see http://www.scienceforthepeople.com.

41. See Nelson Blackstock, *Cointelpro: The FBI's Secret War on Political Freedom* (Atlanta: Pathfinder Press, 1988).

42. Michael E. Brown, *The Historiography of Communism* (Philadelphia, Temple University Press, 2009), 6.

43. Ellen Schrecker, *No Ivory Tower: McCarthyism and the Universities* (New York: Oxford University Press, 1986); Ellen Schrecker, *Many Are the Crimes: McCarthyism in America* (Princeton, NJ: Princeton University Press, 1998); Joel Kovel, *Red Hunting in the Promised Land: Anti-communism and the Making of America* (New York: Basic Books, 1994).

44. While treatments of the meltdown are now legion, and even Alan Greenspan admits that there were flaws in the model, little rethinking of risk management strategies now recognized to have generated such volatility appear to be on offer. For an account of this dynamic, see Gillian Tett, *Fool's Gold: How the Bold Dream of a Small Tribe at J.P. Morgan Was Corrupted by Wall Street Greed and Unleashed a Catastrophe* (New York: Simon and Schuster, 2009).

45. Ned Rossiter, *Organized Networks: Media Theory, Creative Labour, New Institutions* (Rotterdam, Netherlands: NAI Press, 2006), 14.

46. Ibid., 15.

47. Ibid., 162.

48. See Michel Foucault, *The Birth of Biopolitics* (Houndmills, UK: Palgrave Macmillan, 2008), 132.

49. Tellingly, Organizing for America is a portal on the Barack Obama official Web site held over from the campaign; see http://www.barackobama.com.

50. Germinal texts would be Karl Marx, "Critique of the Gotha Program" and "Communist Manifesto" in *Collected Works*, by Karl Marx and Frederick Engels (New York: International Publishers); V. I. Lenin, *State and Revolution* (New York: International Publishers, 1974); Antonio Gramsci, *Selections from the Prison Notebooks* (New York: International Publishers, 1971).

51. See Nicos Poulantzas, *State, Power, Socialism* (London: Verso, 1978), and the recently issued *Poulantzas Reader: Marxism, Law, and the State* (London: Verso, 2008).

52. Stefano Harney, *State Work: Public Administration and Mass Intellectuality* (Durham, NC: Duke University Press, 2002), 5.

CHAPTER 8

1. Frederick Winslow Taylor, *Principles of Scientific Management* (New York: Norton, 1967). Taylor's third principle invites managers to enlist workers' practical knowledge of their laboring activities to enhance efficiency and productivity.

2. Illustrative here is a recent book from one of the avatars of behavioral finance who uses psychology to counter the biologically based irrationality of *homo economicus*. See Hersh Shefrin, *Ending the Management Illusion: Eliminate the Mental Traps that Threaten Your Organization's Success* (New York: McGraw-Hill, 2008).

3. See, for example, Eddie Yuen, Daniel Burton-Rose, and George Katsiaficas, *Confronting Capitalism: Dispatches from a Global Movement* (New York: Soft Skull Press, 2004); Richard Day, *Gramsci Is Dead: Anarchist Movements in the Newest Social Movements* (Ann Arbor: Pluto Press, 2005); George Katsiaficas, *The Subversion of Politics: European Autonomous Social Movements and the Decolonization of Everyday Life* (New York: AK Press, 2006); David Graeber, *Possibilities: Essays on Hierarchy, Rebellion, and Desire* (New York: AK Press, 2007).

4. The publication *Workplace: A Journal for Academic Labor* has sustained both the critique and the engagement. On the prospects and frustrations of such activism, see especially the special issue on the NYU strike, in particular the piece by Elizabeth Loeb, "Making It Work: Audre Lorde's 'The Master's Tools' and the Unbearable Difference of GSOC," *Workplace* 14 (May 2007), available at http://m1.cust.educ.ubc.ca/journal/index.php/workplace/article/viewFile/22/loeb (accessed December 15, 2010). I am grateful to Annie McClanahan whose observations regarding deradicalization in union activism proved quite clarifying.

5. The problems are sharply posed in Rosa Luxemburg's critique of Eduard Bernstein's social democracy in her pamphlet *Reform or Revolution* (1908; rev., New York: Pathfinder [1900] 1970). The notion of revolutionary or nonassimilable reforms was broached by Andre Gorz in the sixties with the rise of the student movement. See his *Réforme et Révolution* (Paris: Seuil, 1969). A pamphlet version was published in English by the *Socialist Register* in 1968.

6. Derrida's remarks were made in the early 1980s at a conference at Columbia University and subsequently published in Richard Rand, *Logomachia: The Conflict of the Faculties Today* (Lincoln: University of Nebraska Press, 1992). See also Simon Wortham, *Rethinking the University: Leverage and Deconstruction* (Manchester: Manchester University Press, 1997).

7. Intersectionality is a concept developed to appreciate the multiple historical and cultural markers that bear upon identity and politics. See Kimberle Crenshaw, Kendall Thomas, Gary Peller, eds., *Critical Race Theory: The Key Writings that Formed the Movement* (New York: New Press, 2001) and more specifically, to electoral politics, Carol Hardy-Fanta, ed., *Intersectionality and Politics: Recent Research on Gender, Race, and Political Representation in the United States* (New York: Haworth Publishers, 2007).

8. Henry Giroux, *The University In Chains: Confronting the Military-Industrial Academic Complex* (Boulder, CO: Paradigm Publishers, 2007), 205.

9. Shannon Jackson, *Professing Performance: Theatre in the Academy from Philology to Performativity* (Cambridge: Cambridge University Press, 2004), 218.

10. Take Back NYU, February 18, 2009, http://takebacknyu.com/demands.

11. Provost David McLaughlin, email message to New York University faculty, February 23, 2009.

12. For reports on these various struggles, see Edu-Factory (http://www.edu-factory.org/edu15). Instances of social centers with activist, publishing, and theoretical interventions are appearing on the U.S. landscape, such as El Kilombo Intergaláctico (http://www.elkilombo.org) in Durham, North Carolina, and Reworking/Rethinking the University (http://rethinkingtheu.wordpress.com) at the University of Minnesota, with its conferences that theorize current activisms and organizing.

13. Antoinette Burton, *After the Imperial Turn: Thinking with and through the Nation* (Durham, NC: Duke University Press), 15.

Index

Randy Martin is Professor and Chair of Art and Public Policy at New York University. He has published, as author or editor, a dozen books, including *An Empire of Indifference: American War and the Financial Logic of Risk Management* and *Financialization of Daily Life* (Temple).